Delhi
A History

Manisha Choudhary teaches at the Centre of Advanced Study, Department of History, University of Delhi. She specializes in Medieval Indian History.

She is also a recipient of the Professor Pema Ram Award 2019 awarded to her at the 33nd session of the Rajasthan History Congress for her paper, titled 'Recruitment, Role and Hierarchy of Khojas–Nadars in the Amber–Jaipur State: A Study of the Rise of Eunuchs'. Presently, she is working on a research project titled 'The History of Thar: Environment, Culture and Society', as Fellow at the Indian Institute of Advanced Study, Rashtrapati Nivas, Shimla.

Delhi
A History

MANISHA CHOUDHARY

RUPA

Published by
Rupa Publications India Pvt. Ltd 2020
7/16, Ansari Road, Daryaganj
New Delhi 110002

Sales centres:
Allahabad Bengaluru Chennai
Hyderabad Jaipur Kathmandu
Kolkata Mumbai

ISBN: 978-93-5333-809-1

First impression 2020

10 9 8 7 6 5 4 3 2 1

Printed HT Media Ltd. Gr. Noida

For Sachin

CONTENTS

Preface   *ix*

Introduction   *xi*

1. The Imperial City   1

2. Twins: Glory and Sink   19

3. The Alive Past   57

4. The Sufis and Elites of *Dilli*   97

5. The Charisma of the City   134

6. The Corn-fit Cultures   147

7. The Aching Struggles   175

8. Conclusion   216

Appendices

I.   The Mistress of Every Conqueror
     by Khushwant Singh   221

II. The City of Scents   223

III. The Rome of Asia   224

IV. The Peacock Throne   225

Bibliography   227

Acknowledgements   232

PREFACE

The American historian, Charles Beard, employed the expression 'That Noble Dream' to refer to the disposition amongst historians to seek 'the objective truth' about the past, and pursue that account of history which would retail perfectly historical events as they actually happened, and be devoid of the historian's own predilections and biases. With this noble dream, he wanted to make a convincing case for the relativity of historical knowledge.[1]

This book aims to provide the reader a glimpse into the general history of Delhi, and attempts to bring together the diverse histories of the city into a major narrative along with an understanding of the discipline. Major interests, politics of the times, economy and social aspects have all been highlighted within a framework of the time, space and knowledge of their occurrences. The purpose behind this effort is to make the reader aware that history aims to explore and understand past processes in the light of changing times and expanding spaces, and that it is not a fault-finding business. The purpose behind assessing and analysing events is mainly to understand the nature of the state and highlight its activities by also considering various other activities that were happening simultaneously at the time. This work will also not eulogize any great historian, as all historians use evidences, and through their arguments

---

[1] C.M.D. Crowder, *Histories and Historians: A Selection of Articles from History Today*, Oliver & Boyd, Edinburgh, London, 1968, p.1.

try to alter general concept of the discipline. The reader is dependent on the historian and the task of the author is to offer the events without any biases. Often the debates in which historians participate guide their metaphors and orient them to choose a direction. An honest effort has been made in this work to stay immune to the present politics of the country, where the state is aiming to attain a monolithic identity, and is trying to set all of history in one single course by burying the heterogeneity which has guided the entire history of the subcontinent.

This work is a simple history of the city meant for general consumption, from ancient times up until the Partition of India in 1947. References are provided in the appropriate places for the interested explorer. Since historians are humans who are writing about the past, while often firmly planted in their present, it is possible that their language and research orientation are silently guided by the circumstances around them. I am also not immune to my current environment. Although I undertook much precaution while researching, I would like to humbly extend my apologies for any errors that may have crept in. The work doesn't aim to hurt the sentiments of anyone. If any such event appears, the mistake is solely mine and no one else is to blame. Finally, I can say with assertion that this work is penned in a simple manner with a great hope and concern for the future of the history of India.

INTRODUCTION

Yeh bhi dilli, woh bhi dilli
Thodi aur dilli, gajab hai dilli

The history of Delhi is unlike the histories of many capital cities such as Baghdad, Cairo and Istanbul. This is because Delhi has seen many rulers and feudatory disputes, especially due to its geographical location along the river Yamuna, whose tributaries were supplying water to various settlements and their activities. Today, Delhi is a cosmopolitan city where people from all walks of life aspire to visit and reside in.

This work is an attempt to write a general history of a city where I have lived for long and one that has groomed me in many ways. Many a time, my own experiences with the city, its monuments and its people have shaped the desire to understand, and hence write about the city. Many of the sections that discuss the behaviour of its inhabitants, as well as its monuments and markets, are my own experiences. I share these with complete consciousness and anyone who holds a contrary viewpoint has the right to discard it totally. I trust that the material collected and presented here will be of interest to the reader, and will be of instructive value in the discipline of history. Archaeological and historical evidences and information are used to arrive at authenticity of events.

The history of the capital city of India goes back up to the Neolithic Age. For more than a millennium, Delhi was at the crossroads of trade, culture and politics. During the medieval times, it was an attraction for both traders and raiders. Nearly all the rulers, invaders, travellers and officials have tried to shape the soul of Delhi, and have contributed to its physical settings, in either an explicit or implicit manner. The stories of its buildings and great historical personalities were told many times before but this book approaches the past of India's capital through its literary, historical and archaeological sources. Various individuals have written about Delhi, but those who have contributed the most were mainly the associates of the Mughal Empire and British officials. Many other writers and thinkers focused on a colourful cast of historical characters while glancing at the political development of contemporary times.

The process through which Delhi reached its present status involved battles, successions and invasions. Its culture also went through a lot of systole and diastole. Many are surprised to know that the language of this city in its heyday was Persian. Or, to put it more aptly, the youth of Delhi (inception during reign of Shahjahan) was adorned by the excellent Persian and the *mushairas* and *mehfils* were the zenith of its probity and delicacy. Despite being first brought to Hindustan by migrant forces, it eventually became an authentic Indian language used both in administration and literature. Regardless of the fact that it was cultivated by the elites in society, it became a widely accessible language of aspirations, expressions and opportunities. It connected India to the wider world, especially to Central Asia. Gradually, the Indian subcontinent, particularly Delhi, became a place for talented poets, scholars and administrators. Many people came in from Turkey, Mosul and erstwhile Persia to make their fortunes. The language was used not only by elites but was also picked by the common man. It attained a very different style which had influences of indigenous vernaculars. Today, traces of Persian can be seen everywhere, but sadly it is no more in use in India as it was during the medieval centuries. Persian was the language of art, culture, literature, academic exchanges and knowledge transmission. It was accessible to all classes and had a great administrative utility. The language is dead today, as hardly any efforts were made to keep it alive. Its decay paved the way for the bloom of the sweet Urdu language, which was, and still is, a significant voice of poetry in India. Despite this, today some institutes are struggling hard to keep it breathing. Urdu emerged in the eighteenth century as part of the military contingents' exchanges and the word itself stands for the *lashkar*—a convoy or caravan. The epistemological derivation of the term 'Urdu' is from the Turkish word 'ordu' meaning army. In English, it signifies a horde.

Evidences of prehistoric sites in Delhi are being investigated by many archaeologists. Many of them have concluded that a majority of the tools that were in use around prehistoric times were mainly manufactured by a technique used $1^1/_2$–2 million years ago, during the Acheulian times. In fact, the remains of the Chalcolithic or the Bronze Age and Iron Age settlements are noticed in and around the city of Delhi. An ancient mound is located in village Mandoli, and its excavation indicated evidences of the Late Harappan and Painted Grey Ware (PGW) culture. Many other locations in the city, such as Dhansa, Timarpur, Majnu ka Tila, Loni, Bankner, Jhatikara, Kharkhari Nahar, Khera Kalan, Salimgarh, Bhorgarh, etc. also indicate the presence of the PGW phase. Today, most of these sites are part of the main city.

Much of the ancient history of Delhi is not well recorded. According to the great epic Mahabharata, this was Indraprastha—the city of God Indra—the magnificent capital city of the Pandavas, which was founded around 3500 BC. The term *prastha* means 'plains'. There were five *prasthas* and Delhi was one among them. The other four *prasthas* were Sonepat, Panipat, Tilpat and Baghpat. Sanskrit texts refer to Delhi as Hastinapur, which means the 'elephant city'. This name was probably given due the availability and presence of elephants in the area. Medieval literature also narrates many instances of the large number of elephants that were kept in the city. Swami Dayanand, in his famous work titled *Satyarth Parkash*, has provided a long list of the dynasties and the families who ruled Indraprastha.[1] According to the historian Firishta, Raja Dhilu laid the foundation of Delhi. The state was established in the year 736 and was an important political centre for many dynasties.[2] Much of the information found in the medieval court histories and travelogues are based on the information that was made available to authors from various sources. Most of them fail to mention their evidences and sources.

Women were always an intrinsic part of the literature of the Indian subcontinent. They were also represented in architecture and other diverse art forms. Women form a major section in diverse sources for the expression of the

---

[1]Swami Dayanand Saraswati, *Satyarth Parkash*, Chiranjiva Bharadwaja (trans.), Star Press, Allahabad. Available at <https://drive.google.com/file/d/0B-ll6TtiictNekFVSy1KekpYTEU/view> (accessed on 21 October 2019)

[2]Refer to <https://en.wikipedia.org/wiki/History_of_Delhi> (accessed on 21 October 2019)

social setups and aesthetics. A similar effect also extends to the site of our research. In fact, Delhi was also named after female ascetics, or *yoginis*. The name Yoginipura and its origin is discussed in Chapter 1 of this book.

The earliest inscription that mentions the word *Dhillika* is the Bijolia inscription, dated *c.*1170. The VS 1383/1326AD inscription confirms the foundation of Delhi by the Tomars. During the tenth century, the same area was included in the domain of Prithviraj Chauhan and the fort of Rai Pithora Garh, or Durg Rai Pithora, was constructed. The wall remnants of the fort indicate that the first walled city of Delhi was established with the construction of the Rai Pithora Fort. In 1192, Prithviraj Chauhan was defeated by Mohammad Ghori at the Battle of Tarain/Taraori near Thanesar in present-day Haryana. The defeat of Chauhans at the battle led to the foundation of the Delhi Sultanate in north India. The winner at the battle left the city under his trusted slave Qutubuddin Aibak and left for Ghor, the capital of the Ghurid empire, and never returned. Revenue was regularly collected and sent to the capital. With the death of Shahabuddin Ghori *c.*1206, popularly known as Mohammad Ghori, the loyal and trusted slave Qutubuddin Aibak attained liberty through a letter of freedom against a large fee and declared his succession. With the declaration of the Sultan-hood, he became the top authority, and informally laid the foundation of the slave dynasty. He announced Delhi (Mehrauli) as his capital city. Thus, it was in 1206 that Delhi became the capital of the Delhi Sultanate, and it was with the foundation of the slave dynasty that Delhi was called a city.

Inscriptions of the eleventh and twelfth Centuries

The developments around the city during the eleventh and twelfth centuries can be highlighted through numerous inscriptions. The inscriptions of these centuries are mainly in Sanskrit. Historian Pushpa Prashad has collected an impressive catalogue of various Sanskrit inscriptions from the early medieval centuries in her work.[3] The Palam Baoli inscription categorically mentions, 'The land of Hariyanaka was first enjoyed by the Tomaras and then by the Chauhans. It is now ruled by the Saka kings.' The date of the Palam Baoli inscription is VS 1333/1274AD, and this was the heyday of the Delhi Sultanate. The names of the city in the inscription are Dhillipura and Yoginipura. The Sarban stone inscription of VS 1384/1327AD also provides a similar kind of description.[4] Interestingly, it differentiates between Dhillika and Indraprastha. According to this inscription, Delhi was nearly 10 km away from Indraprastha. Thus, it can be said that Dhilli is the city that was founded in the eighth century, and it was this city that was going through a lot of upheavals during the early medieval centuries. Indraprastha was a different site altogether. The site of Indraprastha was located around the present-day Purana Qila. Various excavations conducted at this site indicate constant human habitations and activities at the site of the Purana Qila until the coming of the Mughals.

The notes of various British officials and poets also confirm the introduction and derivation of the name Dhilli, prior to

---

[3]Pushpa Prasad, *Sanskrit Inscriptions of Delhi Sultanate 1191–1526*, Oxford University Press, New Delhi, 1990.

[4]B.R. Mani, *Delhi Threshold of the Orient: Studies in the Archaeological Investigations*, Aryan Book International, New Delhi, 1997, p.2.

the coming of the Ghurid invasion. The recordings in Henry Elliot's work[5] and later by Colonel James Tod confirm that Delhi was first ruled by the Tomars, then the Chauhans, and finally by the Mughals and Pathans, as recorded by Edward Thomas.[6]

With the coming of the Mohammedan rulers, a regular tradition of chronological historical writing was established. Writing history became a highly-paid job and the historians were considered as authentic voices. A large variety of the literature, including chronicles, diaries, biographies, memoirs, travelogues, *T'arikh* (history/historiography), *T'warikh* (plural of *T'arikh*) and *T'azkirat* (memorandum/ admonition) became available. Some of the earliest famous historians were Al-Biruni, Ziauddin Barani, Uthbi, Hasan Nizami, Juzjani, Amir Khusro, Ibn Battuta, and Shams-i-Siraj. Although these authors made extensive contributions to the tradition of historical writing, their writings did not make the reconstruction of history easy. At times, they even failed to provide the essential matter required to narrate the past. Yet, they provided enough evidences to locate, associate, relate and co-relate contemporary events, and are continuously helping to understand the effects that these actions had on the socio-political environment of the city in those times.

---

[5]Henry Elliot, *Memoirs on the History, folk-lore, and Distribution of the Races of the North Western Provinces of India: Being an Amplified Edition of the Original Supplemental Glossary of Indian Terms*, John Beames (ed.), Trubner & co., London, 1869, p.294.
[6]Edward Thomas, *The Chronicles of the Pathan Kings of Delhi (Illustrated by Coins Inscriptions and Other Aniquarian Remains)*, Trubner, London, 1871, p.55.

An Imperial City

The city of Delhi attained the status of an imperial city during the tenth century, and the same status continues with this city even today. In this long journey of around 1,500 years, the city has revived itself many a time. The multiple political and cultural collapses could never uproot the spirit of the city nor could they stop the city and its inhabitants from coming back. Surprisingly, the city ingrained multi-effects, ranging from political experiences to cultural shifts, social assimilations, and territorial expansions from each political and cultural jolt and shock it received. Gradually, all of India has found representation within this imperial city, and it is today multi-lingual and multi-cultural, with a vast diverse social setting. The consistent historical layering, assimilation and constant social fusion has made the nature of the city truly cosmopolitan. The political capital city of India holds many cities within itself with all its diversities intact.

Historically, it is evident that from 3000 BC onwards up until the nineteenth century, Delhi has housed numerous dynasties and many cities (see Table 1).

TABLE 1
Overview of Delhi from Prehistoric Times

City	Established in	Ruler
Indraprastha	3500 BC	Indra
Surajkund	9th century	Tomar Dynasty
Lalkot	1052	Tomar Dynasty ruler, Anangpal
Durg Rai Pithora	1180	Prithviraj Chauhan

Siri	1303	Alauddin Khilji
Tughlaqabad	1320	Ghiyasuddin Tughlaq
Jahanpanah	1325	Muhammud bin Tughlaq
Firozabad	1354	Firoz Shah Tughlaq
Shergarh/Purana Qila	1530s	Sher Shah Suri
Dinpanah	1545	Humayun
Shahjahanabad	Construction began in 1638 and was completed in 1649	Shah Jahan
Lutyens' Delhi	Declared capital in 1911	British

However, the foundation of all the cities of Delhi mentioned in Table 1 was not a peaceful process. The history of the city is soaked in the blood of many ambitious, politically active and even innocent masses. A noted author states, 'Destruction is in its foundation and blood is in its soil. It has seen the fall of many a glorious kingdom, and listened to the groans of birth. It is symbol of life and death, and revenge is its nature.'[7] I aside on the nature of this city, but cannot agree that it is indeed a city of revenge. It can be asserted that modern Delhi, or New Delhi, that we know of today, attained its name during the ancient times. During the medieval period, it gained popularity as Dilli. At all times, it was a space of historical ups and downs, even then it was aspired for by many. It houses many distant identities that were contributions made by various foreign and indigenous heritages over a long period of time.

The area of Mehrauli is known as the first city of Delhi. In Ancient India, this place had many temples, which were

---

[7] Ahmed Ali, *Twilight in Delhi*, Oxford University Press, London, 1966, p.2.

dedicated to the sects of *vaishanavism* and Jainism. Most of these were huge structures with large pillared halls. After defeating the Chauhan king Prithviraj, the sultan of Ghazni pulled down twenty-seven temples. He also built the Qubbat-ul-Islam, the first mosque in northern India for the army of faithful soldiers who came with Shahabuddin Ghori. The fading inscriptions, disfigured and demolished figurines of the temples have withstood the test of time and whisper about the unexplored folds of contemporary growth. The columns, pillars and shafts of the temples were reused with the modifications as per Islamic principles to construct the mosque and its surroundings. According to S. Rangacharya, the Qubbat-ul-Islam was originally a Vishnu *mandir* that was reconstructed into a mosque when Prithviraj lost Delhi to Ghori.[8] D.S. Triveda's work states, 'Some ten inscriptions in the Nagari script can be read on the Qutub Minar. They enlist the kings who repaired it at different epochs in history. They are Prithviraj, Malikadian, Govindpala, Alladian, Mohammad Shah, Firoz Shah, etc'.[9] Further, he asserts that the twelve sides of the tower represent the twelve zodiac signs and the seven storeys are symbolic of the seven heavens.[10] The *Yamunastambha* (pillar of Yamuna) as described by Maithalisarana Gupta in his *Bharata Bharati* has also been considered the base of the

---

[8]Staff writer, 'Hindu Temples of Delhi', *The Statesman,* Calcutta, 14 September 1958. Cf. D.S. Triveda, *Visnudhvaja or Qutb Manar*, The Chowkhamba Sanskrit Studies, Vol. XXIV, Chowkhamba Sanskrit Series Office, Varanasi, 1962, p.246.

[9]D.S. Triveda, *Visnudhvaja or Qutb Manar*, The Chowkhamba Sanskrit Studies, Vol. XXIV, Chowkhamba Sanskrit Series Office, Varanasi, 1962, p.243.

[10]Ibid., p.247.

Qutub Minar. In a pamphlet from 1913, AD, Kanwar Sain of Lahore also confirmed the Qutub Manar (Minar) to the Hindu rulers of India.[11] It is interesting to note that Timur was so astonished to see the great mosque and its minar in 1398 that he got its sketch made, and took it with him to Samarkand.[12] He also pointed out that it was originally an observatory tower known as Vishnudhvaja,[13] and the absence of a shadow of the minar on 23 June each year is a testament to this fact.[14] A similar kind of presence at Jantar Mantar— popularly known as Misra Yantra—is also an indication of the southern precession. Both the towers highlight southern precession, 'which is some five degree north of the Tropic of Cancer or Karkarekha'.[15] Thus, the construction of the pillar as per the Hindu astrological principles provides a clear insight into historical events, and indicates to the past purpose of this tower.

Mehrauli can be considered as the oldest of Delhi's cities in terms of the monumental remains. The thriving capital of the Tomar and Chauhan dynasties became the Dar-ul Khilafat of the slave dynasty in the thirteenth century. Its congested lanes and crumbling ruins are the threads connecting history and modernity. In the true sense, the living and the dead are rubbing against each other, the dead and the alive are in neck-and-neck competition to mark their existence in the

---

[11]D.S. Triveda, *Visnudhvaja or Qutb Manar*, The Chowkhamba Sanskrit Studies, Vol. XXIV, Chowkhamba Sanskrit Series Office, Varanasi, 1962, p.243.
[12]Ibid., p.147.
[13]Ibid., p.148 and p.153.
[14]Ibid., p.148.
[15]Ibid.

oldest city of Delhi. Some scholars have tried to describe the
religious diversity of Mehrauli's monuments from the rocky
Qila Rai Pithora to the *dargah* of Khwaja Qutbuddin Bakhtiyar
Kaki, Hauz-i Shamshi and Zafar Mahal. Each monument is the
structure of a living memory for an era that has dissolved in
the underbelly of history. The stones and bricks of Mehrauli
are soaked in the sights and sounds of a bygone era. The
reflections and the illuminations of the Sufi *dargahs*, mosques,
temples and Buddhist monasteries are the voices that need
to be heard before they are flattened by anyone trying to aim
for a state with a uniform population. The enchanting historic
city of Delhi is hypnotizing due to its cultural heritage. All
these monuments shape Delhi from an ordinary settlement
to an imperial city.

Chronologically, the next city of Delhi was Siri. The
city of Siri was found by Allaudin Khilji in 1303. This was a
walled city planned as part of a defence mechanism against
the Mongols. It was oval in shape. The Hauz Khas complex
around the citadel was made to meet the water requirements
for the city. This city was also known as Dar-ul-Khilafat which
means the seat of the Caliphate. The city of Firoz Shah was
Firozabad, today known as Firoz Shah Kotla. Presently, it
houses a popular cricket ground. The Topra Pillar of the third
century BC was erected by the Mauryan emperor, Ashoka.
It was pulled out from its original location at Topra Kalan
in Pong Ghati of Yamunanagar, in present-day Haryana, and
was brought to Delhi under the orders of Firoz Shah Tughlaq.
It was then re-erected in the Firoz Shah Kotla at its present
location in 1356. The Jami Mosque is still visible and in use
inside the premises of the fort. This mosque is a fine example
of Tughlaq architecture. The Chhaburja Mosque is located in

the northern ridge of Delhi, and was a *shikargah*, or a hunting palace, of Firoz Shah. This mosque has two floors with long corridors running around the central pillared prayer hall, and small canopies along the central dome, which adorns the top of the mosque. Many *sarais*, along with water arrangements, were also built for the comfort of travellers, mainly traders, who passed through the city. During the fourteenth century, these efforts made this city a centre of attraction and many sections of society aspired to secure some space in this city.

Asian capital cities were often ruled in such a way that they became symbols of power and influence. Their rulers extended in nearly all directions in order to attain a centre for the capital and protect it from all sides. These cities became the 'sovereign cities', and were miniature empires in themselves. Similarly, Shahjahanabad, the imperial Old Delhi, became a sovereign city. The markets around the city expanded day and night. The Red Fort served as the seat of power. Around the fort, huge markets of varied natures came up and the prolific expansions of the market spaces made this city a much sought-after economic hub. The glamour of Chandni Chowk was known in distant places, and it was a market that supplied nearly everything, from the sword to the needle. The most intricate and luxuriant of goods from around the globe were easily visible at the Mughal Bazaar of Chandni Chowk. The grandeur of the market even attracted royal personalities. It was the most bustling shopping space of the seventeenth and the eighteenth centuries, and one that catered to necessities, rarities and luxuries. Even today, the busy marketplaces have the look of medieval times. The only missing items are perhaps the riches, rarities, intricate luxuries collected from across the globe and the delicacy of the language that was used by the shop owners in the olden days. The market today is a storehouse of wholesale supplies, and holds a special status as a bazaar meant for wedding shoppers. Interestingly, even today, people from parts of Haryana, western Uttar Pradesh (UP) and certainly most of Delhi are dependent on Chandni Chowk for their requirements of fabric and imitation designer clothing. Indeed, the medieval look and feel of the market has kept up with upcoming modern structures and technologies.

While the introduction of Delhi Metro has most certainly destroyed the set-up and the composition of the market, it failed to change much of its internal layout and lane system. The lanes were named after the items that were sold in them. Luckily, even today the same pattern continues. For example, shops in Kinari Bazaar sell various kinds of laces. This lane gets its name from the word *kinari*, meaning lace. Similarly, the Paranthawali Gali is the place to visit in order to satisfy one's appetite for all sorts of *paranthas*, or flatbreads. Indeed, food, clothes and jewellery are the main attractions of Chandni Chowk. The variety of sweets, food and clothes available at this market caters to nearly all sections of society—from millionaires to rickshaw pullers. All modes of transport, from the ancient bullock carts to the modern-day metro rail system, criss-cross each other in this space without contradiction. In fact, even when one mode overtakes the other, it is more with astonishment than anger. Many even admire and aspire to access some of these modes of transport. Bullock carts are prominently visible and are mainly used for transporting load from one corner of the walled city to another. The bullocks are mainly of *Nagori* breed with overgrown horns. The rickshaws, however, are the most popular medium for commuting through the narrow lanes of the walled city.

Motor cars were introduced in India during the nineteenth century. An Indianized version of the motor car was introduced in the walled city during the twentieth century, which was extremely efficient in transporting people from one destination to the other. In no time it became an acclaimed mode of transportation for a majority of the population from east Delhi, who were regularly commuting to the walled city for their requirements of bread and butter. This is the *Phat-Phat Sewa*—literally translated as a 'fast service'. Besides this, the Delhi Transport Corporation (DTC) buses are also used for ferrying a large number of visitors, travellers and workers into this ancient city of Shah Jahan. The visible and loud presence of the Indian Railways can also be appreciated at the Old Delhi Railway Station that has served as an imperial hoarding and inter-connecting station during the nineteenth and twentieth centuries. The twenty-first century brought with it the metro rail which reached Old Delhi in late 2005, and within a decade it has become unequivocally the most effective and sought-after mode of transportation to the mesmerizing Chandni Chowk.

The Sish Ganj Gurudwara, Fatehpuri Mosque and Sunahri Masjid have a magnetic effect on history enthusiasts. Indeed, it is in the lanes that house these magnificent buildings, and in their occupants live the past of Delhi in its present. The Haveli of Ghalib is yet another attraction for students of literature and history. Although the population of the old walled city is struggling for basic amenities, none of them are able to part from the charm of this city and do not wish to move out from these congested areas.

The Jama Masjid holds the believers in its spacious and

extensive lap five times each day along with the special prayers said on Id-ul Fitar (Meethi Eid) and Id-ul Zuha (Bakri Eid). Meena Bazaar serves as a shopping destination for all groups of people who are residents of the walled city, irrespective of their religions, castes and classes. Shops selling a variety of sweetmeats, clothes and accessories encroach upon the each other, but a little hackling is sufficient to settle the matters mutually, hence the popular saying *Dilli dil waalo ki*. Often, the inhabitants engage vehemently to capture resources and to secure a share in the sources of income, save profits and to cut larger margins in their infrequent but sporty incomes. At times these struggles culminate in brawls, but none are carried beyond a robust engagement, and often end amicably over a cup of tea along with some *matthi*, or perhaps some *suji*, when there is an extra bit of generosity involved!

Delhi is equally famous for its street food and cuisines, such as Mughlai and Punjabi, as well as food from other states, and enjoys the reputation of having an all-embracing food culture. In fact, most visitors, workers, shoppers and employers survive on these mouth-watering street food items, which are all a specialty of Chandni Chowk. Many other localities have also developed local eating joints, which have become famous over time.

Lutyens' Delhi is the name given to the central area of Delhi, and it is named after the British architect, Edwin Lutyens, who was the brain behind the architectural designs and buildings constructed in British India. The popular buildings designed by Luytens along with his team of architects include the Rashtrapati Bhawan, India Gate, Rajpath, Viceregal Lodge, Janpath and Connaught Place. The impressive imperial buildings were part of the grandeur and glamour displayed by

British officials.

Despite going through such harsh struggles and many demolitions, Delhi holds a unique aura as a city. Being a historic city without parallel, it culturally contains relatively dominant new dwellers. Another city that holds glamour like Delhi is Kashi-Banaras (Varanasi). While people come to Delhi to build their lives, Varanasi is the chosen one for attaining death. Technically, both the cities stand counter to each other. It is interesting to note here that most people from the Islamic dynasties aspired to build their tombs so they could be remembered in history.

The present city of Delhi is an umbrella cast over the various cities of the ancient, medieval and pre-modern times. Culturally and geographically, the combination of Mehrauli, Siri, Feroz Shah Kotla, Tughlaqabad, Indraprastha, Dinapanha, Purana Qila, Shahjahanabad, Luytens' Delhi and its environs shaped present-day Delhi.

Delhi as a capital city is not devoid of legends and stories, and it is surrounded by many mysteries. The Partition of India in 1947, into the two nations of India and Pakistan, made Delhi a centre of hope for the already broken refugees coming from the newly-formed Pakistan. Partition labelled Delhi as a refugee city. Prior to this, Delhi also housed many refugees during the medieval centuries; the city accommodated them all, and these immigrants became natives in the course of time. None of them were known as refugees. But, this label cannot be applied to modern times, as the modern state truly failed to incorporate them.

The most popular immigration was during the late thirteenth and early fourteenth centuries when Mongol invasions took a heavy toll on life and property in Central

Asian cities such as Mosul, Baghdad, Nishapur, etc. The Mongol threat acted as a push for a large populations and Delhi became a safe haven for them. The attraction of Delhi was due to its economic stability and peace. Scholars, artists, painters and many other people skilled in craft and literature were attracted to Delhi, as the moth is attracted to light. This immigration has benefitted the city in the long run as much of the art and craft of Central Asia travelled down to this economic hub, and flourished under different patrons. Separation is always a painful experience, but luckily, those painful narrations didn't haunt the refugees of the medieval times, and rarely do we encounter any literature that depicts this. Unfortunately, the great Partition of 1947 and its memories are beds with sharp thorns, and it is rare to find people who can hold back their tears as they share their stories. The memories of loss and destabilization are soul-stirring. The sense of loss still shrouds most of them and one must empathize with them. Presently, the concept of the National Capital Region (NCR) is at work, and this is a mechanism to adjust and accommodate the never-resting incoming population that comes to Delhi for livelihood or education.

The city is unique in its gossip as well as its tell-tale culture. Nearly all the *kuchas*, *galis*, *havelis*, forts, mosques, temples, *khanqahas*, *dargahas* and gurudwaras of this city have tales, anecdotes, folklores and stories around them. Many of the monuments lack written stories, but the moment we scratch the surface, numerous anecdotes, myths and gossips pour out profusely. The stories of the *jinns* are available around the Sufi hospices. Similarly, the temples serve as centres to nurture myths. Many self-appointed local guides narrate historical tales with a strong sense of authenticity. In all this, Delhi provides a healthy feed to all its curious investigators, travellers, visitors and myriad tourists. Thus, the task that comes with this received information is that of sorting, believing, feeding and saving memories. Further, the retainer takes back with himself some solitary information and experiences that don't relate to the history of Delhi, but definitely form a part of the memory and landscape within which they are associated with the city, and which, over time, become a part of the history that is created in this city every day. Overall, it can be said that this city is loaded with diverse interactions, which vary a lot in nature.

It can be said that the city of Delhi is holding much of India's history and its social assimilations, cultural interactions and political journeys. The city stands as an evidence of India's culture of acceptance and peaceful co-existence. Most of the struggles were part of historical processes and were inevitable in the contemporary times. Its culture was complimented by many of the civilizations, and Delhi has acted as a basket and received all the interactions prospectively and progressively. This work is, however, not just another book on Delhi. It links the monuments, and many neighbourhoods of the city, with the events of history. Most of the contents are related to the medieval period, though the readers will find scattered references to the dim ancient past peeping out of the archaeological crusts that have been explored in recent years. The character of the city shines in its biography and can be felt in its monuments. The vastness of its history at times glorifies the past and we find that it looms on the dark sides. With all its developments, the city continues to be a seat of imperial power from the tenth century onwards and still hold the crown with its ever-expanding aesthetic glamour and power. This work aims to write a short biography of the city with which I fell in love during my post-graduation days, and I sincerely hope it will serve as the book of the season.

1

THE IMPERIAL CITY

Treacherous games have been played under its skies, and its earth has tasted blood of kings. But still it is jewel of the eye of the world, still it is centre of attraction.[1]

Delhi has been a capital city for many kingdoms and empires. The successive waves of incursions from the North West Frontier and the internecine wars have caused the city many ruins and pushed it into numerous resettlements. Rapid development, along with concentration of resources and political power, has created this urban conglomerate. The concentration of political power in Delhi has also shifted the status of the city immensely, and it has turned into a place which is impregnated with resources and full of opportunities. All these features have made it a protected and majestic city.

Nomenclature of Delhi

The ancient history of Delhi is shrouded in mystery. The absence of any mention of the city's name, Delhi, in early medieval literature helps to indicate that during ancient

---

[1] Ahmed Ali, *Twilight in Delhi*, Oxford University Press, London, 1966, p.2. Many travellers, authors and kings have defined the city of Delhi in most fascinating ways. My favourite regarding the imperial city is the book by Ali.

times, Delhi was not a prominent city, and didn't have much economic significance. Most of the medieval records were used by the British officials as a source for compiling the history of Delhi. The records and reports compiled by various British officials indicate a complete absence of human activity in the vicinity of Delhi in ancient times. Even if anyone tried to indicate any activities in the region, it was doubtful and lacked any verifiable data. According to Carr, 'We are still treading on the speculative grounds...when Delhi succeeded to Indraprastha.'[2] The British Officer of Bengal Civil Service, Henry Elliot, further writes in his *Memoirs on History*, 'It is stated that the name of the imperial city of Delhi (correctly Dilli, Dihli and Dhilli) is derived from the word Dahal, which means quicksand or quagmire. It derived this name because the ground on which it was built was so loose that the tents could not be fixed in it.'[3]

Roots of Delhi's Grandeur

In his extensive work, H.C. Fanshawe provides an illuminating paragraph on Delhi and its imperial status. He writes:

> The present Moghal city of Delhi, which should properly be known as Shahjahanabad, is the most northern and most modern of a number of capitals and fortresses constructed on the above plain between 700 and 1550 of

---

[2]Stephen Carr, *The Archaeology and Monumental Remains of Delhi*, The Civil and Military Gazette and Station Press, Shimla, 1876, p.10.

[3]Henry Elliot, *Memoirs on the History, Folk-lore, and Distribution of the Races of the North Western Provinces of India*, Vol. 2, ed. John Beames, Trubner & co., London, 1869, pp. 293–94.

the Christian era, from the Lal Kila of Rai Pithora at the Kutab Minar eleven miles south-west of Shahjahanabad to the Jahannuma palace and quarter, built by Firoz Shah Tughlak on the ridge, slightly in advance of the Moghal capital.[4]

According to Fanshawe, these old cities from north to south were as follows:

1. Firozabad of Firoz Shah Tughlak (*c*.1360), adjoining modern Delhi on the south
2. Indrapat of Humayun and Sher Shah (on the site of a still older, but doubtless small city), two miles south of modern Delhi (*c*.1540)
3. Siri (now Shahpur), four miles south-west of Indrapat (*c*.1300)
4. Jahanpanah, or the space between Siri and Old Delhi, which became gradually occupied, and was ultimately connected by walls with the cities north and south of it (*c*.1330)
5. Old Delhi, or the Fort of Rai Pithora, the original Delhi of the Pathan invaders in the twelfth century, and containing the Kutab Minar, three miles to the south-east of Siri (1150–1350)
6. Tughlakabad, four miles south-east of Siri, and five miles east of Old Delhi, built by Muhammad Tughlak Shah (*c*.1320)

The author further adds that there were 'some unimportant and still more short-lived capitals at Kilokhri, one mile south

---

[4]H.C. Fanshawe, *Delhi: Past and Present*, John Murray, London, 1902.

of the tomb of the Emperor Humayun, and Mubarikabad, a little further south again, of which there are no remains in the present day.'[5]

Gordon Risley Hearn was a captain at Royal Engineers, and an associate of the Institute of Royal Engineeers. In his book *The Seven Cities of Delhi*,[6] he identifies Delhi as the Rome of India.[7] Hearn states that Delhi has been an imperial city of India for seven hundred years.[8] He further notes, 'Delhi was first occupied somewhere about the year AD 300, that the city was afterwards abandoned, for some cause which we do not know, and that it was not re-peopled until AD 1052 after the final retirement of Mahmud of Ghazni.'[9]

While Risley, Carr and Elliot wrote about Delhi, they did so without turning to archaeological evidences. They collected much of the information either from ethnographical works or from manuscripts and the histories written by different authors during medieval times.

To discover Delhi's ancient past, a careful balance of archaeological evidence and an understanding of literature is needed. This is a difficult task as a scholar has to distinguish between information, evidence and multi-layered myths.

---

[5]H.C. Fanshawe, *Delhi: Past and Present*, John Murray, London, 1902.

[6]Gordon Risley Hearn, *The Seven Cities of Delhi*, W. Thacker & Co., London, 1906. This book was divided in three parts. The first section provides details of the seven cities and their monuments. The second section highlights the archaeology and architecture. The final part gives an insight into the history of the city from the time of Muhammadan conquest till the early twentieth century.

[7]Ibid., p.1.

[8]Ibid.

[9]Ibid, p.73.

Archaeology is the only method which is able to reel the underground and unwind concealed layers of history.

Early History of Delhi

The early historic period of Delhi is jewelled with many inscriptions, which are supported by archaeological excavations. An insight into these literary and inscriptional sources helps to reach some conclusions at least, even if they don't offer definite answers. The main sources to study the early historic period in Delhi are the archaeological evidences of the Northern Black Polished Ware (NBPW). This type of pottery was generally made on a fast wheel as is evident from its fine finish quality. The timeline of NBPW is very vast, ranging from the sixth century BC to the first century BC. A large collection of terracotta figurines have been found at the Purana Qila excavation site. Some dishes have stamped figures of elephants. The punch-mark and cast copper coins also found at the site indicate to their being NBPW. Terracotta ring wells are also significant identifications of the NBPW, which were created using sophisticated technology. All these collectively indicate the presence of vibrant human activity in and around Purana Qila.

Material evidences of the NBPW also overlap in the Mauryan phase. The Major Rock Edicts and Minor Rock Edicts of Ashoka, along with the inscriptions on the Pillar, provide immense data. These edicts form a substantial base to comment on the activities of this period. The inscriptions of the Mauryan emperor Ashoka are scattered throughout the length and breadth of the country. In the absence of a neat historical writing tradition and scattered literary evidences, these inscriptions are important contributions as they form the base of ancient historical writing, and are crucial for understanding the social, cultural, political and economic circumstances of the times.

Arthashastra of Kautliya and *Indica* of Megasthenes are two significant texts and have been constant guides for students of Ancient India. Megasthenes was a Greek historian and an ambassador of Seleucus-I Nicator in the court of Chandragupta at Pataliputra. Although the original copy of the book *Indica* was lost, and is not available in an intact form, it has been recompiled using scattered and fragmented information available in other contemporary sources. Interestingly, the compiled work (taken from Greek and Latin works) provides details of the various places visited by Megasthenes during his stay in India. A full description of the region of Punjab, which was webbed by five rivers, was also provided by our diplomat historian, as this was the region he crossed, while travelling to Pataliputra. This shows that even Megasthenes didn't visit the Delhi area during his stay in India. Similarly, the *Arthashastra*, which is a treatise on statecraft, political system, economic policy, social arrangements and military strategy written in Sanskrit, is also silent on Delhi. Hence, to narrate the ancient past of Delhi, scholars have to deeply depend on archaeological evidences which help to cull out substantial and authentic information. The rock edict of Bahapur in the Sriniwaspuri area of Delhi is very close to the temple of the goddess Kali in Kalkaji, and is the only rock edict in Delhi from the Ashokan times. The inscription was noticed by Shri Jang Bahadur Singh, a contractor of Delhi, who came upon the inscribed rock when it was about to be blasted away for the development of a residential colony. Archaeologists

B.M. Pande and M.C. Joshi visited the spot of the inscription along with Shri Singh and were able to identify the inscription as one of the Minor Rock Edicts of Ashoka.[10] The text of the inscription is as follows:

> Devanampiya (His Majesty) saith (thus). (It has been) more than two and a half years that I became a lay devotee, (but) I did not exert myself greatly (in the cause of Dhamma). It was more than a year after my joining the samgha, and I exerted myself greatly. (Consequently) I could unite with the gods the mortals (who had so far been) un-unified with gods during this period in Jambudvipa (India). (This is the outcome) of exertion. (And) it is not to be accomplished only by the men of importance, (but) even lowly-placed ones if they exert can attain heaven. For this purpose this proclamation (is being made) (so that) both the low and the high (poor and rich) may exert (in the cause of Dhamma) and (those living on and beyond the borders of my kingdom) may also know about this. Let this exertion be ever-enduring and this objective will also be immensely increasing (certainly) to the extent of one-and-a-half fold.

The offerings made to the goddess are usually meat and liquor. She is considered the wild goddess, who has incarnated to demolish the demons. The teachings of the Bahapur inscription are mainly based on the virtues of *ahimsa*, or non-violence. It might have been an effort to introduce the virtue of *ahimsa*

---

[10]M.C. Joshi and B.M. Pande, 'A Newly Discovered Inscription of Asoka at Bahapur, Delhi', *The Journal of the Royal Asiatic Society of Great Britain and Ireland*, No. 3/4 (October 1967), pp.96–98.

to the devotees, who were engaging in the sacrificial rituals to please the goddess, who was believed to feed on flesh and drink blood.

Regarding the edicts found in Kalkaji, D.C. Sircar, an archeologist of global repute, notes, 'This shows that there was a flourishing city in the vicinity of the inscription during Ashoka's time and that it was intended for the people of the said city.'[11] This intervention was crucial not only to establish the tradition of writing Indian history but also to put forth the idea that the history of Delhi doesn't start with the medieval period. In fact, it had a much more complex and intricate history and social life before the much lambasted medieval invasions.

History has witnessed Delhi as the imperial city of many kingdoms. Archaeologists have dedicated the archaeological findings at Purana Qila to the Mahabharata's city of Indraprastha. The destruction of Hastinapur by a flooding of the river Ganga was also proven by remote-sensing. The destruction of the cities led to migration from these areas. On several occasions, there was resettlement that helped to cope with the unpredictable mutations of the time, and this has been a survival technique throughout history.

The second century is dedicated to tribal movements in Central Asia, which led to the migration of many groups into the Indian subcontinent. Many Greeks, Bactrians and Persians came to India at this time. Later, the Shakas, Parthians and the Kushanas entered India and carved out their empires. There was

---

[11]D.C. Sircar, 'New Delhi Inscription of Asoka', in *Readings in History, Delhi: Ancient India*, (ed.) Upinder Singh, Social Science Press, New Delhi, 2006, pp.126–27.

an influx of a large variety of ethnic groups who had more than just political significance and influence. These interactions led to the emergence of various cultural dimensions. The Gandhara School of Art is a remarkable example of this, where Buddhist themes from India were incorporated into the Graeco-Roman styles that flourished under the Kushana rulers during the third century AD. The collapse of the Kushanas led to the emergence of many smaller monarchical and non-monarchical states in northern India. The popular tribal republics of Arjunayanas and Yaudheyas in the surrounding areas of Delhi might have also exercised some control over Delhi. These tribes and their states were not able to make a mark in history. But their inscriptional evidences, literary collections and archaeological remains highlight the turbulent political history of the region, continuity in its settlements and occupations, and provide a picture of an area expanding as urban centres and flourishing in trade activities.

The etymological derivation of Delhi has been suggested by Stephen Carr from the name of Raja Dalip.[12] But, in the very next paragraph, Carre notes, '...the ground of his opinion don't appear to me altogether satisfactory....'[13] Even Cunningham didn't trust these derivations. Instead, he credits Anang Pal II for the establishment and habitation of Delhi between *c.* 1052 and *c.* 1060. His city was around the Lal Kot area, near Mehrauli. The Palam Baoli inscription dated AD 1274 categorically states, 'The land of Hariyanka was first enjoyed by the Tomaras and then by the Chauhanas. It is now

---

[12]Stephen Carr, *The Archaeology and Monumental Remains of Delhi*, Ludhiana, 1876, p.11.
[13]Ibid., pp.12–13.

ruled by the Saka kings.[14] The name given to the city was
Dhillipura and the alternative suggested was Yoganipura. Thus,
in a nutshell it can be said that Lal Kot and its surroundings
were known as Dhilli or Dhillika after the foundation of the
city by the Tomars. B.R. Mani, a noted historian of ancient
Delhi, suggests,

> The evidences of the 8th–9th century sculptures [and]
> inscriptions—including iron pillar inscription and
> architectural fragments from the Qutub Archeological
> area suggests that during the Gupta, Post Gupta and
> Pratihara periods, the area comprised a temple complex
> and was called Yoginipura and only later it became
> famous as Dhilli or Dhillika.[15]

Further, he expands to distinguish between Dhilli and
Indraprastha. Thus, he clearly establishes Lal Kot as the earliest
fort in Delhi that was constructed in the middle of the eleventh
century by Anang Pal II, the Tomar ruler. The Rajput phase of
Delhi history began with the coming of the Tomar dynasty. As
per the historical evidences deciphered and located till date,
Anang Pal II was the undisputed ruler of Delhi from *c.*1050
onwards till the Chauhans took it over in *c.*1155. The two
Rajput clans who were associated closely with Delhi were the
Tomars and Chauhans of Ajmer (Rajasthan). The writings of
Rajput histories have depended much on bardic oral traditions
and *Raso* literature, which are eulogies highlighting the brave

---

[14]Pushpa Prasad, *Sanskrit Inscriptions of Delhi Sultanate 1191–1526*,
Oxford University Press, Delhi, 1990, pp.3–15.

[15]B.R. Mani, 'Excavations at Lal Kot 1991–92 and Further Explorations
in Delhi', *Puratattva*, No. 22 (1991–92), pp.75–87.

acts of rulers. Many a time, traditional bardic lores were recorded as inscriptions. A twelfth century inscription found at Bijholia in Rajasthan points out that Dhillika was conquered by King Vigraharaja. Some other inscriptions found around Delhi also associate and establish links to the history of this city. The Palam Baoli inscription of the thirteenth century reads, 'Uddhara, a householder of Dhilli, constructed this *baoli* [step well]'. This inscription further brings to light the chronology of the Tomar and Chauhan dynasties as stated previously.

Another name of the city as per this inscription is Yoginipura. An inscription from the thirteenth century found in the Sonipat district of present-day Haryana records the construction of a well in the village of Suvarnaprastha, and states that Dhillika in Hariyana was ruled by the Tomaras, Chauhans and Shakas, respectively. The Sarban village inscription from the fourteenth century records four stanzas about the past of Dhilli. Another fourteenth century inscription found at Naraina, in west Delhi, also refers to a great province of Hariyana, wherein the city of Dhilli lay. Thus, it may be said that the name Dhilli or Dhillika were much in use from the eleventh century onwards, and it was also the capital of different ruling classes.

Many inscriptions prove that the Chauhana king Vigraharaja IV took Delhi from the Tomars. The inscriptions which speak about his success are the Delhi-Topra inscription, the inscription of Bijholia in Rajasthan, Palam Baoli inscription and the Sonepath inscription. The Rai Pithora Garh is associated with Prithviraj Chauhan, who is one amongst the most revered Rajputs in Indian history. The struggles of Muhammud Ghori and Prithviraj were eulogized by Chanderbardai, who was a Bhatt at the latter's court. This epic is known as *Prithviraj Raso*. Thus, it can be propounded that Prithviraj who got the kingdom as a successor, was ruling over Delhi during the twelfth century and laid the foundation of Rai Pithora Garh over Lal Kot. Besides these, as per the recorded opinion of noted scholar Sayyid Ahmad Khan, the first storey of the Qutub Minar was a 'Hindu monument' built during the time of Prithviraj Chauhan and subsequently the Turks added storeys to it. Anyone on a visit to the Qutub Minar can say that the first level shows evidence of stones that were placed at a later stage and there is an inscription of a bell-and-chain motif on the very first floor, which is typical of the Hindu temples. Additionally, the inscription on this pillar is similar to that of Qutubuddin Aibak, the first slave sultan of India. Also, Mu'izzuddin, who was the chief of the Islamic army, invaded Delhi and defeated Prithviraj Chauhan. It was his conquest over the temple area that led to the restructuring of the temple into a mosque. From these various facts, it can be argued that the first floor is Hindu in origin. There is nothing odd in the fact that epitaphs were inscribed over the idols. It is well today known that stones with the praises of King Rai Pithora were replaced with inscriptions in the name of Mohammedan kings and Quranic verses. Putting together these facts, it can be said with assertion that Rai Pithora was a fort and had a temple that was later converted into a mosque. More evidences from the Chauhan period over Delhi need to be located through excavations in order to arrive at a more appropriate version of facts.

Qila Rai Pithora was larger than Lal Kot as is evident from the fortification wall. The entire circuit is not traced but the identified fortification wall indicates that the wall of the fort was 5–6 metres thick and 18 metre in height, and had several gates, out of which only a few survive. This has been revealed by the excavation of 1957–58. An inscription of Qutubuddin Aibak over the eastern gate of the Quwwat-ul-Islam mosque states that it was built from the ruins of the twenty-seven temples.

Many Jain texts talk about the importance of Yoginipura and Dhilli. Yoginipura is the name of an ancient and medieval settlement. After the defeat of Prithviraj Chauhan, Qila Rai Pithora was occupied by the victorious Turks. The sultans of Delhi continued to rule from here till the early fourteenth century, until Alauddin Khalji built a new capital city in Delhi at Siri.[16] All these remains are fast losing their face value to urbanization and constant human activities in the areas. Therefore, it can be said that in order to know the ancient past of Delhi, excavations are the only authentic way forward, and a meticulous study of the ruins will help rewrite the history of Delhi.

Al-Biruni's Delhi

Al-Biruni came to India with the Ghaznavid invaders and continued to write in Arabic, or *Arbi*. Later, he learnt Sanskrit. The Gaznavids were a Persianate Muslim dynasty of Turkish mamluk origin, who ruled over a large part of Iran, Afghanistan and Transoxiana. The shift of Ghaznavid's base from Arabic to the Persian language was a result of the Ghazna–Lahore

---

[16]Upinder Singh, *Ancient Delhi*, second edition, Oxford University Press, New Delhi, 2010, p.99.

interaction.[17] Delhi was flourishing under the Chauhans when it was captured by the Mahmud of Ghor in 1192 after the Battle of Tarain. An interesting description of the Indian subcontinent and romanticized description of its richness by Al-Biruni signifies the wealth of India and its attraction amongst the various invaders. He states:

> [T]he Turkish invasions and conquests in North India were a *goldrush* stands out most glaringly. By all counts, the amount of booty in the form of bullion, gold and silver, and coins was staggering...next to money the Turkish slave element is conspicuously predominant in North India....[18]

The administrative institutions of the Delhi Sultanate evolved largely in Persian lands, and in many ways the Delhi court became a replica of the Sasanid Court. The slave king Balban resorted to the *darat-i-salatin-i-ajam*, which highlighted 'the lustre of the Persian kings...Persian–Sasanid tradition... completely transformed Islamic dominion...over wholesale in the Delhi Sultanate.'[19] Delhi rose to become the *Darul Khilafa*— abode of king/caliph—of the Sultan Qutubuddin Aibak and Iltutmish in the first decade of the thirteenth century. From Ghiyasuddin Balban onwards up to Khurram, Delhi was constantly evolving, and as many as nine cities evolved, which, in some point in time, became known by the name of Delhi.

---

[17]Al-Buruni, *Al-Hind: The Making of the Indo-Islamic World, Early Medieval India and Expansion of Islam, 7th–11th Centuries*, translated, Andre Wink, Vol. I, Oxford University Press, New Delhi, 1999, p.21.
[18]Ibid., p.23.
[19]Ibid., p.22.

Other popular establishments and independent projects that were made with the intention of developing a city but were not full-fledged cities were Mehrauli, Kilughari, Siri, Tughlaqabad, Jahanpanah, Firuzabad, Khirabad, Mubarakabad, Dinpanah (Humayun), Salimgarh or Rurgarh, Shergarh or Hazarat Delhi and Shahjahanabad. Today, all these constitute the city of Delhi.

The economy of early medieval India in the tenth and eleventh centuries was flourishing due to trade activities. The vast presence of coins as described in the literary sources indicates an upward movement in economic activities. The coins in use were *rupaka, suvarna, dinara, nishka, karshapana* and *pana*. The Kalacharis were the first to revive the gold coinage *c.*1015–40. They were followed by the Candellas rulers (*c.*1060–87) and the Tomars of Ajmer (1019–49); this was prior to the coming of Muslim rulers in north India.[20] The Arabic sources repeatedly mention the use of gold and silver coins by the kings of Al-Jurz (Gujarat or the Gurjara dominion), the *tatariya dirham*—each dirham weighs a dirham and half of the royal currency—and ingots of silver as the instruments of commercial exchange. Many of these coins continued to be in circulation under the early Muslim rulers in other parts of the subcontinent. But, in Delhi, most of the mints (if not all) were eventually converted from the coins of the Hindu rulers into coins with the names of the sultans stuck on them. Thus, it can be said that Delhi was a flourishing town when Islamic forces invaded and looted it. The immense wealth of the city and its capacity to generate constant revenue and wealth made

---

[20]Al-Buruni, *Al-Hind: The Making of the Indo-Islamic World, Early Medieval India and Expansion of Islam, 7th–11th Centuries*, translated, Andre Wink, Vol. I, Oxford University Press, New Delhi, 1999, p.300.

the looters desirous to hold it. 'Remonetization of the Hindu coinage but also of immobilized wealth, as we know, greatly strengthened the Muslim urban economy.'[21]

With the accession of new sultanates, Delhi was constantly expanding and becoming a living example of glory and power. With accession, each new sultan started building afresh the city and its complexes. But, this was done almost always after demolishing the existing structures, and willingly allowing a few to decay. According to H.C. Verma, the course of the decline of the old city and setting up of the new city was so much in trend,

> [that] Delhi lost much of its charm and glory and finally went into oblivion as a capital city when Sikander Lodi made Agra his *Darul Sultanat* in 1506 and it remained so till Shah Jahanrestored to Delhi its former position by laying the foundation of Shahjahanabad in AD 1639.[22]

The ever-expanding Delhi remained loyal to its needs. An interesting feature to note in the expansion of the building activities of the medieval era is that all constructions were on the north and the north-eastern side of the Purana Qila and were near the course of the river Yamuna, the only water source for the population of the imperial city. The architectural style of nearly all buildings and forts were as per Indo-Sasanian art. The aesthetics of the buildings improved

---

[21]Al-Buruni, *Al-Hind: The Making of the Indo-Islamic World, Early Medieval India and Expansion of Islam, 7th–11th Centuries*, translated, Andre Wink, Vol. I, Oxford University Press, New Delhi, 1999, p.302.

[22]H.C. Verma, 'Delhi', *Historic Delhi: Indian History Congress*, 52nd Session, 1992, pp.25–27.

with the introduction of Persian art. The state was engaging in a lot of building activities to expand its influence, and to extend protection to travellers who were forming the spine of the economic state. Throughout the year, merchants and traders used to travel in order to enhance business. Further, specialized transporters made transportation a regular activity throughout the length and breadth of the subcontinent.[23] The *sarais* were mainly outside the walled cities and were centres for offering facilities to the travellers. The services of the *sarais* were mainly availed by those individuals and groups who reached the city after sunset. Mosques also provided lodging facilities, and were used for prayer and other religious activities. They were mainly built to showcase the faith of the ruler and to demonstrate the significance of the religion. The *Kahnqas*, or the Sufi hospices, were also pivotal points of religious activities and served as a parallel platform for spreading the message of Islam. These structures are identical to contemporary structures. Today, the popular Sufi centres in the city include the Nizammuddin *dargah* and the *dargahs* of Mai Sahib, Baktiyar Kaki, Jamali Kamali, and others. All these centres started flourishing during the medieval era, and even today carry a lot of significance for sectarians and believers. The most popular *malfuzat*—written records of audiences and question-and-answer sessions of notable scholars or Sufis, providing historical context, teachings and attitudes, which are typically dated and presented in a chronological order— of the medieval times was that of Nizammuddin Awaliya. Prior to settling down at Ghiyaspur, Nizammuddin lived

---

[23]Manisha Choudhary, *Trade, Transport and Tanda: Shifting Identities of the Banjaras*, Manohar Books, Delhi, 2018.

at various places in Delhi. Ghiyaspur was a locality in the neighbourhood of Delhi, and it was chosen by Nizammuddin due to its distance from the noise and hustle of city life. The *malfuzat* was compiled and recorded by Amir Hasan Sijzi, who was a *murshid*, or disciple, of the *pir* Nizammuddin. These compilations were created after proper consultations and many rounds of discussions with Nizamuddin Awaliya. This collection became popular as *Faud-ul Fawad*. Nizamuddin was also a different type of Sufi saint as he never worked in the imperial arenas and was constantly challenging the sultans of Delhi. His truly abided by the credentials of the Chistiyya Order which encouraged living a humble life revolving around discussions of the Almighty, and away from lavish pursuits. He is the only Sufi saint who saw twelve sultans on the throne of Delhi. In fact, he was called a parallel sultan of Delhi, who ruled without the *taj* (crown), and so, was the *betaj badshah!*

2

TWINS: GLORY AND SINK

The glory and fame for which the city of Delhi is known today were attained during the medieval times. The buildings of the city, its markets and its residential layouts were the means to organize the city. The houses of the city of Mehrauli were built from stone and bricks, and the roofs were laid with wooden logs. The floors were paved using stone slabs. The city of Siri was a walled city and was mainly constructed to put up a defence mechanism in place, and to protect its inhabitants against Mongol invasion. The foundation of Siri was laid down in 1303 by Alauddin Khilji, who was the nephew and son-in-law of Jalaluddin Khilji. The ruins of the city wall and its structures can still be seen in the Siri Fort Asian Village Complex and the Siri Fort Auditorium. During the reign of Alauddin Khilji, the city of Delhi attained a cosmopolitan culture. It became home to a cluster of learned scholars, who were attracted to the safety and security that Delhi offered as well as the immense opportunities in reading and writing. The attraction of the scholars to the city of Delhi made for the popular proverb: 'Delhi is like a candle that attracts moths.' Besides being an able military general, Alauddin Khilji was also the first sultan to ensure regular supplies of necessities, mainly grains, to the city. This was done by collecting produce at the centres of production, and subsequently organizing the transportation of these diverse products by hiring the robust and well-equipped banjaras. These efficient banjaras were popularly known as *carvanis* during the medieval times. A noted historian testifies, 'The provisions were supplied to the city largely by 10,000 to 20,000 load-cattle per day under the control of the Naik.'[24] A proper lifting mechanism and regular supplies helped to ensure a better organization of the markets, which were classified into four categories. Price reforms were also undertaken along with the standardization of weights and measures. Alauddin Khilji introduced four markets: Galla Bazaar-Mandi for grains, a market for manufactured goods and imported commodities specially cloth (Sarai-e-Adal), a market for the sale of slaves and animals, and lastly, a general market. Other measures introduced include the appointment of a market controller who assisted with the anti-hoarding measures, daily reporting, state-run granaries and price-fixing. In addition to all these provisions, spies were also appointed to collect news from the markets. These spies reported the day-to-day activities of the markets directly and only to the sultan. Thus, with the efforts of Alauddin Khilji, Delhi attained the status of an economic hub, and was admired by all traders and merchants.

The city of Firoz Shah Tughlaq was Firozabad, and this was the first city with a different layout as it was divided into two complexes. The first was occupied by the royal personas (the royal building/royal apartments) and the second was the general city divided into wards or *mohallas* that were further extended and organized as *kuchas* (lanes) and cross-lanes. Firoz Shah patronized various mosques and water works

---

[24]H.C. Verma, 'Delhi', *Historic Delhi:* Indian History Congress, 52nd Session, 1992, pp.25–27.

which were mainly meant for the purpose of irrigation. Before him, other sultans too made efforts towards constructing various water reservoirs for public utilities. The popular and surviving examples of these include Hauz-i-Shamshi or Hauz-i-Sultani built by Iltutmish *c.*1229 and Hauz-i-Alai which was patronized by Alauddin Khalji *c.*1296. The officer-in-charge of the construction, repair and maintenance works was known as Shahna-i-Imarat. A lot of building activities were carried out by the state. Abundant supply of labour from the countryside ensured regularity in construction activities. The changing milieu of the city and its shifting material culture led to a greater concentration of mansions, architects, engineers, artisans, craftsmen, traders and merchants in the city. The city was tuning itself to changes, and weaving, carpentry, paper manufacturing, building activities and distillery became the order of the day. Mohammad Habib, a historian of Medieval India, propounds that the thirteenth and the fourteenth centuries were the ages of the 'Urban and Rural Revolution' due to the efforts of the Delhi sultans who constantly engaged in public works and established markets as well as other necessary structures to facilitate movements. The rapid growth of Delhi under the Turkish sultans reflects the change that was taking place all over the country. The Turkish rulers imitated native rulers and the styles of their palaces and establishments, and these in turn became models for the Turkish governing class. Much of the revenue collected in the form of surplus was spent in the markets of Delhi. John Dowson and H.M. Elliot argue in their book *The History of India, as Told by Its Own Historians*: 'Delhi by the end of the thirteenth century had come to occupy a unique position in the Asian world.'[25] This idea was also critically studied by Irfan Habib, who offered more empirical evidences and a better understanding of the period.[26] There was an upward movement in the economy of the city and the subcontinent in general. Being the capital city, Delhi was always the first to harvest the best and was under the direct supervision of the sultans. The sultans acted through the various officials who were always available at their disposal. The city was protected day and night, and its population was always under watch. The large concentration of population and the industries in the city were fed by neighbouring villages. The surplus production of distant lands such as Bengal, Awadh and Malwa and the raw material from these distant areas, which were specialities of the lands (where they produced) were brought to the city. This kind of a system was at work until the middle of the seventeenth century when Delhi was the most advanced city of the time, and was an all-rounder in its growth pattern. Along with expansion of Delhi's frontiers, agricultural expansion and production of artisanal goods also became huge and diverse. The water arrangements for the city along with irrigation facilities for the agricultural lands and gardens were also marvellous. Amir Khusro was credited for the creation of *Hindavi*, which was a raw mixture of Hindi and Persian words, and up until the fifteenth century, people spoke diverse versions of this language, pushing it to the status of

---

[25]Henry Miers Elliot and John Dowson, *History of India as Told by Its Own Historians*, Vol. II, Cosmopolitian, Aligarh, 1952, p.43.

[26]Irfan Habib, 'Economic History of the Delhi Sultanate: An Essay in Interpretation', *The Indian Historical Review*, Vol. IV, No. 2 (January 1978), pp.287–303.

the 'language of masses'. Later, during the time of the Mughal Empire, the introduction of Persian as the state language led to the widespread use of Persian, and it became the language of the masses. So, Delhi represented excellence until the shift of the imperial capital to Agra by Sikander Lodhi in the true sense.

The intermission in Delhi's glorious past, which set in with the shift of capital to Agra, was rested, and once again the story of excellence started moving in Delhi which began with the declaration of the foundation of the city of Shahjahanabad, by the Mughal emperor, Shah Jahan during the seventeenth century. The capital of the Mughal Empire was at Agra, and all the emperors from Babur till Jahangir ruled from there. However, this did not mean that the Mughal emperors never came to Delhi and its vicinity, until Shah Jahan thought of shifting the capital. Babur entered the city of Delhi on 24 April 1526 after winning the Battle of Panipat. While describing the interaction of the Mughals with the city of Delhi, Hearn notes:

> Of his visit to Delhi he gives an account in his most interesting memoirs; he mentions the shrine of Nizamud-din Aulia, that of Kutb-ud-din, the Hauz-i Shams (which is close to the latter), and the Hauz Khas. Babur also visited the palace of Ala-ud-din and his minaret, the sepulchers and gardens of Bahlol and Sikandar. He then embarked on a boat, and dropped down the river to Agra, drinking 'arrack', which presumably he tasted for the first time.[27]

---

[27]Gordon Risley Hearn, *The Seven Cities of Delhi*, W. Thacker & Co.,

The visits of Humayun to Delhi were few and mainly in between the travels.[28] The battle between Akbar and Hemu concluded at Panipat in favour of the Mughals, who gained sovereignty over Delhi after this success. However, Delhi was never made the seat of power by Akbar. He denied the status of *Takht Dilli* to Delhi but was constantly visiting the city to meet Maham Anga, who was his foster mother. The environs of Delhi—Palam, Rewari and Sonepat—were one amongst his favourite hunting grounds. In 1563, Akbar paid a visit to the college of Maham Anga and encountered a deadly experience where he was shot at with an arrow in his left arm.[29] Jahangir too passed through Delhi on many occasions, and paid visits to Humayun's grave where he read the prayer—*fatiha*. He also paid homage to the shrine of Nizamudin Awaliya, which is next to Humayun's tomb. Unlike any other Mughal emperor, Shah Jahan (grandson of Akbar) had a long association with Delhi. He secured shelter in the vicinity of Delhi (in present-day Faridabad) when he was in rebellion against his father. The imperial army and the rebellious troops encountered each other opposite Tughlaqabad. After the succession, Emperor Shah Jahan stayed mostly at Agra and turned his attention to Delhi only *c.*1638. Prior to him, his wives constructed a few mosques around Delhi. The vast narratives available in manuscripts indicate that the site for the walled city was chosen very carefully. In 1639, Shah Jahan instructed his engineers, architects and astrologers to choose a location with a mild climate somewhere between Agra and Lahore

London, 1906, p.212.
[28]Ibid., pp.213–18.
[29]Ibid., p.222.

(now in Pakistan). According to Francois Bernier, a French physician and traveller, the excessive heat of Agra during the summers rendered it unfit for the residence of a monarch. According to *Amal-i-Salih or Shahjahan Nama* written by Mohd Salih Kambo, other reasons for the shift include the broken ravines that ran through Agra city, want of space inside the fort, the narrowness of the streets, and the inconvenience caused to the inhabitants due to the large crowd of troops, elephants and retinues of the emperor and his *umara* (noble, plural of Amir).[30] An Italian traveller and writer Manucci also wrote about the comfortable weather of Delhi, and the desire of the emperor to build a city therein. The astrologers and *hakims* were entrusted with the task of locating the site for the construction of the fort. The location of choice was on the western bank of the Yamuna and at the north of Purana Qila. Historically, it was known by many names, such as Qila-i-Mubarak, Qila-i-Shahjahanabad and finally Qila-i-Mualla during the reign of Bahadur Shah II. Today, it is popular as Red Fort, the site associated with India's Independence, and each year on 15 August, the prime minister of the country gives his speech from the terrace of this illustrious monument. According to Shah Nawaz Khan, the noted author of *Maatiru-al-Umara*, the fort was constructed in nine years, three months and a few days. After the completion of the structure on 19 April 1648, Shah Jahan entered the fort and his new capital, Shahjahanabad, from its riverfront gate. A grand festival was organized around the event and many nobles were promoted as per the court culture and custom

---

[30]Gordon Sanderson, *Delhi Fort: A Guide to the Buildings and Gardens*, Asian Educational Services, New Delhi, 2000, p.2.

of the Mughal administration. The city wall had many large gates that acted as entrances and exits to the city. The names of some of the gates are Lahori Gate, Kashmiri Gate, Ajmeri Gate, Mori Gate, Kabuli Gate and Akbarabadi Gate or Dilli Darwaza. Named after important destinations and cities of the empire, these gates indicated the direction of the places they were named after. The city walls also have gates and entrances towards the banks of the river Yamuna. Over these walls, there were *chowkis* (posts) at regular intervals for security personals who were posted for keeping watch. These *chowkis* were adorned or beautified, with canopy tops. This made the *chowki* efficient and guarded posts were mainly designed to protect the posted soldier from any direct attack. The smaller gates were constructed beside the big entrances to keep the flow of the communication active. These were the feeders to the city, and most of the postal collections were done at these smaller entrances known as *moris.* There is no doubt that the structure of the city was built to meet the requirements of the time, and its aim was to organize the city space in the best possible way.

To make water arrangements for the city, the Yamuna Canal of Firoz Shah that was initially extended to water the Hansi-Hissar region was further stretched up to 125 km and entered the city from the north-west side near the Kabuli Gate. Then, it was called Nur-i Faiz. It was a matter of pride that Chandni Chowk got its name from the reflection of the moon that shone over the waters of the Nur-i Faiz flowing between the Red Fort and the Fatehpuri Mosque. A *chowk* was created in the centre of the canal and this was called Chandni Chowk. The bazaars around the *chowk* had nearly 1,500 shops, and the popular bazaars of this place were Urdu Bazaar, Jauhari

Bazaar and Fatehpuri Bazaar. The *havelis* of the nobles were constructed on the road that connected the Kashmiri Gate to the fort. The Dilli Darwaza housed the Fazila Bazaar. The entire city was dotted with lights at regular intervals. The only hillock in the walled city was the area where the Masjid now stands. The *kucha* and the *kalans* were the centres of trade and catered to large crowds.

Indeed, the fort complex was the seat of the state and represented the empire. A close perusal of the structure which was occupied by the royal family and their attendants is necessary to understand this. The Lahori Gate provides an exit to the Chandni Chowk and was the principle entrance to the fort. This gate opens in a square courtyard and a covered running corridor connects it to the royal structures of the fort, which were the palaces. This massive square-hall served as the *Naubat-Khana*, and housed many shops on both sides of the corridor and served the most expensive and luxurious items meant for royal consumption. Beyond this were the security structures and edifices for armed retainers. Further, the royal apartments, pavilions and palaces enhanced the beauty of the complex. The cost incurred for the construction of the fort was a hundred lakh rupees—half of this was spent on the walls and the other half on the buildings within. Aurangzeb added the barbicans to the fort at the Delhi Gate. During this time, Shah Jahan was imprisoned at Agra, and at this addition to the fort he wrote to his son, 'You have made the fort a bride, and set a veil before her face.'[31] To appreciate the architectural marvel of Emperor Shah Jahan, the historian Elphinstone said,

---

[31]Gordon Sanderson, *Delhi Fort: A Guide to the Buildings and Gardens*, Asian Educational Services, New Delhi, 2000, p.9.

'Shah Jahan's greatest splendour was shown in his buildings', and the Red Fort and its intricate designs and architectural principles stand witness to it. The architectural excellence and the specifications of the fort will be discussed in Chapter 3, which is dedicated to the monuments of Delhi.

With the newly established lavish fort, extensive and highly classified and organized markets, the fortified city of Delhi re-attained its *abad* (honour) once again. The economic activities of this time were immense and traders around the city renewed their connections with the city. Much of the population was also living inside the walled city, and it soon became a huge and extensive centre for artisans. The markets, *kuchas* and *kalans* of the city became the hub for designing, drawing, preparing and producing the masterpieces of this age. All kinds of accessories related to clothing, jewellery, shoes, utensils, food and other consumable items, and beautification items were available in the lofty and attractive shops inside Meena Bazaar which is in front of Jama Masjid. Delectable kababs with a variety of chutneys and flavoured *biryanis* offered with *raita* and raw salads were the most sought-after food-items for both shoppers and shopkeepers. The city was impartial to all the wanderers who were in search of something or the other. Even today Shahjahanabad is striving hard to keep its cultural glory alive.

Manucci offered an interesting description of the city and its activities. The city became a centre of cultural synthesis. The literary development of Urdu is one of the best examples of this. Several renowned poets such as Arzoo, Sauda, Abru, Tek Cand and Mazmun wrote their poetic expression in Urdu, and were freely picking up from the Persian and *Hindavi* dialectic currents. *Brajbhasa* was yet another medium of expression.

Coffee houses known as *kahwah-khanas* were the hives for the intellectuals of the city along with members of trade guilds and clubs. These like-minded groups made the coffee parlours the bowls for discussion where exchange of ideas took place, along with discussions on politics and matters of business. The gossips which surrounded the elites also sensed labour camps here (originated) and further breathed a new life in the markets of the city. *Mushairas* were also popular assemblage points, and they were organized regularly at the *havelis* of the elites and important people of the city. Music lovers would gather in different setups according to their taste, such as a preference for *dhrupad, khayal* and *gazals*, or *qawwalis*. The state also patronized various artists and the writers by confirming titles and salaries.

Intermixing and exchanging with each other was not limited to the culture of the elites. It was also filtered down to the general populace due to the imperial influence. Joint celebrations of festivals were a unique way of intermingling. For instance, the festival of Vasant Panchami[32] was a popular occasion for both Hindus and Muslims to celebrate alike. Diwali too was an awaited festival for the city-dwellers who keenly waited to watch the *roshni*, and it was celebrated at the tomb of Nizamuddin Awaliya and Chirag Dilli. The *dargahs* of the Sufis were also popular among all sections of society, and everyone held reverence for the saints and their mystical and healing powers. The Jain Mandir of Chandni Chowk located in front of the Lahore Gate of Red Fort is another monument that reflects the culture of peace and cohesive co-existence that dominated the time.

---

[32]Other names of the festival are Vasant and Basant.

The Decline of Mughals

The city of Shah Jahan was thriving until its revenues were diverted by his successors. Aurangzeb acceded to the throne of the Mughal Sultanate at Shalimar Gardens in c.1658,[33] and spent a considerable time in Delhi. His favourite sister Roshanara also lived there until her death, and their elder sister Jahanara also joined them c.1663 at Red Fort, Delhi, after the death of their father. Circa 1661, there was a dreadful famine in the city, and many of its inhabitants perished despite the relief measures that were extended by the state. Aurangzeb's inclination towards the Deccan, and the shift of imperial activities from Delhi to Aurangabad (in present-day Maharashtra) claimed its toll on the city. In 1680, Aurangzeb left the city and never returned.[34] Constant expeditions in the Deccan were proving expensive for the state. Further, the overgrown size of the empire was becoming unmanageable due to corrupt officers and over-engagement of the emperor in the affairs of Bijapur and Golconda. Rebellions against the state were also on the rise. According to noted historian Jadunath Sarkar, rebellions by the Jats, Marathas and Sikhs were part of the 'Hindu reaction', and these reactions swept away the Mughal Empire. Historian Satish Chandra also propounds that the empire declined due to the Jagirdari crisis. The same decline of the state has been put forward as the 'Agrarian Crisis' by the noted scholar and historian Irfan Habib in his highly acclaimed thesis at Oxford University.

---

[33]Hearn, *The Seven Cities of Delhi*, p.228.

[34]H.C. Fanshawe, *Delhi: Past and Present*, John Murray, London, 1902, p.4.

Between the death of Aurangzeb in 1707 and the Mutiny of 1857 it is nearly 150 years. Many have wondered, 'What were the Mughals doing in this time until the coming of the John Company?' Turmoil and raids haunted the city during these years. The weak successors to the Mughal throne were engrossed in wine and women, and spent the accumulated wealth of the empire without thinking about generating new sources of income. Further, the disinterest of the emperors in state affairs made the officials freebooters. The exploited and starving population of the empire was not getting audience, and the absence of strict state action on the ground made the peasantry devise their own means of struggle. Thus, the absence of results from state-oriented action pushed the peasants to resort to everyday forms of resistance.

Besides the unstable matters of the state, the crumbled and decayed internal affairs of Delhi were exposed to invaders. As a result, the city was ransacked, looted, raped and murdered by the ruthless invaders and the new tax collectors. Circa 1739, Nader Shah ransacked Delhi for several days and took back a large sum as fine, amounting to nearly two crore rupees. This fine was levied on the people of Delhi. The keys of the royal treasury were handed over by Muhammad Shah to the invader and the Peacock Throne which was carved out after hard labour of seven years[35] was lost to Nader Shah. The much-desired throne of Shah Jahan thereafter served as a symbol of Persian imperial might. Amongst a treasure trove of other fabulous jewels, the Koh-i-Noor (Mountain of Light) and Darya-i-Noor (Sea of Light) diamonds were also taken away. Many slave girls, eunuchs and servants also formed a

---

[35]Hearn, *The Seven Cities of Delhi*, p.227.

part of the large booty.

Bahadur Shah was the successor of Aurangzeb and he died after serving for five years. The fight for the *taqat* (throne) and *taaz* (crown) was a usual phenomenon of Mughal succession. Thus, the struggle amongst the brothers after the death of Bahadur Shah was a natural occurrence. In the contest for the throne of Delhi, two brothers, Kam Baksh and Azam Shah died, and the survivor ascended the throne and assumed the title of Jahandar Shah. He appointed Zulfikar Khan to the post of Wazir. Besides this, he resigned to degrading pleasures and promoted the relatives of a dancing girl, who was also his favourite mistress, to the highest honours in the state. At this time Farrukhsiyar was the viceroy of Bengal and an active administrator. Seeing the weakness of Jahandar Shah, he and his army of seventy thousand men defeated the emperor in the neighbouring Agra. Zulfikar Khan was executed along with the emperor, who reigned for six months only. Farruksiyar ascended the throne *c.*1713. His advancement was indebted to the efforts of two brothers—Hussain Ali (the governor of Behar) and Abdoolla Khan (the governor of Allahabad)—who were generally denominated as Sayyids to denote their descent from the Prophet. While Abdoolla was advanced to the post of vizier (wazir), Hussain was appointed commander-in-chief. They were both men of talent and valour and were able to monopolize all power. They were able to secure for themselves the title of 'King Makers'. A convention with the Marathas led the troops of Hussain Ali to march from the Deccan to dethrone Farrukhsiyar. Advised to disallow the treaty, the breach between the emperor and the Sayyid brothers became wider. Accompanied by Balaji Vishwanath and ten thousand noted Maratha horsemen, Hussain Ali hurried to the capital to restore his family's ascendancy. A confederacy comprising the prominent ministers of the state was formed by the emperor to destroy the brothers, but this enterprise did not succeed. Therefore, Hussain Ali was able to march into the city with nearly no opposition. Farrukhsiyar, who made hopeless submissions, was dragged from the recesses of the seraglio where he had taken refuge and assassinated privately in 1719. The next two puppets who were made to sit on the royal throne of Delhi were Rafi-ud-Darajat and Shah Jahan II respectively, and both were poisoned to death by the Sayyid brothers. Rustom Khan was grandson of Aurangzeb and he was instituted on the throne with the title of Muhammud Shah.

The young emperor was fretting under the yoke of the Sayyids. To release himself from their power, he formed a combination among the nobles of his court under the discreet guidance of his mother. The plot, which involved some of the most eminent courtiers, could not be concealed from the brothers; however, they were distracted by the difficulties which surrounded them on every side. During this time, the Nizam of the Deccan revolted and captured the fort of Asgir. After a lot of thinking it was finally decided that Hussain Ali should march against the Nizam, taking the emperor with him, and that Abdullah should return to Delhi. After commencing the five-day march, Hussain Ali was killed when Kalmuk, a servant, approached his palanquin on the pretext of presenting a petition and stabbed him in the heart. On hearing about the loss of his brother, Abdullah decided to take revenge.[36] In the conflict which ensued, the partisans of the

---

[36]J. Talboys Wheeler, *India and the Frontier States of Afganistan, Nipal and Burma*, Peter Fenelon Collier, New York, 1819, pp.251–52.

emperor were victorious, and the victorious army marched back to Delhi. Although Hussain Ali was killed, his brother's life was spared, in consideration of his august lineage.

Fifty-eight Days of Violence by Nader Shah

Eventually, Muhammud Shah became popular as Muhammud Shah 'Rangeela'. Circa 1737 Muhammud Shah summoned the Nizam-ul-Mulk of Deccan to Delhi, nominally, to assist the emperor in streamlining the conditions of state affairs, but in reality it was an action to disgrace him.[37] Saadat Khan of Awadh and Nizam-ul-Malik reached a negotiation, and decided to invite Nader Shah to teach the emperor a lesson. Qoli Khan also known as Nader Shah of Persia set out in the latter part of the year 1738 with an army of thirty-six thousand horses. The army of Muhammud Shah marched out of Delhi and the two forces camped in the plains of Karnal. The march to Karnal to repel the invasion was a failure, as the emperor met a fatal defeat. Since he was without any means of resistance, he proceeded immediately to the Persian camp, and threw himself at the mercy of the conqueror. The objective of Nader was wealth, not conquest, and this was affirmed when he was ready to retire on receiving a contribution of two crores rupees. None of the state associates extended to contribute to the ransom money. As the invader was determined not to go empty-handed, in March 1739, he entered the city in the company of the emperor in order to levy the extractions. He was well-received in the royal palace. A *khutba* was read

---

[37]Hearn, *The Seven Cities of Delhi*, p.232.

in his name in a mosque as was done for Timur.[38] So, the reading of a *khutba* in the name of the invader was not a new happening in the city of Delhi. The next day, a rumour of his death was spread. The citizens arose and a thousand Persians perished as the mayhem continued throughout the night. The next morning, as Nader went ahead to restore order, the first thing he saw was his soldiers' mangled corpses. Just then, he was attacked with missiles from windows, and a favourite officer was struck dead at his side. His fury knew no bounds and he issued orders for a general massacre of the city's inhabitants. The metropolis of India saw hours of violence and bloodshed, leaving thirty-thousand dead. Every sword was sheathed the moment he issued the order. Nader Shah despoiled the emperor and his nobles of all their treasures and jewels, and every house was searched and ransacked. No cruelty was spared to extort wealth. The governors of the other provinces were likewise put under heavy debt. After putting Delhi under fifty-eight days of ruthless violence, and exhausting the country's wealth, Nader Shah was set to depart with loot that added up to thirty-two crore rupees, along with thousands of elephants, a hundred masons and two hundred carpenters. Before his departure, he re-seated Muhammud Shah on the throne.

The Mughal Empire that had been in a state of rapid decay for more than thirty years since the death of Aurangzeb received its death blow with the attack of Nader Shah, and the ransacking of the capital ensured its instant collapse. Its prestige was irrecoverably lost, and its various provinces

---

[38]Bamber Gascoigne, *The Great Moghuls*, B.I. Publications, New Delhi, 1971, p.245.

ceased to yield any but a nominal obedience to the throne of Delhi. Another Afghan who continued to invade the Mughal Empire was Ahmed Shah Abdali. Proving true to his element of the tribes (plunder, loot, raids and murders for collecting resources of livelihood), he constantly raided Delhi and took away enormous wealth in each raid. Between 1748 and 1767, he invaded India seven times and each time Delhi was forced into political darkness.

The Mughal Emperor Ahmed Shah Bahadur (r.1748–1754) was a successor of Muhammud Shah and he built a wooden mosque called Chobi Masjid, located between the Diwan-i-Aam forecourt and the imperial gardens. His successor Alamgir II witnessed the crippling invasion of Shahjahanabad by Ahmed Shah Durrani and then by the Marathas, who were becoming immensely powerful in the eighteenth century. He was virtually kept as a prisoner in his palace by his prime minister, and was finally murdered in 1759. In these seditious surroundings, his son Ali Goher escaped from the fort by descending along the huge walls of the Red Fort using a rope, and fled to the sandy riverbank. The insolvency of the Mughals had already set in by this time, and the area around the Shah Burj had become a cramped living quarter for adult princes who did not have the means to support themselves. The vacuum created by the weakening Mughal throne inspired the Marathas and the Jats to seize the opportunity, and they attacked the fort. Heavy gunfire damaged the buildings that were located on the eastern wall of the fort. The plundering armies stole precious decorative items from the palaces located in the Red Fort. In the meantime, Ali Goher proclaimed himself as Emperor Shah Alam II. He tried to assert control over his erstwhile territories and win allies but was defeated *c.*1761 (at Bihar), *c.*1764 (at Buxar) and finally *c.*1765 (at Kora) by the British. This defeat was the final nail in the coffin of the Mughal Empire, and with these consecutive defeats, the emperor was forced to sign a treaty on 12 August 1765 with the British, which gave the John Company the *diwani* rights of Bengal, Bihar and Orissa, and put the emperor under British protection. This is known as the Treaty of Allahabad. In 1771, Shah Alam II succeeded in recapturing Shahjahanabad by joining hands with the Marathas. In order to acknowledge the services and support extended by allies, he gave away a bulk of his territories to them. With the relinquishing of territories to the Marathas, Shah Alam II was left with a small area limited to the vicinity of Delhi. The forces that were constantly confirming and asserting their power in the eighteenth century were Rohillas, Jats and Marathas, and they continued to attack Shahjahanabad. An imaginary frontier was at work which made the emperor believe that only trading rights had been extended to the company. However, in reality, the company was effectively controlling all the political and economic matters of the subcontinent.

British Rule

After politically establishing itself in the eastern provinces, the British East India Company realized that capturing political power would maximize trade profits, and they started working to gain control of the same. In 1803, Shah Alam II approached the British for help to counter the Marathas, and his request was followed by the declaration of the Battle of Delhi. The British emerged successful in the battle while the Marathas lost. Prior to this, Shah Alam's

authority and image also received a severe blow from a
Rohilla Afghan known as Ghulam Qadir, who had dug up
the floors and gardens of the imperial quarters in the belief
that immense treasure lay beneath. Furious at being unable
to locate any treasures, he blinded Shah Alam in the Diwan-
i-Khaas and imprisoned him in the Salimgarh Fort. While
the Mughal emperor's inability to protect his private quarters
from intrusion had already been demonstrated, this incident
showed that the emperor was now incapable of protecting
even his own person from assault.

This humiliation was followed by the succession of Akbar
Shah. He acceded to the throne in 1806 and introduced
several changes in the outer periphery of the Red Fort. He
built British-style masonry bridges over a moat surrounding
the Lahori Gate and Delhi Gate barbicans. The Asad Burj,
which had fallen due to bombardment, was also rebuilt.
This period witnessed a simultaneous decay, damage and
overcrowding in the court. Smaller gardens and imperial
private quarters, or harems, also fell into neglect due to the
paucity of resources. With the Battle of Delhi, a new phase
was inaugurated in the history of the Red Fort and northern
India. The success of the British at the Battle of Delhi made
the empire accord the victorious commander Lord Gerard
Lake with ceremonial honours, and titles were bestowed
upon him in the Diwan-i Khaas. In the past, Diwan-i-Khaas
was the platform for crucial decisions of the state, with a
long history of political and cultural significance. Now, it
was transformed into a site where the indispensability of
the British power for the survival of the doddering Mughal
rule was recognized. The emperor's civil and criminal
jurisdiction was now confined to the Red Fort. The British

took over the administration of the Mughal territories and installed a 'resident' at the Mughal court. This resident was entrusted with the tasks of the state, and all stately matters and communication were under his surveillance. Nothing was done without his permission. The Mughal ruler was now renamed the 'King of Delhi' rather than 'Emperor', and became dependent on a pension from the British. Colonel R.H. Phillimore, a British officer, confirms:

> By treaties signed at the close of war, the Marathas withdrew from the area north-west of Delhi surrendering the districts of Gurgaon, Karnal, Rohtak and Hissar. The old blind emperor, Shah Alam II, was granted a pension and allowed to govern the city of Delhi and a small area around it.[39]

The palace became overpopulated and minor buildings were built within it to accommodate the large numbers of princes and other dependants who had no resources to live independently. The imperial private spaces also lost their sanctity and opulence. The reputation, control, etiquette, mannerism and hierarchy were lost to the extent that nearly every European visitor and traveller had a freeway to the Diwan-i-Aam. The highly guarded private domain of the Mughals was now thrown open to visitors, while the members of the royal family were still living in it. The protocol of the state was no more in place and the apartments were open arenas.

However, British control over the Mughals slowly improved the rough state of affairs under the latter in the

---

[39]R.H. Phillimore, *Historical Records of the Survey of India 1800 to 1815*, Survey of India, Dehradun, 1950, pp.58–59.

Shahjahanabad area. There was an efflorescence of culture
in the half century that followed, and interaction with the
Europeans who had begun to settle in the city, opened up. This
period was marked by uninhibited interaction between British
officers and missionaries and the people of Shahjahanabad.
According to Narayani Gupta, European facades and upper
storeys were added to buildings along arterial roads, even as
the ground floors built in Mughal style were retained, leading
to a curious mix in architecture.

Urdu flourished and evolved as a literary language and
a medium of communication. In the midst of all this, court
patronage to the arts continued, though on a smaller scale.
In 1837, Akbar Shah was succeeded by his son Bahadur Shah
II, known for his love of poetry and who wrote under the
pen name Zafar. The renowned court poet Asadullah Khan
'Ghalib' also wrote and composed Urdu verses in Delhi at this
time. The growth of printing presses had made books cheaper
and easily available, promoting this literary efflorescence and
the circulation of newspapers in Urdu. The Delhi College was
set up to impart Western scientific education through the
medium of Urdu, and nurtured several bright scholars who
rose to fame all over the world. With the building of English
gardens and churches, as well as a bank, a hospital and a tank,
the appearance of Shahjahanabad gradually changed in a way
that detracted from the original principles of symmetry and
hierarchy that had positioned the Red Fort at the height of
visual and spatial landscape. The Mughal ruler, though a mere
figurehead, continued to reside within the Red Fort at Delhi.
Contemporary descriptions and British official documents
indicate that the living quarters inside the fort were bursting
at the seams with several generations of male and female royal

descendants living there. Many construction activities were under play, and vast areas of the fort, notably the southern half, took on the appearance of an overcrowded, poor locality. With the British controlling the revenues of the Mughal territories, the royal descendants were surviving on the stipends that were paid by the company. The impoverishment and humiliation were both working hard against the decaying Mughals.

The British built a garrison at Daryaganj, and a magazine and powder room near the Kela Ghat Gate of the city to fulfil military needs. The riverfront area, which housed residences and gardens of Mughal nobles and princes, was replaced with European-style utilitarian buildings. Shahjahanabad, approached by boat in this period, now had a mix of structures and styles. A part of the British army also began to live in the palace. When Akbar Shah's son tried to murder a British resident, the British at once found an excuse to build permanent accommodation for the British Commandant of the Palace Guard. According to Shekhar Mukherji, 'two separate social and cultural systems began to function inside the palace— the British and the Mughal.'[40] While the rooms on the top of Lahori Gate now accommodated British guards and their commanders, the verandah and arcades were left empty. With this, surveillance over the Mughal occupants was achieved as the top of Lahori Gate offered a bird's-eye view of the entire palace. British manning of the main ceremonial entrance into the Mughal ruler's palace was another stark demonstration

---

[40]'Comprehensive Conservation Management Plan, Red Fort Delhi', A Collaboration Project of ASI and CRCI, March 2009, p.13. Available at <https://www.scribd.com/document/235187712/History-of-Delhi> (accessed on 7 September 2018).

of the controllers and their real political power. However, Bahadur Shah Zafar did manage to undertake some new construction and repairs in this period, such as the Chhatta Bazaar, Hayat Bakhsh gardens and two pavilions—Zafar Mahal and Hira Mahal. The architecture and the planning of Hira Mahal testify to the highly diminished power of the Mughal Empire and their exhausted resources. According to contemporary official correspondence of the British, there was much suspicion and anxiety about possible conspiracies among the 'classes of sullateens' staying in the fort. The British felt that this fort was a hotbed of intrigue and served as a threat to the stability of the British enterprise. The high fortification walls and commanding location of the Red Fort made it a stronghold if the rebels seized control of it. Thus, they decided to shift out the royal descendants from the fort premises. Suggestions were also made to remove the king and his retinue from the fort to the Qutub area. The official correspondence is evidence to the shrewd planning of the governor general, who, through an agreement recognized Prince Mirza Fakhruddin as the heir to the throne as early as 1852. One clause of the agreement stated that the king and all the residents of the palace would vacate it. The British attitude towards the Mughal king and his palace became increasingly impatient, often verging on insolence. Overt and covert means employed by the British made it apparent that they didn't wanted to restore the health of the Mughal rule. Often, requests made by the Mughal ruler were declined and officials breached the court etiquette. In one such instance, the Acting British Resident, Francis Hawkins, went into the forecourts of the Diwan-i-Aam and Diwan-i-Khaas on horseback. Several Europeans are also reported to have entered the Jami Masjid and the Diwan-i-Khaas with their shoes on and seated themselves on the crystal seat therein. This was highly offensive to the authority and religious beliefs of the Mughal emperor and humiliation of the highest order for the populace of Shahjahanabad. In 1835, Thomas Metcalfe recommended a sum of five thousand rupees for the maintenance of the Red Fort but the council of the company was not willing for the same.

The Mutiny of 1857 and the British Capture of Shahjahanabad

The fears of the British proved correct with the uprising of 1857. The residents of Shahjahanabad were infused with anger and humiliation and therefore quickly drawn in the Great Uprising of 1857, a major watershed for the Indian subcontinent. The Mughal emperor was made a symbolic leader of the resistance, and the Red Fort, his residence and the erstwhile palace of the Mughal dynasty emerged as the heart and soul of the revolt. The uprising against the British yoke broke out in Meerut on 10 May, and its flames engulfed other towns rapidly. Not just soldiers but people from all walks of life came to Shahjahanabad and acclaimed the Mughal emperor Bahadur Shah Zafar as their sovereign on 12 May 1857. Shouting slogans in praise of the emperor and in favour of the Mughal Empire, the masses congregated on the banks of the Yamuna. Captain Douglas, the British resident, looked from the balcony of the fort and instructed them to leave. Somehow, they managed entry into the fort and the soldiers met the king. The soldiers were able to convince Zafar to join the revolt and accept leadership. Being helpless, Bahadur Shah Zafar had no choice and the events that unleashed made circumstances much more difficult. In the absence of any proper guidance, the agitated soldiers made all possible efforts to make the revolt a success. However, their actions were highly bifurcated. They killed Captain Douglas and Commissioner Simon Fraser and drove out all the other British officials and gathered them on the north ridge. The Red Fort remained the nerve centre of the uprising for several months. In the Battle of Badli-ki-Sarai, the soldiers inflicted heavy causalities on the British. The artillery was placed in the Diwan-i-Aam and the cavalry in Mehtab Bagh.[41] These military and defence developments damaged the buildings and gardens and beyond it, overstepping the boundaries between private and public spaces. The propertied classes were unsympathetic to the cause of the rebels and ordinary citizens were fed up with the chaos and breakdown of law and order, and preferred the restoration of British authority.

The British attacked Delhi in September 1857 with the intention of re-conquering it. They broke in the city through Kashmere Gate, and seized a large section of the city on 20 September. The fort was the last defence against the British onslaught. Both sides resorted to firing. The southern part of the Red Fort was bombarded and the imperial apartments faced cannonballs. The rebels responded with gunfire from the bastions of the fort. The military secretary wrote to the chief commissioner of Punjab saying: 'The king is reported to be in the Palace still—if so, his residence must be a very warm one, for our shells are pouring into the whole length of it from

---

[41]Anisha Shekhar Mukherji, *The Red Fort of Shajahanbad*, Oxford University Press, USA, 2003, p.192.

North to South."[42] Eventually, the British made their way into the fort through the Lahori Gate. There they found significant arms and ammunition and soon conquered the fort. Being certain of the British victory, the emperor escaped with his sons and took refuge in Humayun's Tomb. With the capture of the Red Fort and thus of Shahjahanabad, the British won a powerful, strategic and politically symbolic victory, which ensured that all businesses were in their hands and the Mughal emperor was clearly and completely under the subordination and subjugation of the John Company.

The Red Fort was the abode of the Mughal emperors for more than two centuries, where even the slightest action was not beyond the notice of the emperor, and further they controlled all the happenings of the city and palace, but now all of this was evaporating. The uprising gave the British an excuse to implement exactly what they had planned in order to take control of Delhi. This time they wanted to secure it fully. The Mughal king was captured as he was trying to escape, and brought to the Red Fort where he was put on trial. Ironically, the Diwan-i-Khaas served as the venue of trial. The king was declared guilty of treason, rebellion and murder and banished to Rangoon in Burma along with his retinue, where he died in 1862 after a prolonged illness. The palace was looted; this was sanctioned officially by the appointment of 'prize agents' who assessed and systematically removed valuables from the palace and the city. The destruction caused by the mutineers and the events during the revolt were recorded in extensive details by Gordon Risley Haren.[43] The British were now the

---

[42]National Archives of India, S.C., 30 October, 1857, No. 81.

[43]Hearn, *The Seven Cities of Delhi*, pp.262–94.

unchallenged rulers of vast territories, and they declared erstwhile Calcutta as the capital of their empire.

The Indian empire was directly governed by the British Crown from 1 November 1857. This was a major change in the politics of the state and various dimensions began to work in parallel. Official correspondence of the period indicates that the British realized that the location of the Red Fort on an elevation, along with its sturdy high walls, gave it a commanding position over the city and therefore it was especially suited to be a garrison. The Red Fort was considered by the British army as a strategically valuable possession.[44] Circa 1863, the British demolished vast tracts of buildings outside and inside the fort. Inside the fort, only a handful of buildings were retained and those too mainly along the central axis and the imperial private chambers. These were the Shah Burj, Diwan-i-Khaas, Moti Masjid, Hammam, Rang Mahal, Mumtaz Mahal, Asad Burj, Diwan-i-Aam, Zafar Mahal, Sawan and Bhadon pavilions, Hira Mahal, Naqqar Khana, Lahori Gate, Delhi Gate and the fortifications. The courts, arcades and water features that connected and characterized these buildings were done away with. It was not just the overcrowded living quarters that were demolished but even the stables, the royal kitchen, the harem, the colonnades and the canal were engulfed by the demolition drive. Colonel R.H. Phillimore testified:

> The ancient Mughal canals that watered the country to the right and left of the Jumuna had been allowed to fall into disrepair and disuse during the period of Maratha supremacy. And not long after the British occupation of

---

[44]National Archives of India, S.C., 18 December 1857, No. 439, pp.21–31.

Delhi the Resident at Delhi was authorized to have them put into order.[45]

The buildings that survived were looted and stripped of every last valuable item. The cruelty of greed knew no limits. The gilded copper domes of the Moti Masjid and Musamman Burj and the *chhatri* tops at the Diwan-i-Khaas were pulled down and sold. The fort and its palaces that were a marvel of art, architecture, craftsmanship, rarities, wealth and intricacies of the Mughal Empire for nearly two-and-a-half centuries were now reduced to an artistically dry military fortification. Subsequently, numerous barrack structures were built within the fort premise. Mosques, *sarais* and gardens which were symbols of Mughal power, grandeur and glory were demolished, and supporters of the uprising were persecuted and the loyalists to the British were generously and favourably rewarded. The Shahjahanabad of Shah Jahan was restructured and renovated to give it a new appearance. The clock tower at the centre of Chandni Chowk and the town hall on the main street of Chandni Chowk stood as the typical symbols of Victorian towns of the period and reflected the glory of the British, who had recently taken control of Delhi after suppressing the revolt. Within the Fort, in the area north of the Chhatta Bazaar, buildings were constructed to house families of British officers. Barracks and wash houses were set unimaginatively. The fort walls had workshops and godowns of the executive engineer and the barrack master. Chhatta Bazaar became a market for the soldiers' supplies. The Naqqar Khana became a quarter for staff sergeants and the Diwan-i-Aam

---

[45]Phillimore, *Historical Records of the Survey of India 1800 to 1815*, p.67.

served as a lounge for officers. The Rang Mahal served briefly as a mess for the soldiers; Mumtaz Mahal first housed a prison and then was converted into a mess for sergeants. According to Mukherji, photographic evidence points to the use of the Musamman Burj and Shah Burj as barracks. The Zafar Mahal became a swimming pool for officers. Wash houses and urinals were built in front of the Sawan and Bhadon pavilions. Circa 1864–65, there was further demolition within the fort and the city owing to the introduction of railways in Delhi. The railway line entered the city through Salimgarh Fort, crossed a newly constructed bridge—popularly known as Loha Pul, or the iron bridge—and cut across the northern area of the fort and its walls to enter Shahjahanabad.

Preparing for King George V's Coronation

To the British, the Red Fort was a reminder of their success in 1857. Perhaps, due to these associations, the Red Fort has always remained integral to British coronation *darbars*. Circa 1877, a *darbar* was held in Delhi to welcome the Prince of Wales to India. As part of the celebrations, a ball was organized at the Diwan-i-Khaas. In the first decade of the twentieth century, much work was done to arrest the decay of the fort and restore its past glory to whatever extent possible. In 1901, an official of the company, John Marshall, prepared recommendations for the conservation of the fort. He suggested that the eastern row of buildings be taken from the military and protected, and gardens be laid out in the open spaces. The Archaeological Survey of India (ASI) was established in *c.*1902. Thus, when preparations for the *darbar* of 1903 were being made, these recommendations were kept in mind. There were extensive festivities around the fort.[46] During this *darbar*, the buildings of the Red Fort saw numerous ceremonies and functions that celebrated the virtues of the British Empire. However, Marshall's suggestion that interventions be limited to preservation as far as possible was not adhered to. Instead, a policy of restoration was adopted. When an earthquake struck in 1904, the Shah Burj was damaged and was rebuilt by the ASI. The suggestion of an ASI official, Gordon Sanderson, to plant shrubs to mark the boundaries of courtyards was implemented. By 1906, the city had changed so much that it became difficult to recognize it as it was twenty years ago. The expansion of the city in the early decades of the 1900s was explained as a 'miraculous change' by Lord Hardinge.[47] The Coronation Darbar of 1911 (for coronation of King George V) and laying of the foundations of a new capital city in Delhi were major events in the history of the Red Fort. Since the fort was about to be a platform for many ceremonies and celebrations associated with the *darbar*, efforts to conserve and preserve it received a new vigor, and generous grants were allotted. A grand garden party was planned at the fort and military structures were removed from the Hayat Bakhsh. Besides this, the Nahr-i-Bahisht was revived, excavations were speeded up and a revitalization of the gardens took place. The courts in front of the Rang Mahal and the Diwan-i-Khaas were also excavated. Rang Mahal got ample fill from

---

[46]Fanshawe, *Delhi: Past and Present*, Leaflet of the Darbar, pp.2–7.

[47]Narayani Gupta, *Delhi between Two Empires 1803–1931: Society, Government and Urban Growth*, Oxford University Press, Delhi, 1981, p.175.

conservation work and the Mumtaz Mahal was turned into
a museum.

The King and Queen of England arrived in Shahjahanabad
by the railway via Salimgarh. They disembarked in the fort
and gave *darshan* from the Musamman Burj balcony just as
the Mughals used to do. Crowds had gathered on the river
bank to catch a glimpse of the visiting monarch, just as they
had done during the Mughal times. Thus, the city that was
torched, looted and stripped of its valuables was again pulling
up its socks and tying up its laces to engage in the marathon
which the new monarch and government was about to launch.
This underlines the significance of the Red Fort to the British
due to its imperial past as the palace of the emperors of India.
In 1921, the Red Fort witnessed the last colonial ceremony
when the Duke of Connaught, Prince Arthur, inaugurated a
Permanent Chamber of Princes in the fort. From the 1930s to
1947, some buildings in the Red Fort were used as high security
cells for alleged war criminals, and the fort was used to house
political prisoners illegally. Today, the ongoing construction of
New Delhi (Lutyens' Delhi) and the concentration of wealthy
and powerful persons there (south of Shahjahanabad) have
greatly eroded the vitality of the walled city.

Next Stop: New Delhi

New Delhi came into being due to the increasing need for
space felt by the administrators living in the city of Delhi. Even
today New Delhi is popularly known as Lutyens' Delhi—a name
that was given to recognize the efforts of the British architect,
Edwin Lutyens, who designed the city. The capital of the British
Empire in India was at Bengal since 1751. The shift of the

capital from Bengal to some other part of the country was considered only after 1905, when the situation in Bengal grew intense after the declaration of the Partition of Bengal. Delhi became the imperial capital of the British Empire in 1911. In addition to the financial, cultural and engineering pressures, the social and political implications of the transfer were very great for Delhi. Only a few state activities and celebrations were conducted at the Red Fort before the capital was moved to Delhi. With a shift of the imperial machinery into the city, a requirement for space was felt. It was then that the New Delhi capital, along with the many political buildings, was designed.

At this time, Delhi was also a centre for the freedom movement, and people like Mukhtar Ahmed Ansari were active enough to make the inhabitants of Delhi aware of the British imperialist yoke through newspaper writings. The Rowlatt Act was introduced in 1919 and was labelled as a draconian legislation by all the parties as it allowed certain political cases to be tried without juries and permitted internment of suspects without trial. Delhi inaugurated the Non-Cooperation Movement by observing *hartal* on 1 August 1920. In pursuance of the Calcutta and Nagpur Resolution of the Congress, people of Delhi voluntarily surrendered honours and awards bestowed upon them by British India.[48] In its later stages, however, the movement acquired an ugly shape with much bitterness between Hindus and Muslims of Delhi. Repeated incidents of violence erupted. The Civil Disobedience Movement was launched on 12 March 1930 and it had a broad base in Delhi. Students, women, labourers,

---

[48]Uma Rani Gupta, 'The Freedom Movement in Delhi, 1911–1942', *Historic Delhi* Indian History Congress, 52nd Session, 1992, pp.34–36.

peasants and many traders participated actively. Besides all these political upheavals, the British government was dedicated and committed to the cause of its imperial capital by posing massive structures to reflect their valour and glamour and advertise their civilization.

A town-planning committee was formed, which made recommendations for the acquisition of large areas for the construction of imperial buildings, keeping in mind the extension of the existing city and sanitary measures for Delhi and New Delhi. The idea was to build the city along civil lines. During the *darbar* of 1911, the king laid the foundation stone for this project at a place north-west to the Kashmiri Gate. The town-planning committee was headed by Edwin Lutyens, and he was provided full freedom to choose the site for building the new British imperial city. The site location was finalized after much deliberation by the committee. According to official documents, it was stated, 'The new site must be Delhi, i.e., an area in close physical and general association with the present city of Delhi and the Delhis of the past.'[49] The town-planning committee was inclined to a site in southern Delhi, but a case was made out by Bradford Leslie—a committee member for the northern site—and the committee was pushed to reconsider its decisions. Looking at all these developments, Fleetwood Wilson said, 'The battle of the site is becoming positively bloody'.[50] However, the decision of the committee succeeded and the area south of Shahjahanabad was finalized for raising the structures of the imperial capital.

A second round of meetings was conducted for preparing

---

[49] *First Report of Town Planning Committee*, 1913, p.1.
[50] Ibid.

the plans of the city apparatuses and for building the official structures of the imperial capital. In this, the first task was to locate the space that will suit the architectural specifications of the colonial power. In this process, Lutyens and Baker felt:

> [T]he fact that half the population of the town live outside the walls in irregularly developed suburbs made the work of co-ordinating New Delhi in balanced perspective with the present city a hard task.[51]

Between 1911 and 1916, three hundred families were evicted from Raisina and Malcha villages under the Land Acquisition Act of 1894, thus clearing about four thousand acres of land to begin the construction of the Viceroy's House (now Rashtrapati Bhawan). Herbert Baker designed the Secretariat Buildings (North and South Block) and bungalows on the then King George's Avenue for high-ranking officials. Other members of the team of architects were Robert Tor Russell, who built Connaught Place, the Eastern and Western Courts on Janpath, Teen Murti House, Safdarjung Airport, National Stadium and several government houses. At the beginning of 1912, the city that was called Dilli through the ages became Delhi and was juxtaposed to New Delhi. Shahjahanabad attained the title of Old Delhi. This colonial frame is so stuck in memories and landscape that even today nearly every person who visits the walled city refers to it as Old Delhi, rather than identifying it as Shahjahanabad, which represented the zenith of medieval architectural excellence. It might have served as a model for many future buildings. Despite all the ironies, Shahjahanabad still attracts the maximum number of visitors who want a deep

---

[51]*First Report of Town Planning Committee*, 1913, p.1.

dive into the history of the medieval times, but a few hear and a miniscule understand the whimpers of this monument, which now serves as the symbol of Indian Independence. The journey of Delhi between 1911 and 1931 was full of adventure where it travelled from being a city, to a province and finally grew to represent the nation.

The Indian subcontinent was divided on the eve of Independence as per the two-nation theory. Lord Mountbatten was entrusted with the task to work out the details of Partition. The declaration of Partition carved out a new nation on the north-western frontier of the Indian subcontinent, which was called Pakistan. This was to be an Islamic nation based on the idea of a Muslim-majority republic. Partition did not do any good to either of the newly-defined nations. Mass migration became the plight for months to come after August 1947. Hordes of Muslims moved to Pakistan to claim their rights and avail the benefits that the newly-formed state promised to offer. The migration camps on the frontiers were hubs of crime and the unhygienic conditions took a toll on innocent lives. Similarly, many Hindus came out of the popular trading centres of Lahore, Multan, Islamabad and Karachi, most moved out with their movable wealth, and were looted on the way. The constant encounters between Hindus and Muslims who were advancing towards their respective destinations of India and Pakistan led to the eruption of communal violence and unleashing of hate crimes. Millions lost their homes, families and family members and had no resources to sustain themselves in the new lands. Partition maltreated Delhi and took away its humility, brotherhood, communal harmony and peaceful coexistence. Shaken and traumatized Delhi was unable to overcome the effects of terror and shock. The raids, invasions, and plunder and loot of Delhi in the past were more material in nature, and after each shock, the city rose from the dust efficiently and effectively to re-attain its glory. Partition, however, took away the soul of Delhi.

A few months after Partition, Delhi became a massive refugee camp. The necessity to settle the incoming migrants was constantly growing larger. Along with the arrangements of food and shelter, medical requirements were pressing. The need for sanitation and hygienic living conditions in the camps was also increasing. The government, however, was engaged in the paperwork that was required to mark the refugees, so sufficient benefits could be extended. Delhi was in a sorry state! Refugee camps were created in Vijay Nagar, Hudson Lane, Outram Lanes, Model Town, Lajpat Nagar, Rajouri Garden, Moti Nagar, Raja Garden, Janakpuri, and so on, to accommodate the constantly incoming crowds. Even today, much of the same composition which set in during the post-Partition period is visible in these areas.

On 15 August 1947, Jawaharlal Nehru stood on the bastions of the Red Fort to deliver a historic speech announcing India's first steps as an independent nation. This historic speech still echoes, and many leaders still draw inspiration from it. Post-independence, the fort transformed from being the preserve of a single imperial entity into a precinct with single ownership but multiple managements and occupants. While the area notified in 1912 continued to be under the jurisdiction of the ASI, the Chhatta Bazaar area came under the Municipal Corporation of Delhi, and the Red Fort was occupied and managed by the Indian Army. Many new structures were made during the second half of the twentieth century in the army-occupied area. The outer areas of the fort, too, were actively used as a seam between the fort and the residential and commercial areas of Shahjahanabad. The forecourt of the Red Fort continues to be used on the two most significant national events, namely the Independence Day on 15 August and on 26 January when the Republic Day parade culminates here. The Red Fort is not only an indisputable national icon but also a symbol at a global level. The immense value of the site lies in both its tangible and intangible heritage. The great challenge that lies ahead is for the conservation of this national symbol, and further revitalizing it so that visitors can experience the rich layers of history and also sense the harmony within the tangible and intangible stories at this site. This is the only monument that has withstood the test of time and is most remarkable in many aspects, especially in relation to the history of all the imperial dynasties that came into Delhi.

3

THE ALIVE PAST

While Chapter 2 gave a sense of the political history of the city, this chapter is an effort to study some of the important monuments of the city and to extend the political, economic and cultural significance of its buildings along with the uncoiling of the slow death that had engulfed their glamour, grandeur and history.

With the proliferation in the network of trade routes and markets, the towns and cities became vital centres of exchange. These also became models of development and were imitated on a large scale. Cities such as Ujjain, Aurangabad, Varanasi, Gwalior, Ajmer and Jaisalmer located at the crossroad of many trade routes, were becoming hubs of conglomeration, and soon many became either administrative centres or attained the status of capital cities.

Since ancient times, Delhi has been at the crossroads of the routes that connected northern India with southern India, and it was also a centre for traders who were moving from the eastern side of the subcontinent into the north-western frontiers, and vice versa. Due to its strategic location, Delhi served as a clearing house for the whole province during medieval times. The appearance of cities has changed and undergone a lot of alterations with the changing reigns. Historian K.M. Ashraf made a brief comment on the changing

appearance of the cities.[52] According to him, all cities had a
population of 20,00,000 or more.[53] It is significant to mention
here that till date cities of India have not been historically
well explored. If at all any effort was made, it was gradually
diverted towards the circles of power. Some seminal historical
works have been conducted on monuments describing the
physical features of the buildings. The constant degradation
and decay of the monuments is worrisome. The information
available on these monuments from the time of their existence
is in the form of *qalam*, noting art pieces, historical dates and
literary writings. All this heritage will be lost and damaged
irreversibly, if not restored.

Delhi gets its strategic significance due to its peculiar
geographical location. It lies in the corridors of trade routes
and gains its importance due to its proximity with the river
Yamuna. The environment, especially water sources, has
always played a crucial role in shaping the histories of cities.
The Gazetteer of the Delhi District 1883–4 introduces the tract
of Delhi as '...though exhibiting none of the beauties of the
mountainous districts, possesses a considerable diversity...'[54]
Many monuments still stand tall to narrate their sad stories
and remind us of their glory and splendour. The unfailing
interest of monarchs have contributed immensely to the
landscape of the city, and nearly every ruler from the tenth
century onwards added either, a minor or a major building

---

[52]K.M. Ashraf, *Life and Conditions of the People of Hindustan*, 2nd
edition, Munshiram Manoharlal, New Delhi, 1970.
[53]Ibid., p.198, p.200, p.205 and p.275.
[54]*Gazetteer of the Delhi District*, 1883–84, 2nd edition, New Delhi, 1988,
p.1.

such as mosques, *sarais*, wells, *baolis*, etc. in the vicinity of Delhi. The extensive territories of this city were further being expanded with each new massive plan and various public works that were undertaken by individuals of diverse backgrounds. Each new ruler was also kind to consider the contribution made by their predecessors, and none allowed the previous cities to decline. Public works and their utilities were exploited to the fullest for making arrangements that would benefit the inhabitants. Revenue was certainly an attraction. Constant engagement with the previous cities further expanded the population, along with the new inflow of people who came to cities to earn wages. Also, the constant state activities—military and building—made human resource a necessity for the new conquerers. Nearly all the capitals cities were connected and acted on the model to constantly expand the frontiers to further add to the revenue of the state. The detail of the revenue that was attracted into the royal treasury indicates a wide variety of revenues.

I would further propound that the constant inflow of revenue was creating surplus in the royal treasury. Therefore, the rulers felt motivated to patronize some of the structures, and subsequently the officials and the royal family members also contributed to the building activities. The construction of public utility buildings was an attraction for all patrons, as it kept the population stable in the city, which was furthering economic growth of the city to the next level.

The city of Delhi has seen many capital cities that were built by different rulers in different times. Some of the rulers were kind enough to acknowledge and renovate some of the buildings that were built by the earlier dynasts. Qutub Minar stands as the most robust example of this, and it was lucky enough to attract maintenance and contribution to its structure from nearly all the dynasties that followed after its patron. The interesting feature of the building is that the topmost column was added by the British administrator Charles Theophilus Metcalfe in the nineteenth century.

As this section of the book is dedicated to monuments and buildings in the city, it is important to mention that heritage monuments that dot the landscape of Delhi are mainly contributions from the twelfth century onwards, with the exception of the fortification of Lal Kot and Rai Pithora. Along with these fortifications, the pillars and the rock edicts of Ashoka, as well as the iron pillar at the Qutub Complex are amongst the most ancient contributions. These will also be discussed in detail in this chapter.

The Qutub Complex

One of the earliest works available on the monuments of Delhi was a contribution by Surendranath Sen, which starts by considering the Qutub Minar as the oldest structure in the city. The structures found during excavations at the Purana Qila site are much modern in nature, so, to his understanding, they do not qualify as the ancient past of the city. The excavations conducted at the Purana Qila during 1970 to 1975 and later in the decade of the 1990s clearly indicate to past activities, and even take it back to pre-historic times. The crown and the title of the earliest building in the city were bestowed upon the Qila Rai Pithora (built c.1143), and it is termed as the earliest Muslim capital.[55]

---

[55]Surendranath Sen, *Delhi and Its Monuments*, A. Mukherjee & Co. Ltd,

The fortification wall of the Qila Rai Pithora, the fort of Prithviraj Chauhan, still exists in ruins. It was used by nine Muslim sovereigns of Delhi, namely, Qutubuddin, Aram Shah, Iltutmish, Ruknuddin, Razia, Muizuddin Bahram, Alauddin Masood, Nasiruddin Mahmud and Ghiyasuddin Balban, all of whom are known as the slave rulers of the Delhi Sultanate. This same complex now houses the Qutub Minar and the Quwwat-ul-Islam located inside the Qutub Complex. The latter is the living symbol of power and force that was founded by the Turks and the Afghans to carry forward the banner of faith and empire further into the east and the south. The generosity of a few sultans added new arches, domes and gateways to the mosque. The conqueror, Qutubuddin Aibak, was in hurry to build a prayer house that would be worthy of the conquering forces. Therefore, twenty-seven Hindu and Jain temples were pulled down to provide the raw materials for the prayer hall of the faithful! This prayer hall was called Quwwat-ul-Islam. The pillars in the mosque still bear the symbols of the disfigured sculptures and figurines of the animals and humans that were an integral part of both faiths (Hinduism and Jainism), representing the cosmology and the indefinitely powerful, the Almighty. The disfiguration of the figures and the idols was essential before using them in the mosque, as the use of these representations is forbidden in Islam as per the Quran. The floral depictions have not been destroyed and disfigured, as there is no specific instruction for this in the holy script of Islam. According to Surendranath Sen:

Calcutta, reprinted 1954, p.5.

The pillars still bear all the traces of their origin, and sculptured representation of men and animals, forbidden by the Quran, tell their own story. On some of the pillars are found female figures mounted on lions, on other human faces and *kirtimukhas*. The Muslim over seers who supervised the work of Hindu masons and work-men had no time to efface from the stone slabs the figures of Brahma, Vishnu and Shiva, and some of them still retain sculptured depictions of scenes from Krishna's life [...] every obnoxious figure down below, which might distract their attention or offend their sense of decorum was ruthlessly chiselled off.[56]

The explanation of the celebrated architect and art connoisseur James Fergusson also indicates that the slabs were taken down and put up again. The extensive plan of the building and its complex is provided with specific physical details. The mosque was begun by Qutubbudin Aibak in 1191. The rectangular court of the mosque is 142 ft × 180 ft which is open from the top. The iron pillar of king Chander stands in the centre of the mosque as an ornament, which definitely meant something significant for the then rulers. An inscription placed on the top of the northern gateway states, 'The building was commenced by the high command of Muhammad-bin-Sam, ally of The Amir-ul-Mumenin.'[57] The aim was to have semi-circular arches and pointed minarets on the western end of the mosque to give it a look like the Ghor mosques, following the style of a popular art form that originated in Afghanistan.

[56] Surendranath Sen, *Delhi and Its Monuments*, A. Mukherjee & Co. Ltd, Calcutta, reprinted 1954, p.5–6.
[57] Ibid., p.7.

But due to the inability of the Hindu workmen to understand this particular design, the same could not be achieved. These arches were preferred due to their load-bearing capacity, and their well-defined principles of using arches have been described in a work published nearly two decades ago.[58] The Romans preferred round arches while the Arabs had an inclination for pointed arches. The arch that was developed by the Indian artists to make the entrance of the mosque was called the Sham arch.[59] The Sham arch is a mix of both, the round and the pointed arch. The popular buildings that were patronized during this time include the Qutub Minar, tomb of Sultan Ghari and Adhai-din ka Jhopra (next to tomb of Moinuddin Chishti Ghareeb Nawaz at Ajmer) and the arches of all these monuments were made in the same Shams style or the style of the slave kings.

The Quwwat-ul-Islam mosque stands very close to the Qutub Minar. Many successors aimed to expand this mosque in order to make it a massive structure to showcase the glory and power of the Islamic rulers and their faith. This mosque was the Jama Masjid (conglomeration mosque) for the sultans of Delhi. Iltutmish was determined to expand the mosque, and added three arches on each side. So, in total, six new arches were added. The total extension on both the north and south was one hundred and nineteen feet.[60] By this time, many artists also came from Persia and they were put on the task of construction. The difference of the architectural designs

---

[58]Percival Spear, *Delhi: Its Monuments and History*, Oxford University Press, Delhi, 1994, p.102.
[59]Ibid., p.103.
[60]Sen, *Delhi and Its Monuments*, p.7.

is visible in the carving of the arches. The Indian artists depended on flowers, trees and the climber designs whereas the Persians used geometrical designs to decorate the arches and the pillars. After securing success in south India, Alauddin Khilji brought a lot of wealth to Delhi and decided to further expand the mosque. His plan for the extension of the mosque started from the tomb of Iltutmish, and he wanted to add six more arches to the mosque. The gateway was built near the Qutub Minar and it was called Alai Darwaza. He desired to make two more such gateways, but his wish was not fulfilled. The death of Alauddin Khilji stalled the entire mosque project. The half-complete Alai Minar is a proof of this. The minar in the complex appealed to many rulers and was also able to demand a contribution from some of them, but the mosque could not attract much attention, even from the Muhammadan rulers of the city. Timur, born in 1336 in Transoxiana near Kech (present-day Uzbekistan), visited the Quwwat-ul-Islam *c.*1398 when he invaded Delhi. It was only much later that Lord Dalhousie gave orders for the repair of the arches at the request of Thomas Metcalfe's daughter. The visit of Lord Curzon to the mosque in 1904 proved most beneficial, and it was on his suggestion that the ASI took charge of the building and its areas. Since then, the ASI is responsible for conserving the fragmented remains of this complex.

The Alai Darwaza was the entrance gate to the mosque built by Alauddin Khilji in 1310. This is an example of the beautiful ornamentation in which early Muhammadan rulers delighted. Later, it gave way to several designs such as the blending of marble and red sandstone visible in the exterior decoration, the pierced screens to the windows and the diaper pattern inside. In 1828 this gateway was in a sad state of decay, but it was attended to and the upper part of the exterior was built up and plastered over. This maintenance, rather than making the gate look beautiful naturally, spoils its effect. The inside structure is still beautiful and retains its original style, although some of the sandstone is flaking away. The diaper ornamentation ceases abruptly at the commencement of the dome, but this leads the eye to notice the very effective pendentive arches by which the corners are spanned and the square building is brought to an octagonal shape. The horseshoe arch of the Darwaza is a remarkable addition in contrast to all the other arches of the complex. The greatest advantage is in the light of the morning sun when it shines like an exquisitely jewelled casket as stated by Surendarnath Sen. The beauty of the gate and its arch stands the test of time and it testifies for the aesthetic sense of the patron. The physical features and details of the measurements about these buildings are available with the ASI and any interested person can avail them.

Qutub Minar

The next most significant monument in the Qutub Complex is the Qutub Minar after which the complex attains it name and fame. The status attained by the Qutub is representative of the 'Original Delhi' as recorded by an official, and describing it, he states, '... in the original Delhi are situated the Kutab Minar, the Kuwat-ul-Islam Mosque, the Alai Darwazah, the tomb of Altamash, and the Dargah, or shrine of Khwaja Kutab-ud-din...'[61] Qutub Minar is made of red and buff sandstone and

---

[61]H.C. Fanshawe, *Delhi: Past and Present*, John Murray, London, 1902, p.8.

it is the highest tower in India. It has a diameter of 14.32 m at the base and is about 2.75 m on the top with a height of 72.5 m. Its spiral staircase contains three hundred and seventy-eight steps.[62]

Many argue that stairs were not made on the topmost two levels. One needs to ask the purpose. While some think and propagate that it was meant to call for prayers, others believe it to be the tower of victory, as many similar kinds of minars were built in other regions as well. One such minaret is the Minaret of Jam, and it is located next to the river Hari in a remote and nearly inaccessible region of the Shahrak district of Ghor Province, Afghanistan. It is a sixty-two metre high minaret and was built around AD 1190. The entire structure was made of baked bricks.

Qutubuddin Aibak laid the foundation of Qutub in 1199 and raised the first storey. Three more storeys were added to it *c.*1231 by his successor and son-in-law, Shamsu'd-din Iltutmish (r.1211–1236). With these three floors added by Iltutmish, Qutub became a minar with four sections. All these levels are surrounded by a projected balcony encircling the minar. These balconies are supported by stone brackets, which are decorated with a honeycomb design, more conspicuously done in the first storey. In 1368, Firoz Shah added one more storey to it, and finally a dome or a cupola was added in 1803.

Numerous inscriptions in Arabic and Nagari characters are visible in different places of the minar and they testify to the history of Qutub. According to the inscriptions on

---

[62]The first level contains 156 stairs, the second level has 78 stairs, the third level has 62 stairs, and there are 41 stairs each on levels four and five.

its surface, it was repaired by Firuz Shah Tughlaq (r.1351–1388) and Sikandar Lodi (r.1489–1517). Major R. Smith also repaired and restored the minar in 1829. The iron pillar in the courtyard bears an inscription dating back to the fourth century AD, which is written in Sanskrit language and Brahmi script. According to the inscription, this pillar was set up as a *Vishnudhvaja*—standard of god Vishnu—on the hill known as *Vishnupada* in memory of a mighty king named Chandra. A deep socket on the top of the ornate capital indicates that an image of Garuda was probably fixed to it. According to G.R. Hearn, author of *The Seven Cities*, we owe the completion of Qutub to Altamash.

The lowest section of the minar is decorated with alternating circular and square engaged columns. The spherically engaged columns enhance the second section. The square columns are on the third section, while the top two round sections add to its aesthetic value. The structure is made entirely of red stone, except in the fourth level where white marble is also used. It is often thought that Sultan Shamsuddin Altamash (r.1211–1236) constructed this column, and this information is often seen in history books. The epitaph of Sikandar Bahlul on the entrance also confirms the same. While in some history books, the monument is identified as a mosque's minaret to call for prayers, others believe it is the pillar of Sultan Mu'izzuddin Gauri (r.1173–1206). Many disagree that it was used to call for prayers as the door of the column or entrance is north-facing, similar to the entrance of a temple—the doors of minarets are always east-facing. This justification appears logical as the minar, which was started by Alauddin Khilji next to it (Alai Minar), has an east-facing door, which is common in mosque constructions, and it is also built on a plinth. This use of the plinths as a specific feature is missing from Qutub Minar. The first level of structure also shows evidence of stones being placed at a later stage, and there is evidence of the bell-and-chain motif of Hindu temples on the first floor. Additionally, the inscription on this pillar is similar to that of Qutubuddin Aibak and Mu'izzuddin's conquest through which temples were demolished and mosques were made out of the demolished stone material after organizing the material, as per Islamic principles. Hence, it can be argued that the first floor is Hindu in origin as claimed by various scholars. It is not unusual to note that epitaphs were inscribed by chiselling off the intricate idols that were once enhancing the charm of the pillars and slabs with human, animal, floral and artistic expression of the figurines.

Interestingly, all these evidences help in continuing the belief that Raja Bikramjit (Vikramjit) had built this pillar along with the Rai Pathora Fort and temple in 1200. As discussed in Chapter 2, some historians consider this to be true based on the theology that the daughter of Anagapal was a sun worshipper. As per mythology, Yamuna (or Jamna) was the daughter of the Sun and the sister of Yama (lord of death). Therefore, visiting and worshipping river Jamna was considered an important obligation. From this point of view, the pillar was first constructed at a location from where the river could be worshipped.

As per the epigraphs upon the monument, Fazl-ibn Abul-Ma'ali was appointed as the caretaker and his name is inscribed near the entrance. The expansion by Iltutmish is also documented on inscriptions embedded in the wall. Since then the column has been called a minaret, with inscriptions on every level referring to this identification, including those of the call to prayer, and the name of the architect behind this expansion was also inscribed on the minaret. On the fifth level, there were doors on all four sides, and on top of that a *chhatri* was placed to form the seventh level. Firoz Shah, who built the seventh level in 1378, wrote at the time of construction that he had the column's height raised from the existing level and got the details of construction inscribed upon a door on the fifth level. In 1782, due to a severe dust storm and earthquake, the uppermost levels fell to the ground. Stones from the original construction also fell and the minar had cracks in some places. There was more damage to the column in 1798. Restoration of the column was undertaken in 1803 by Major Smith, under the orders of the British government. The column 'appeared so incongruous that Lord Harding ordered its removal in 1848'.[63] He replaced the crenellations with stone railings and a beautiful brass railing on the fifth level. The sixth level was replaced with a beautiful stone *burj* with eight windows, and the seventh level was cut away to place a wooden *burj*. Unfortunately, neither of these towers remained intact. The stone *burj* was taken down from the column and placed on the ground below, and the wooden *burj* no longer exists. The same column that has been removed from the top can now be seen in the lawn near the dak bungalow. Thus, the original balustrades and contributions were removed and his contribution is aptly described as 'an illustration of "the present flimsy style of garden architecture".'[64] This is the story of the tower known as Qutub Minar, which, according

---

[63]Refer to <https://www.cse.iitk.ac.in/users/amit/books/sen-1954-delhi-its-monuments.html>

[64]Sen, *Delhi and Its Monuments*, p.11.

to Fergusson, was 'the most beautiful example of its class known to exist anywhere.'[65] With this long history of the construction of this minar, we need to ask ourselves, 'Why did this minar acquire the name of 'Qutub'?' Regarding the name of this minaret, many think it is named after its patron, the but in fact, it is named after a famous Sufi saint Qutbuddin Bakhtiar Kaki, who came from Osh in Central Asia. He was the disciple and successor of Ghareeb Nawaz Moinnudin Chishti. The monument has been adorned and repaired for its massive structure and historical value. And surprisingly, this is the only monument in the city of Delhi along with the Red Fort to attract the attention of the crowds across wide socio political sections.

The *Dilli* of Khiljis: Siri Fort

With the death of Ghiyasuddin Balban *c.*1287, Old Delhi (Mehrauli) lost its glory. The new capital was built by Alauddin Khilji, son-in-law and successor of Jalaluddin Khilji, and this capital was called Siri. Siri was also called Dar-ul-Khilafat, which stands for the Seat of the Khilafat. Before Alauddin Khilji, during the reign of Kaiqubad, the centre of power shifted to Kilokheri—between present-day Okhla and Maharani Bagh— but the status of the capital continued to hang on Mehrauli.

Siri was famous as it had a thousand pillars. Much of this fort is now in ruins, and hardly any pillar can be seen. At the western end of the new town, Alauddin built a huge tank over an area of seventy acres. It was later repaired by Firoz Shah

---

[65]James Fergusson, *History of Indian and Eastern Architecture*, John Murray, London, 1876, p.506.

Tughlaq. Fanshawe explains in detail the stay of Timur on the banks of this tank after looting Delhi. He notes that Hauz Khas is the place where Timur first rested and encamped after defeating the troops of Delhi, and received the congratulations from his *amirs* on the recently gained victory over Delhi by defeating Firoz Shah. Of Hauz Khas, Fanshawe writes, 'This is a reservoir which was constructed by the Emperor Firoz Shah, and is faced all round with cement. Each side of the reservoir is more than a bow-shot long, and there are buildings round it.'[66] It is a significant example of the public work carried out by the state for the benefit of the city people. This tank is known as Hauz-i-Khaas. A *madarssa* and a college was also made within the walled city for the propagation of *dini* (religious) and *duniyabi taleem* (wordly education) as done by a previous Muslim king in the Qutub Complex. This indicates the essence of education during the sultanate times. The destruction of the fort is attributed to Sher Shah Suri, who removed the stones, bricks and other artefacts of the fort for building his own city inside the walls of Purana Qila, the fort of the Afghan king.

Historian Spear describes Siri as:

> [T]he walls in some places are quite complete and you can walk right round them. There are a number of towers and gates. They are about a mile and half round. Inside there is today nothing but fields and crops. But once there was the great palace of Alauddin Khilji...Mongols invaded India and marched right to Delhi...Alauddin determined that they should never plunder the suburbs and gardens again. So he built the fort of Siri to protect

---

[66]Fanshawe, *Delhi: Past and Present*, p.254.

them. No one could plunder the suburbs unless they first took the fort of Siri. Inside the fort Alauddin built a palace. In it was a hall which was famous throughout India and was called the Hall of a Thousand Pillars.[67]

It was built in 1303[68] and had seven gates.[69] It was also the place where Malik Gafur, the loyal slave of Alauddin, showcased the wealth that was collected by looting south India. Thus, it can be said that Alauddin was a great patron and greatly desired to contribute towards public work. Safety was an initial concern while designing the city, but the later development of many other buildings for education, water arrangement, etc. clearly indicate the farsightedness of the ruler, Alauddin Khilji.

Tughlaqabad

Ghiyassudin Tughlaq (r.1320–1325) was the founder of the Tughlaq dynasty in India and was crowned at Siri but chose not to stay in this capital. He laid the foundation of Tughlaqabad but his rule was cut short in the fifth year of his reign due to his death. Stones of huge size were used in the walls of this city. The path through the main Tughlaqabad gate leads to a large reservoir hewn in the rock, and beyond it to the north-west are ruins of the palace, stables and of a mosque complex. On the west, there used to be a very deep *baoli* for the use of the defenders of the citadel, and all around were underground

---

[67]Spear, *Delhi: Its Monuments and History*, p.67.
[68]Gordon Risley Hearn, *The Seven Cities of Delhi*, W. Thacker & Co., London, 1906, p.103.
[69]Fanshawe, *Delhi: Past and Present*, p.255.

passages, which led to the quarters of servants and slaves of the king. An extremely fine view towards the north and east could be obtained from the top of the citadel. On clear days, the domes of the Jama Masjid in Shahjahanabad and curves of the river Yamuna (Jumna) were clearly visible. The description of the fort by Fanshawe is extensive and gives a sense of the location, and also reflects the massiveness of this structure. He writes:

> [A] fine view of the western portion of the citadel of Tughlakabad is obtained from the point where the road makes a sudden turn towards it from the south, about three-quarters of a mile on the Kutab side of the tomb of Tughlak Shah.[70]

The ruins of the wall and the bridge that connects the fort with the mausoleum of later are also evident. He also certifies the dates of the city and citadel construction between 1321 and 1323, and its desertification by Muhammad Shah Tughlaq in favour of Daulatabad. Missing in between is the city of Jahanpanah (of Muhammad Tughlaq), as per him the latter was finally superseded by Firozabad. For Muhammad Tughlaq, the main causes of desertification were not the sloppy and sporadic thoughts of the ruler. Fanshawe puts forward the idea, '...the real cause of its permanent abandonment was no doubt the badness of the water and general insalubrity of the site, as in the case of Fatehpur Sikri.'[71] Fanshawe was conscious enough to respect the general saying that was part of the popular culture of Delhi then. The saint who cursed the

---

[70]Fanshawe, *Delhi: Past and Present*, p.288.
[71]Ibid., p.288.

city was the most respected saint Nizamuddin Awaliya, and was also known as 'the Sultan of Sultans who rules without the crown'. Then, another popular saying of his directed for Ghiyasuddin Tughlaq was, *Hunooz, Dilli dur ast!* (Delhi is far yet!) Later, the ruler could not reach Delhi as he died by falling from a wooden platform built by his son to welcome him after the success over Laknauti (Bengal). The same saint also cursed the city of Muhammad Tughlaq, saying, *Ya base Gujar, ya rahe ujar* (Be it the home of the Gujar, or else it shall remain deserted). Today, the saying appears to be doubly fulfilled as most of the area inside the city wall lies utterly desolate, and covered in ruins. There are also two small Gujar villages inside the fort.

After the death of Ghiyassudin, the search of a suitable place for the capital city took Muhammad Tughlaq towards the south, and Adilabad was the chosen site for the capital building. Now, only the bastioned wall of Tughlaqabad stands and narrates the story of its harsh and unkind past. The massive sloping walls indicate a hardy fortress. At present, much of the structure is ruined, and ironically even the patron ruler was not able to pay attention to it due to his constant engagement in wars. Later, he deserted the city and built the Jahanpanah.

Jahanpanah

The word Jahanpanah is etymologically derived from the Persian language, and it literally means 'the Refuge of the World'. Jahanpanah was the fourth city in Medieval Delhi that was established 1326–27 by Muhammad bin Tughlaq (r.1321–1351), the son and successor of Ghiyasuddin Tughlaq.

It was mainly built to deal with the constant threat that the Mongols posed to Delhi. The fortified city of Jahanpanah was erected and enlarged to subsume the Adilabad Fort that had been built in the fourteenth century, and also all the other establishments that were lying between the other two capital cities, Qila Rai Pithora and Siri Fort. Neither this city nor the fort has survived. The only surviving structure of the city is Bijay Mandal, the palace of Muhammud Tughlaq. Spear's description of the Bijay Mandal makes the city come alive. He talks about the ruler walking around the Bijay Mandal. The gates which were made were used for taking water inside the fort, the lakes of the city, the *zenan*, the *hamam*, the pavilion, *chabutras*, Diwan-i-Khaas, the hall of a thousand pillars, and the mosque.[72] As per the information collected by an English official, there were six gates in the western wall of the city and seven in the eastern.[73] According to another official, '[Jahanpanah] has thirteen gates, Siri has seven gates'.[74] He also confirms the mosque, the well, and the fortification walls of Siri as well as the close proximity of this capital with Qutub. Today, only the Maidan Gate on the west near an old *idgah* can be identified. The most authentic source for reconstructing the history of Muhammud Tughlaq and his times is the work of Moroccan traveller Ibn Battuta, who stayed in the court of Muhammud Tughlaq for eight years. According to him, the thousand-pillar hall was a spacious hall with a thousand columns of varnished wood that supported a beautifully

---

[72]Spear, *Delhi: Its Monuments and History*, pp.71–73.

[73]Hearn, *The Seven Cities of Delhi*, p.104.

[74]Fanshawe, *Delhi: Past and Present*, p.255.

painted wooden roof. The thickness of the fortification wall as suggested by Ibn Batutta was seventeen feet.[75] Timur also visited the city as he visited many other old cities of Delhi.[76] The city and its ruins are not visible. Many reasons have been offered for such a situation. The most popular one of them is the idiosyncratic rule of Mohammed bin Tughlaq who inexplicably shifted the capital to Daulatabad in the Deccan and much of the population was forced to move from Delhi to the new capital. Many lives were lost during travel, and soon after, they came back to Delhi. Thus, in a nutshell it can be said that efforts were actually initiated for the safety and security of human resources and the protection of all the cities that were inhabited. The design and the architecture were made while keeping in mind the requirements and necessities of the city population, military and administrative hierarchies, apparatuses and demands.

Firozabad

Firozabad was the city of Firoz Shah Tughlaq, and it lies to the south of modern Delhi. It is nearly five hundred yards beyond Delhi Gate. Kotla Firoz Shah was built in 1350–70 on the banks of the Yamuna which contained the Buddhist *lat* (pillar) and Jama Masjid; only these two monuments have survived through time. The fortress of Firozabad was also referred to as Kushk-i-Firoz. Kala or Kalan Masjid was probably the principal mosque of the city of Firozabad, which extended on the west of the distinguished citadel and its two-

---

[75]Hearn, *The Seven Cities of Delhi*, p.103.
[76]Ibid., p.120.

storey building. It is reached by a steep flight of steps, and like other mosques built in the 1380s by the two great *wazirs* of Tughlaq. The mosque consists of a courtyard, surrounded on three sides by a simple arcade, borne by plain squared columns of quartz stone, with a dripstone over the arches, and on the west side by a mosque chamber of three rows of similar columns, each carrying five arches. The corner towers and outer walls of the mosque are all sloped inwards; there are no minarets, and probably the call for prayer was made from the roof of the terrace. As per Bishop Heber's journals, it appears that for a long time prayers were not held in this mosque.[77] The wall of the fort also accommodates the graves of the founder and his father. These graves were destroyed during the Great Uprising of 1857. On the left side of the road, opposite to the mosque, is the tomb and cemetery of Turkman Shah, after whom the Turkman Gate of the city is named. He was a militant saint and died in 1240. It can be said that Firozabad is a collection of suburbs, without a wall running around it. Even archaeological explorations are unable to confirm a containing wall for the city. This was a constantly expanding city. According to Fanshawe:

> The city of Firozabad extended, as has been seen, as far west as the Kalan Masjid, now enclosed by the walls of Shahjahanabad, and probably spread two miles north and south—the chronicler says it reached from Kasbah Indrapat to Kushk-i-Shikar, and was thus a larger city than its later rival.[78]

---

[77]Fanshawe, *Delhi: Past and Present*, p.66.
[78]Ibid., pp.224–25.

The absent walls around Firoz Shah's *shikargah* (hunting park) located in the northern ridge and around Kotla highlights the gap between the ruler and the ruled and that segregation was not aggressively attempted.

Scarcity of material could be the other reason for not building the wall as is noted by Fanshawe in case of Sher Shah. He notes that had there been enough material for a wall, it is not likely that Sher Shah would have despoiled Siri and Jahanpanah of their walls, in order to surround his city and raise the walls of the Purana Qila. Again, as there was no wall of defence, it was not difficult to occupy Firozabad. When Timur invaded Delhi in 1398, the walled cities of Siri and Jahanpanah were the locations where the general population and the royals preferred to hide. Circa 1407, Muhammud was besieged in Firozabad by a noble named Khizr Khan who rose in revolt, but could only hold out until the siege was raised for want of supplies. Again *c.*1411, while Firozabad was again seized by the same enemy, Muhammud decided to shut himself up, but this time in Siri.[79] This supports the idea that Firozabad was not a walled city. If we accept the fact that Firozabad had no outer walls, we can say it was quite natural for Sher Shah to build up defensive walls by looking into the lessons offered by history.

The *lat* which is placed in the centre of Firozshah Fort is the Topra stone pillar of Ashoka. In 1354, the two stone pillars of Ashoka from 300 BC were removed from Topra, seven miles south-west of Jagadhri (Ambala district) and Meerut, respectively. The Topra pillar was erected by Firoz Shah in the fort and the Meerut pillar was erected at the northern ridge

---

[79]Hearn, *The Seven Cities of Delhi*, p.204.

near the Bada Hindu Rao. The description of *lat* can be noticed in the works of many visitors. Timur felt a special admiration for the *lat* that was noticed in an interesting account by the chronicler Ziauddin Barani, who narrated how the pillar was brought to Delhi. The event progressed like this:

> Directions were issued for bringing parcels of the cotton of the Simbal [silk cotton tree]. Quantities of this silk cotton were placed round the column, and when the earth at its base was removed, it fell gently over on the bed prepared for it. The cotton was then removed by degrees, and after some days the pillar lay safe upon the ground.[80]

After examining the pillar, a square base was found at the bottom that was taken out. To save it from damage, the pillar was encased in reeds and raw hide from top to bottom. A special carriage supported by forty-two wheels with ropes attached to each wheel was made to transport the pillar. The pillar was placed on the carrier and strong ropes were fastened to each wheel, which were pulled by two hundred men. With the simultaneous excursion of many thousand men, the carriage was moved and brought to the banks of the Yamuna. The sultan came to see the pillar and it was then shifted on boats that had the capacity to carry nearly five to seven thousand maunds of grains. Then, it was taken to Firozabad, from where it was conveyed to Kushk Shikargah with indefinite labour and skill.

The speculations around the pillar of Topra ranged from depictions of Bhim, the powerful character from the

---

[80]*Cf.* Fanshawe, *Delhi: Past and Present*, pp.222–24.

Mahabharata, and went up to the Greek language which it was recorded in. All the speculations rested, as James Prinsep, an epigraphist, deciphered it as the pillar inscription of Ashoka.[81] The height of the pillar, above the platform, is thirty-seven feet and the circumference at the base is nine and one-third feet, and at the top, six and a half feet. The four inscriptions of Ashoka are still wonderfully and clearly visible on the pillar. Corresponding to the *lat* platform is the Jama Masjid of Firoz Shah, which must once have been a fine structure as is reflected through the ruins. Many other mosques of the same period consisted of arcades in several rows, with arches that round up or open up in the central court or hall of the mosque. The finest-standing example of the same type of structure can be seen in the Charbhuja Mosque, which was also serving as the *shikargah* for Firoz Shah in the northern ridge. Timur visited the mosque on the last day of 1398, for the purpose of paying devotion and obedience after returning from carnage and rapine in Old Delhi, and moved on further to raid and plunder Meerut and Ambala.

A twentieth-century collection about the monuments of Delhi represents a clear picture of the city of Firoz Shah. 'From the platform of the pillar a fine view is obtained of the ruins of the Firozabad Citadel, of the Purana Kila, and Humayun's Mausoleum, and of the remains of still older cities and buildings right up to the Kutab Minar.'[82] The walls of most of the houses of Firozabad finally disappeared when building materials were needed for Shahjahanabad. A few buildings of the city did survive when Fanshawe was moving around

---

[81]Sen, *Delhi and Its Monuments*, p.17.
[82]Fanshawe, *Delhi: Past and Present*, p.225.

Delhi to collect material for his work. According to him, the most notable structure amongst them was the picturesque mosque, Chausath Khambha, or the sixty-four pillars located at the back of a jail. Even today, locating and marking the boundary wall of Firozabad continues to be an equally difficult and tedious task as it was in the nineteenth and twentieth centuries. The seventh and last city was built in 1648 by Shah Jahan and he pulled down what was left of Firozabad and took off much from the walls of Sher Shah's city, to build up the walls of his own city, Shahjahanabad. William Finch, an English merchant, visited Delhi in 1611, and mentioned, 'The city is two *kos* between gate and gate, begirt with a strong wall, but much ruinate. About two *kos* without Delhi is the remainder of an ancient mole (*mahal*), or hunting-house, built by Sultan Berusa (Firoze).'[83] This clears the distance of the Kotla from the ridge and its Charbhurja mosque.

Firoz Shah Tughlaq was a more stable ruler than his predecessors. A cousin of Muhammad bin Tughlaq, he was a prolific builder of medieval times and extended his city from the old Indraprastha to the ridge and made a palace or the citadel in the near centre of his city boundaries. The other buildings he patronized were the Khirki Masjid, tomb and *madarssa* at Hauz Khas, Kalan Masjid, Chausath Khamba, Begumpur Mosque, Bijai Mandal and Bara Khamba. These are the notable buildings and have been conserved well. He must also be credited for building several hunting lodges in the forests of the ridge. Among these lodges, Bhooli Bhatiyari ka Mahal, Pir Ghalib and Malcha Mahal are still surviving. Firoz Shah also completed the mosque of Jamali Kamali and

[83]*Cf.* Hearn, *The Seven Cities of Delhi*, p.121.

Kamali's tomb at Mehrauli.

The rich heritage of buildings patronized by Firoz Shah brought much glory and fame to the capital city. He invested in many public works until he died in 1388. The growth and the urbanization was in full bloom when it was cut short during the last decade of the fourteenth century by the catastrophic attacks and plunders of Timur, who reserved for himself all the stone masons. He entered the city and took possession of twelve rhinoceros, and the remainder of the menagerie, which were collected by Firoz Shah. Timur also walked into the city of Firozabad, inspected the mosque and was delighted. Here, he was presented with two white parrots, supposed to be seventy-four years old, which had been transferred from one king to the next since the days of the Tughlak Shah dynasty. Finally, Timur returned to Samarkand.[84] This also marked the abrupt end of the Tughlaq dynasty. The Tughlaq buildings had minimal ornamentation, strong and thick sloping walls that evolved proportionately along with the structures that were decorated with lotus motifs and square pillars. A few of these buildings are still standing intact. Large parts of the designs are lost, but the structures are significant to get a sense of the building marvels. The best maintained Tughlaq structure is the invincible fort of Daulatabad, located at district Aurangabad in Maharashtra.

Purana Qila

The capital built by Sher Shah was called Shergarh. It was made on the remains of the old city of Inderpath/Indraprastha. With

---

[84]*Cf.* Hearn, *The Seven Cities of Delhi*, p.203.

this establishment, the settlement of the erstwhile Inderpath came to life once again. The ruins of the previous cities were pulled together by the Pathan king to design his new city. The foundation of another city Dinpanah was laid by Humayun in 1530, and later the same was demolished by the Pathan king Sher Shah after defeating and pushing Humayun into exile in 1540. According to G.R. Hearn:

> Farid-ud-din, having driven out Humayun, ascended the throne in AD 1540 with the title of Sher Shah. Although Agra was his capital, he commenced to build a wall... To Sher Shah, also, are attributed the Kila Kona Mosque, and the Sher Mandal, both in Humayun's Fort.[85]

Shergarh was laid on the same site of Dinpanah and the foundation of Purana Qila. Sher Shah reigned for five years and was able to complete the construction of the fort and the city. Therefore, nearly every building in the fort is named after him, such as Sher Mandal, Sher Shah Mosque, and so on. A huge well is located in the centre of the fort. The mosque of Sher Shah is another building that attracts the attention of any visitor. It is said that 'This is one of the most beautiful mosques built in Delhi before the time of the Mughals.'[86] The beauty of the structure is highlighted through the use of Arabic text and by employing different kinds of stones of varied colours, mainly red, black, grey and white. To the south of Mubarakpur is the Moth ki Masjid, a fine mosque built in 1488 by Sikandar Khan Lodi, which served as a model for Sher Shah's mosque

[85]Hearn, *The Seven Cities of Delhi*, pp.215–16.
[86]Spear, *Delhi: Its Monuments and History*, p.30.

in the Purana Qila.[87] Another significant building inside the fort is Sher Mandal, which is an octagonal building with steep steps. This building was used by the founder as a mosque. Later, in 1545, Humayun regained his empire and started ruling from the same building that was made by Sher Shah. The reverence for art and craft did not allow the former to demolish the buildings made by his rival, even though the norm of the day was to demolish the older structure and build a new one in its place.

Humayun occupied Shergarh and started ruling over India from the same place. The building of Sher Mandal was used by him as his library. The shelves that were made for keeping books are still intact. This is the very spot from where Humayun fell to his death as he slipped from the steep staircase, as he was rushing out for his prayers on hearing the *azan*. For some time Akbar stayed in the same palace and later shifted to Agra with the intention of making the city his own. Some brick structures are also visible, which served as the *hammam* or the royal bath. The wall of Purana Qila has been called 'extremely picturesque'.[88]

Shahjahanabad

Shud Shahjahanabad az Shah Jahan abad
[Shahjahanabad came to life through the efforts of Shah Jahan.]

This was a chronogram composed by Mir Yahiya Kashi on the completion of the fort. The only city made by the Mughals

---

[87]Fanshawe, *Delhi: Past and Present*, p.245.
[88]Ibid., p.227.

in their heyday in Delhi was Shahjahanabad. The founder of this massive city was the Emperor Shah Jahan, as is evident from the name of the city. Since the history of the city has been discussed in Chapter 2, this section will concentrate on the buildings located within the premises of the Red Fort and the later sections on the monuments that have adorned this city and were buildings of popular use. Although most medieval rulers built their cities due to the Islamic belief that the foundation of a city is an act of piety,[89] piety was not a motivator for Shah Jahan. The heat of Agra was not suitable to the Mughal emperor, and therefore, with the help of the *hakims* and astrologers, the new city was to be built on the banks of the Yamuna. This city came up in close proximity to Firozabad, which was the city of Firuz Shah Tughlaq.

According to Sir W.W. Hunter, who edited The *Imperial Gazetteer of India*, Shahjahanabad was founded in 1638 by Emperor Shah Jahan (r.1627–1658). The palace was built first, followed by the walls of the city, and finally the construction of Jama Masjid took place. Raw materials were largely taken from the half-deserted cities of Firozabad and Shergarh. Much of the construction work was still in progress when the emperor fell ill and was carried off to Agra by his eldest son, Dara Shikoh. This was because, in 1658, he was deposed of by his youngest son, Aurangzeb, who succeeded to the Mughal *taqt*.

The collection of Sir Syed Ahmed Khan on the monuments of Delhi is also very crucial. The most impressive work so far on the Red Fort is a book by Gordon Sanderson. It is a mine of information on the fort, and nearly records every single historical building that was located in it. The exhaustive list

---

[89]Spear, *Delhi: Its Monuments and History*, p.27.

of contents includes the Nubat or Naqqar Khana, Chhatta Chowk, Rang Mahal, Mumtaz Mahal, and so on.[90]

Lal Qila

The Red Fort is a massive structure and many labourers were involved in building this fort along with artists, craftsmen, architects and astrologers. The use of the 'pietra dura' in the building made Sayyid Ahmed Khan believe that some Italian architect was also employed.[91] A huge amount of material like stones and mortar was collected from various governors and the officials of the state. The task of providing the material lay on the *rajas* of the territories where these items were available and obtainable. The raja of the Nagaur area was to supply marble, famously called *makrana* after the name of village Makrana (in district Nagaur) where it was mined. Similarly, Jodhpur was the area where the red stone was available in abundance, and this was supplied by the kings of Jodhpur. The state didn't incur any cost while collecting these resources as they were available in the territories that accepted subjugation to the Mughal state, and were in the service of Mughals at the time of construction. The amount of money that went into making the fort was one hundred lakh rupees. Out of this, fifty per cent was used for the buildings and the other half was invested in making the wall of the city.

The fort is an irregular octagon in plan with its two long sides on the east and west and six smaller ones. Fanshawe

---

[90]Gordon Sanderson, *Delhi Fort: A Guide to the Buildings and Gardens*, Asian Educational Services, New Delhi, 2000.
[91]Ibid., p.5.

writes in his book:

> The present city of Shahjahanabad extends for nearly two and a quarter miles along the right bank of the Jumna...northern wall, so famous in the history of 1857, extends just three quarters of a mile...In the north wall are situated the famous Kashmir Gate and the Mori or Drain Gate, in the west wall are the Kabul, Lahore, Farash Khana, and Ajmir Gates—in the south wall the Turkman and Delhi. The gates on the river side of the city were the Khairati and Rajghat, the Calcutta and Nigambod—both removed; the Kela Gate, and the Badar Rao Gate, now closed.[92]

From this information, it is evident that much of the fort that was made by the Mughal emperor was intact until the late nineteenth century. It was only after the Battle of Delhi (*c*.1803) and the uprising of 1857 that the fort lost its original extent. As per Hearn:

> It was not until after 1804 that the city wall was extended, in the bed of the river up to the moat around the palace; Shahjahanabad the wall along Daryaganj was probably built at the same time. That no wall was originally made along the riverside we know from the writings of Bernier, the French physician, in 1699, and of Captain Francklin, who visited Delhi in 1793.[93]

Thus, the wall of the city was completed by the efforts of many. The contribution of the British made the city safer. The

---

[92]Fanshawe, *Delhi: Past and Present*, pp.5–6.
[93]Hearn, *The Seven Cities of Delhi*, pp.134–35.

Mughals kept the riverside open because the rivers were the main means of transport, as it was fast and incurred less cost. The wall had its faith through the centuries but the remnants speak a lot about the marvels and the excellence that were engaged to make an invincible defence wall around the city, which was emerging as a bustling market of luxury products and necessities and was amongst the most effluent trade hubs of the times.

The entry to the fort is through the Lahore Gate which is next to the platform from where the prime minister of India delivers his Independence Day speech every year. This raised venue, which is now used for delivering speeches, was built by Aurangzeb as part of the two barbicans he added to the existing fort. These barbicans were called 'veil of the fort' by the founder, Shah Jahan. The fort has been referred to by many names by different rulers. The founder named it Urdu-i-Mu'alla, while his eighteenth century successors, Akbar Shah and Bahadur Shah, called it Qila-i-Mu'alla.[94] Amongst the outlasting structures, the most revealing is the Diwan-i-Khaas. After entering from the Lahori Gate, another gate appears immediately along the bastion wall, and it is from here that the entry to the fort begins. Crossing through the Lahori Gate, one passes through the Chhatta Chowk, which is named after a cavity in the ceiling through which the sky can be seen. Various shops make the entire Chhatta Chowk look like a market where buyers can haggle with stubborn shopkeepers. Further off the market lies the entrance to the various palaces and other structures like Diwan-i Aam, etc. This entrance was called Naqqar Khana, which refers to the

---

[94]Spear, *Delhi: Its Monuments and History*, p.1.

drum houses where drums were played on the entry of nobles and officials who sought audience with the emperor or the court. After crossing through the Naqqar Khana, one walks on a pavement with huge gardens on both sides, leading to the Diwan-i-Aam, or the hall of public audience. This is the place where the emperor would come to listen to regular matters of the empire. It was also the venue to receive travellers and ambassadors to the state as well as a place to review the troops and to conduct day-to-day business. The general entry into the fort ahead of this point was prohibited during the medieval times because the personal space of the king began beyond this point. Only officials of the top hierarchy, spies and eunuchs—who were personal attendants of the emperor—were allowed entry, to discuss pressing matters of the state. The movement of the officials and the spies was also restricted up to the Diwan-i-Khaas or the area where the emperor preferred to interact with them. The eunuchs, or the Naders, as they were called, were the only free movers who had access to the private chambers and the harem. They were responsible for controlling and regulating the movements of the officials who were visiting the fort. It is significant to note that only the eunuchs knew how to maintain the cleavage of 'private' and 'public' in the royal mansions, and it was solely their responsibility to keep it intact.[95] Most of the eunuchs fulfilled their duties without fail.

Important guests and elites of the empire who visited to consult about the affairs of the state were received in the next

---

[95]Manisha Choudhary, 'Recruitment, Role and Hierarchy of the Khoja-Nadars: A Case Study of Eunuchs of Amber-Jaipur Kingdom', *Proceedings of Rajasthan History Congress*, 32 session, 2018.

building, the Diwan-i-Khaas. The special guests and the state officials were always under surveillance of the Nadirs. The fine line of the private apartments started from here, and beyond this point the only males who were allowed were the Emperor and the prince (under regulated guidance). Beyond this were royal mansions—the Shah Mahal with its silver roof, Imtiyaz Mahal with its bedroom known as the Burj-i-Tala (The Golden Chamber), Rang Mahal, Khaas Mahal and Daulat Khana, as well as the Hayat Baksh Garden. All these venues were for exclusive guests, and entry to these zones was strictly under the control of the emperor and was possible only with due permission granted by him.

The arrangement of this building and its layout were made with the rarities of the times. The roof of the central room is supported by twelve pillars, forming three openings on each of the four sides; the room is therefore *barahdari* or twelve-doored. The pillars and the upper walls are covered with gold paint and contain inlaid work of precious stones. Above the end arches on both the short sides of the central room is inscribed the famous couplet: *Agar fardos ba rue zamin ast, Hamin ast o! Hamin ast o! Hamin ast o!* (If there is heaven on earth, its here! It's here! It's here!)[96] The grandeur of the fort led effluent writers to comment or compliment on this grand structure. Muhammad Tahir has referred to the fort as the 'edifices resembling paradise' and 'wherever artificers could be found, carpenters, by the mandate worthy of implicit obedience, they were employed in work.'[97] The grandest

---

[96]Hearn, *The Seven Cities of Delhi*, pp.150–51.
[97]H.K. Kaul, *Historic Delhi: An Anthology*, second impression. Oxford University Press, Delhi, 1998, pp.42–43.

building of the contemporary times was before everyone and was worth the display. The aura of the structure continues in the present times as none from the ruling class are able to detach themselves from it.

The debate on whether to keep the fort at the centre of the British imperial city of Delhi helps understand that much effort was made by the new rulers to keep the fort in close proximity of the new seat of power. Grandness is not attained by structures but by roles, as has been the case with this building which has been a stage for all kinds of dynamic economic and political activities of Indian history.

Lutyens Delhi

After the Revolt of 1857, the vestiges of Mughal control in and around the city were uprooted, and the majority of state affairs went into the hands of the crown. The crown converted the fort into a military cantonment and in parallel developed certain portions of the city from where they regulated its movements. The Town Planning Commission of 1912 took the decision to abandon the site of the northern ridge which was unoccupied, dry and fever-free land as compared with the south which was the site with many graves and contained many deserted sites, and yet was crowded and housed ruined mosques and tombs in deplorable condition. The officials and the architects at the task of building the city were living with much pressure in the winter of 1913, 'wondering how a beautiful city could arise from what Lord Curzon described as the deserted cities of dreary and disconsolate tombs'.[98]

---

[98]Kaul, *Historic Delhi: An Anthology*, p.47.

The plan and the site for the city were fixed as per the advice of specialists who were supposed to draw the blueprints of the city and its structures to suit the processional needs and segregate the regular and the Special Forces. Within the Special Forces also, the status of individuals was determined by their seats and the various levels of sitting and standing orders. The expansion of the city was a task in the hands of the officials. In 1902, the waterworks and the drainage scheme came to Delhi along with the electricity, as discussed by Fanshawe. Trams were introduced in the city *c.*1905. Historian Narayani Gupta mentions,

> [...] thus has Shah Jahan built, for a doomed empire. The town-planners wanted the main features of the new city as interesting...the planning of the new city as an extravaganza in classical architecture...of the utmost imperial importance that should be done on a big scale, something which will impress the Indians with our determination to stay here.[99]

Later, in 1914, Patrick Geddes sympathized with the town planners whose schemes were discarded by the close-minded callous and contemptuous city bureaucrats. The plan of Herbert Baker and Edwin Lutyens was to incorporate all the earlier cities in the new city. The planning of the city was getting into trouble as the need to connect both the cities— Shahjahanabad and New Delhi—was proving to be difficult, as each of them were independent entities. The desire to run a processional way from the new city into the old walled

---

[99]Narayani Gupta, *Delhi Between Two Empires 1803–1931*, Oxford University Press, Delhi, 1981, p.179.

city was desired through the Dilli Darwaza. Another path was planned around the lanes of the Jama Masjid. But none was possible without planning and manipulation on ground as construction of these ways required the building of new structures and demolition of some of the old ones that were in the way. Patrick Geddes—a biologist who is more popular for innovative thinking in town planning—wrote a paper on the problems of building a new city adjacent to an older city. The incentives of the Town Planning Act of 1909 were mainly to design any city for a specific purpose, not frustrate old cities or exhaust their spaces of culture, business and trade opportunities. Another issue was that the medieval cities were not guided by the principles of symmetry and the layout of the new city was supposed to be symmetrical. Therefore, all planners strongly felt the need for a buffer zone in between the old city and the new site. Gupta writes, 'The combined fear of the old town encroaching on and spoiling the symmetry of the new, and of the "Indian Town" polluting the imperial one led to the first serious attempt at long-term town planning for Delhi's urban area.'[100] Most of the localities around the municipal areas of Hudson Lane, Outram Lanes, Kingsway Camp and Civil Lines developed during the early decades of the twentieth century. Many of these areas were residential zones for the British officials. The extension of the city took place after finalizing the site on a hill where the president's estate stands today, along with the two superimposing extensions—the North Block and the South Block.

---

[100]Narayani Gupta, *Delhi Between Two Empires 1803–1931*, Oxford University Press, Delhi, 1981, p.181.

The western extension area originated with an idea to use the area of Karol Bagh as a site to provide accommodation for construction workers. This was also in close proximity of Sadar Bazar and Jhandewalan which would connect the imperial city with Old Delhi (Shahjahanabad). The city wall from Kabul Gate to Ajmeri Gate was demolished and the moat and ditches were filled. This entire extension was controlled by the imperial government under the guidance of the Deputy Commissioner, Colonel H.C. Beadon. Many properties were bought around Paharganj and Sadar Bazaar to develop the model mohallas. A class distinction was made evident by segregating the new residential areas for the British officials from the overpopulated mohallas meant for Indians, and these were developed differently. The activities around the British quarters were extensive and the wide roads that connected these areas to the main city were the main focus of the government. Two new roads were planned at Jhandewalan and Idgah.[101] The burden of developing the city was felt deeply by the officials and the team of town planners. It was not only limited to the collection of the material and the planning, but further extended to the possession of the properties from the *nazul* (royal estate) and various other private properties. The changes that tapped Chandni Chowk and the Red Fort areas have been explained in this chapter, along with the development plans executed for the areas on the northern side, such as Idgah, Karol Bagh, the route that led to northern Delhi via Faiz Road, and Paharganj. The city was expanding fast, incorporating its old features into its fold in order to attain a novel look for the imperial city of Delhi with utmost effective utility.

---

[101]Gupta, *Delhi between Two Empires 1803–1931*, p.191.

Since only municipal zones and notified areas were given grants from the imperial treasury, some areas remained neglected and lacked even basic amenities. The extension of the southern and western parts of the city as proposed by the Town Planning Committee were slowed down due to the First World War (1914–1919), which was extracting much of the British resources. The other changes that stuck to the city during the early twentieth century were inflation and mass migrations. These were all effects that were setting in due to the shift of the imperial capital, just like moths reached for the light. People came in for education and business opportunities; others from far away came looking for jobs in the new imperial setup. For many it was a shift guided by the wishes of family members and relatives who wanted to try their fortunes in the newly emerging capital of the Indian subcontinent. Educational institutions were also set up, mainly to prepare a class of people who would 'serve the crown' and 'extend its goodwill'. Overall, it was to highlight that the crown is given to the welfare of the citizens of the city. St Stephen's College and Hindu College were set on the maiden voyage of building up a service class that would support the apparatus of the crown. The task of the state was not complete without providing safe working areas and offices for those who were engaged in the mission of the state!

All the cities mentioned in this chapter were created by individual rulers to serve their own requirements. While some were able to respect the creations of the deceased rulers, other hardly paid any attention to the earlier rulers and their contributions. Interestingly, none of them demolished the previous cities. The walls of all the preceding cities were pulled down to build the defence wall and the surroundings of the new cities. Perhaps this served as a significant reason for citizens to leave an area and inhabit other new walled cities for greater safety and security. This is an interesting feature to notice and serves as an eye-opening fact for anyone, as the state didn't do much to inhabit the new cities. Due to a vast network and extensive trade practices during the medieval centuries in India, the number of cities and territories of the existing cities were constantly expanding. Delhi was no exception to this process, owing to its resources and strategic location. Thus, it attracted many rulers, and subsequently the city structures and its limbs. Together, all these bejewelled Delhi.

4

THE SUFIS AND ELITES OF *DILLI*

The monuments discussed in this chapter, which were (are) revered due to their spiritual sanctity, were also the centres of cultural confluence. Sufi saints were attracted to Delhi but not for political benefit. The Sufi *dargahs* of Delhi are the most significant centres to understand the struggle between the crowned sultans and the uncrowned 'real sultans', or *betaj badshahs*, as Sufi Saints ruled over the minds and the hearts of their followers, and not just territories. During the medieval centuries, the Chistiya Order was a dominant Sufi Order in the vicinity of Delhi. The sultans of the Delhi Sultanate and the emperors of the Mughal Empire maintained contact with these Sufi saints. This was due to the belief that all the saintly and ascetic communities constitute 'the army for the prayer', which was the most crucial requirement for the blessings and positive will of the Almighty. Later, the Mughals made them regular retainers of the state and allotted them grants—the *madad-i-mash* and *suryaghal*—to ensure that they prayed for the well-being and longevity of the empire.

Bakhtiyar Kaki

Bakhtiyar Kaki was a disciple of Moinuddin Chishti, and the founder of Sufism in India. The latter was popularly known

as Baba Ghareeb Nawaz. The tomb of Qutubuddin Bakhtiyar
Kaki is at Mehrauli and it is the oldest *dargah* in Delhi.
Being immersed in learning and the application of wisdom,
Qutubuddin Bakhtiyar Kaki's *pir* (teacher) decided to send
him to Delhi, in order to spread the message of Sufism. He
is credited for establishing Sufism and the Chishti Order in
Delhi. The tomb is located in the oldest surviving area of
Delhi popularly known as Mehrauli, which served as the
capital of the Delhi Sultanate during the twelfth and thirteenth
centuries. The landscape of Mehrauli is scattered with old
ruins and residues of the past. The *dargah* of Bakhtiyar Kaki
is located at a short distance from the towering Qutub Minar
and it is a peaceful sanctum amidst the meandering lanes and
by-lanes of Mehrauli. The tapering road leading to the *dargah*
is lined with eateries and restaurants. The lane that leads to
the *dargah* is full of shops that fan out to sell the *chadar,*
tabaruk, niyaz, ittar and *ziyarat* flowers. All these form the
basket of offerings for the *mazar.* The gate of the complex
is a huge structure decorated with crushed tiles. Even today,
the *dargah* houses many spiritually minded people and many
of them are visitors from far-flung areas of the country. The
rituals of the *dargah* such as *chiragi, roshni, dua* and *niyaz* are
same as they are for many other Sufi *dargahs* and *fatiha* for
the revered soul that lies buried. The complex of the *dargah*
resembles a graveyard as many graves are scattered around.
These are mainly graves of the disciples who wished to be
buried next to their *pir* for the ultimate union.

The management of many *dargahs* do not allow women to
enter the main shrine where the grave of the saint is housed.
The *dargah* of Bakhtiyar Kaki is no exception to this norm.
As the main shrine of the saint Kaki is closed to women,

they can only view it from outside through a marble lattice boundary, and tie their wish threads on it. Devotees on the site often share how their wishes were fulfilled, reflecting an overwhelming respect for the saint.

Qutubuddin Bakhtiyar was a renowned Sufi saint and scholar of the Chishti Order living in Delhi. The original name of Khwaja Qutbuddin was Bakhtiyar, and Qutbuddin was his title. The suffix of 'Kaki' was attributed to him to hint at the virtue of a miracle performed by him. Popularly, he is also called Khwaja Kaki and Hazrat Qutub Saheb. Kaki is not the name of the saint, rather it is the epithet attached to his name, with an interesting story to go with it.

The life that Qutubuddin Bakhtiyar chose for himself also affected his household. Due to this, his wife was forced to beg. Once, when she was begging for some bread from a baker's wife, the baker's wife reduced her to tears, throwing taunts and jeers at her husband's inability to feed her. On hearing this, Bakhtiyar ordered his wife to take bread (*kak*) from his prayer alcove. According to a legend, this alcove miraculously filled up and remained filled, no matter what quantity of bread was taken out from it. Henceforth, he became known by the title of 'Kaki'.

Even today, the *langar* (free meals for the poor) at the *dargah* primarily constitutes of *kak* (roti, or Indian flatbread). Sufi saints found a large number of followers belonging to many faiths due to the egalitarian nature of their teachings. They also became popular as they emphasized on a frugal lifestyle and helping the needy. Qutubuddin Kaki was appointed as the *khalifa* by Moinnudin Chishti and was the most respected saint of the time. Being caliph, his hospice became a great centre of Islamic learning, theology and mysticism. As per the tradition of Sufism he enrolled disciples who were called *murshid*, and trained them in the practices and sciences of the Chistiya Silsilah. His most famous disciple and spiritual successor was Fariduddin Ganjshakar, who, in turn, became the spiritual master of Delhi's noted Sufi saint Nizamuddin Awaliya, who was in turn the spiritual master of Amir Khusro and Nasiruddin Chirag-e-Delhi. Bakhtiyar's *dargah* in Mehrauli is also the venue of his annual *Urs*, which attracts many spiritual-minded people. Sufi *dargahs* are not places for selective crowd assemblages. The believers of the saints come from all walks of life, irrespective of their class, caste and religious distinctions.

The *dargah* of Kaki is a centre for cultural syncretism. Hindus and Sikhs too are a part of this culture, and this is manifested annually in the form of a festival of flower sellers known as *phool walon ki sair*. This tradition began in 1812 after the wife of Mughal Emperor Akbar Shah II promised to offer a *chadar* and a flower *pankha* if her son Mirza Jehangir returned from exile in Allahabad. The prince came back, and thus the act that was started as a wish-fulfilment gesture became a tradition, and it continues to this day. People from different walks of life participate in this annual festival to seek the blessings of the saint.

There are three gates besides the main entrance to the *dargah*. They are unceremonious as any other public space. The footfall to Kaki's *dargah* is less in comparison to the hospice of Shaikh Nizamuddin Awaliya. The Ajmeri Darwaza opens into a courtyard where one can usually see children playing different traditional games. Towards the left is an entrance to the Moti Masjid built *c*.1709 by Shah Alam Bahadur Shah I. There is an entrance to the mosque from the side of the *dargah* and it has been put to disuse. Beyond the courtyard lies Zafar Mahal, built by the last Mughal Emperor Bahadur Shah Zafar.

The influence of Qutubuddin Bakhtiyar Kaki over Sufism in India was immense. He developed the traditional ideas of universal brotherhood and charity within the Chishti Order in India and lived up to it. With this, a new dimension of Islam, hitherto absent, opened up in the Indian subcontinent. He contributed significantly to the Sufi movement which gradually attracted many people to Islam in India during the thirteenth and fourteenth centuries.

Hazrat Nizamuddin Awaliya

Shaikh Nizamuddin Awaliya was born *c.*1238 in Badaun, Uttar Pradesh. Hazrat Syed Ahmed Bokhari and Bibi Zuleikha were the parents of this saint. His father died when Awaliya was just five years old and his mother took it upon herself to ensure that her son got the best education. She placed him under the training of Maulana Allauddin Usooli of Badaun under whose guidance the boy excelled in studies. The young boy Nizamuddin mastered the seven ways of reciting the Holy Quran, studied Arabic grammar, *ahadith* (traditions of the Prophet Mohammed), *tafsir* (commentary on the Quran), mathematics and astronomy. He was an excellent student of grammar and various other religious scriptures. He also evolved in the art of debating. When he was around sixteen or seventeen years old, he heard of the Sufi saint Fariduddin Ganjshakar, popularly known as Baba Farid. He developed respect for the saint and his intense desire to seek training from the saint led him to Ajodhan (part of then-Punjab and present Pakpattan Sharif in Pakistan) at the age of twenty. There he enrolled as a disciple of Baba Farid. The word 'Pakpattan' means the town of purity. After receiving training in the thoughts of Chistiya School of Sufisim, Nizamuddin was asked to settle in Delhi and explore Sufi ideas and study theology. Simultaneously, he started Sufi devotional practices and prescribed litanies along with studies. He visited Ajodhan each year and spent the month of Ramadan in the attendance of Baba Farid. On his third such visit, Baba Farid made him his successor and asked him to be in Delhi itself. After living at various places in Delhi for years, he finally settled down in Ghiyaspur, a village near the city. There he built his *khanqah* which attracted people from far and near, hailing from all walks of life. He was passionately committed to helping the needy, feeding the hungry, and being sympathetic to the oppressed. His kitchen was always open and large hordes of hungry and needy people survived on it. He was very generous towards the poor, although he personally maintained a very austere lifestyle. His diet consisted of a small piece of bread and a small bowl of vegetable soup. Being in Delhi, he enrolled a large number of disciples who took his message to the far-flung corners of the subcontinent and beyond. He was very different in his approach from the previous Sufi *khalifas* and gave a lot of authority to his own disciples to propagate their spiritual lineage. Nasiruddin Chiragh Dehlavi and Amir Khusro were the famous disciples of Awaliya, and the former was declared his spiritual successor. The poet Amir Khusro was Awaliya's most loved disciple. The day-to-day audience of the Sufi believers became a major source for knowing the attributes of life that were propounded by the saint, and these were compiled in the form of anecdotes by Amar Hasan Sijzi.

This compilation was titled *Faud-al-Fawad* and is a major source to explore the life and times of the saint.

The personal history of the saint speaks a lot about his personality and the struggles he faced. The history of the saint forms an interesting reading to understand and know the political history of the times. Awaliya never aspired for funds from the state, and whenever the state approached him with wealth, he denied it. He chose poverty over support from the state. Many instances of his denial to state funds appear in the contemporary *tawarikh* and *tarikh* literature. In fact, the denial of the material gifts by the saint had offended many sultans. His refusal of the offering extended by the state angered the sultan Ghiyasuddin Tughlaq, and he decided to kill Awaliya. When this news reached the Sufi saint, he responded by saying, 'Hunuz, Dilli dur asat!' (Yet, Delhi is far!)

Moving forward from the persona of Awaliya, one needs to see the intricacies of the shrine complex that are marked with many medieval and early modern monuments and sites. The *neela gumbad* at the crossing of Mathura Road is an interesting monument. It is a juncture between New Delhi (via Zakir Hussain Marg) and the cities and monuments of medieval Delhi. The *gumbad* is also a landmark that divides the visitors going towards Humayun's Tomb on the left and the *dargah* of Nizamuddin Awaliya on the right. The Nizamuddin police station is on Mathura Road and next to the lane that leads to the shrine. This lane is an unorganized cluster of many hawkers and shopkeepers who sell a large range of goods, from sweetmeats, sweets, dates, meat to *miswaq*, *itar*, utensils, slippers, religious literature and clothes such as *burqah*, skull cap, scarf and *janamaz*. Walking through these narrow lanes, one can also see many butcher shops who serve *halaal* meat. Goats and sheep also claim space in these lanes that form the surroundings of the Nizamuddin Basti, and live in perfect harmony with the constantly walking crowds by rubbing along but with a few instances of recklessness. In the evenings, *kabab* stalls pop up on the lanes which serve as fast food options for visitors and labourers. The smoky fume of animal fat which is used to cook the *kababs* fills the air and attracts lots of food tasters. Luckily, goods are available in every kind of price range, and the quantity too is flexible, based on the spending capacity and consuming will of the customer. The sulphuric perfume of *loban* and sweet smell of *guldavadi* flowers and fresh roses blend to create a healthy spiritual world in these suffocating crowded lanes. Beautiful beaded strings of different hues hang on the walls, and pictures of religious centres and other items are also visible on the shelves. The innumerable *paan* (betel) shops around the corners are always crowded. Many hang out for buying cigarettes and other kinds of splendorous refreshments. As one enters the lane from Mathura Road, the huge *jamati* mosque on the right hand side can be seen. This is Markaz Masjid or Banglewali Masjid. This mosque is well known for the origin of *Tablighi Jamaat*—an Islamic religious movement based on the principle of 'the work of the Prophets'—and functioning as a global centre for the sect. Here, pan-world followers of the sect are accompanied and trained by religious scholars to pray and preach the teachings of Islam. This mosque houses many *jamatis* who come here to learn Islamic theology in order to serve the purpose of faith. This crowd is a confluence of many Sunni communities. By moving a little ahead, without leaving the lane, one gets to see a large gate that leads to the Urs Maidan, where a number of celebrations are organized, not necessarily related to the annual *Urs* of Nizamuddin Awaliya. The building adjacent to the *maidan* is the Ghalib Academy which is a major centre for the readers of Urdu literature. Next to this is the *mazaar*, or the grave, of the great poet Mirza Ghalib. The grave is recently encircled by a latticework of red stone. Sadly, all these monuments are lying in a deplorable condition. The populace using them just carries on as a matter of right, without bearing even a single shred of responsibility towards these historical structures.

The lane gets increasingly narrower as one moves towards the *dargah* and the *baoli*. The second-level entry can be classified by the covered corridor that leads to even narrower lanes after the grave of Mirza Ghalib. The shops are also like small shelves in the walls, and along the corridor some shops are double-storeyed. The smaller shops are at the top and staircases lead down to storage areas. The elevation of the roads makes one realize that the shops are scattered on a little risen platform in comparison to the level of surroundings. Further on, the hospice is at a lower level that can be sensed from the staircase that drops in the main complex. And after going down a large number of stairs in different brackets, one reaches the front of a white marble tomb that houses the grave of Amir Khusro after crossing a huge arched gate. One has to jump carefully through the many stone-concealed graves before reaching the mausoleum of Amir Khusro. Ziauddin Barani, the great historian who wrote *Tarikh-i Firuz Shahi*, also rests near this most-loved disciple of Shaikh Awaliya. Another set of stairs takes visitors to a lower level where the marble tomb of Nizamuddin can be seen shining with gold work, which initially becomes visible from the tomb of Khusro. The look, however, changes completely as one comes to the square arena where Awaliya is resting. This area is very different from the entire Nizamuddin basti. The whole structure here is made of white marble, and decorated with floral patterns drawn in red and green colour, which are further enhanced with golden paint. The tomb structure is not the result of a one-time job by one person, but rather it attained its present grandeur through the contributions of many wealthy believers in different times, who had respect and love for this Sufi 'Sultan of Delhi'.

On the western side of the tomb is the Jamat Khana Mosque, which was constructed during Khilji's rule. It is a mosque par excellence due to its architectural style and decorations, and is considered unique by art historians as it is the only building here with intricate carvings and hangings. This mosque is finest in term of its latticed stone screen and pendentives, which are the most beautiful specimen of early Muslim craftsmanship. The mosque was built by Khizr Khan, who was a disciple of the saint and the eldest son of Alauddin Khilji. Ferishta confirms the same without providing many details. As per Sir Syed Ahmed Khan only the centre hall was built by Khizr Khan, and the two extensions on either sides were contributed by Muhammad bin Tughlaq, and repaired by the Mughal Emperor Akbar in 1572–73. The contributions made at different times kept the mosque alive, and allowed it to survive through various phases of history. The lane on the northern side of the tomb takes one to another narrow lane that leads to the Nizamuddin basti *baoli*, where water runs down and gets collected from all the sides of the basti. The narrow lanes which lead to the *baoli* are dotted with many verandahs and halls. These lanes serve as working centres of religious leaders engaged in religious counselling and amulet-making. The halls and shelves are constructions that were made during medieval times. The *baoli* is made of red sandstone and serves the water requirements of its surroundings.

Reverence towards the saint led many to contribute to the tomb and its surroundings, and this is evident from the extensions, embellishments and various phases of renovations around the original building. Muhammad bin Tughlaq built a cupola over the grave. Firuz Shah added the arches and the sandalwood lattices. In 1562, Fariduddin Khan rebuilt the tomb, and later, in 1608, Farid Murtaza Khan constructed a lovely canopy of pearl and wood. At around 1882–83, Khurshid Jha of Hyderabad built a marble balustrade around the grave. The Nizam of Hyderabad also made a generous donation in the twentieth century to re do the faded paintings of the tomb. Besides these concrete and objective material constructions, many devotees made some philosophical contributions to the grave of the revered saint. In 1652–53, Alamgir II made a devout offer to express his respect through an inscribed tablet that declared that the saint is 'the royal crown of the whole world' and 'the kingly crown of Hind'.[102] Also, in front of the saint's tomb is the resting place of princess Jahanara, the elder daughter of Shah Jahan who sided with Aurangzeb in the war of succession. There is no tomb over the grave of the princess. However, there is a marble surrounding of latticework which segregates the grave from general interaction. The complex is open on the top, and is made of fine marble with beautiful carvings all around it. Other noted personalities who got space in the spiritual surroundings of the saints' tomb were

---

[102]Surendranath Sen, *Delhi and Its Monuments*, A. Mukherjee & Co. Ltd, Calcutta, reprinted 1954, p.21.

Muhammud bin Tughlaq and Mirza Jahangir, the eldest son of Akbar II. The saint and his hospice is a place for spirituality, blessings and peace. Thus, many tried to ensure their share.

Nasiruddin 'Chirag Dilli'

Nasiruddin Mahmud 'Chirag Dilli' (Dehlavi) was the disciple of Nizamuddin Awaliya as well as his successor. The shrine of this saint is located in the village of Chirag Delhi and is approachable from the Outer Ring Road. Born *c.*1274, he was the last recognized *khalifa* of the Chishti Order in Delhi. His father was Sheikh Mahmud Yahya and the family was settled in Ayodhaya (Awadh) where they flourished in the trade of woollen goods. So, this *murid* (disciple) hailed from a well-to-do family unlike his *pir* Nizamuddin Awaliya who had a humble background. His father died when Nasiruddin was just nine years old. According to the famous texts, *Siar-ul-Aulia* and *Mirat-ul-Asrar*, Nasiruddin came to Delhi at the age of forty-three and joined the circle of Hazrat Nizamuddin Awaliya's *murids*. Initially, he was educated by Maulana Abdul Karim Sherwani, and later he enrolled under the guardianship of Iftikhar-ud-din Gilani. Later, being the *murid* of Nizamuddin Awaliya he attained much respect and was able to establish himself as a distinguished Sufi saint of Delhi. He left for his heavenly abode in 1356. As an avid follower of Nasiruddin, Firoz Shah Tughlaq constructed his tomb to honour him. The rectangular structure was made of rubble stone. Later, Muhammud bin Tughlaq added the chambers and two gateways on either side of the mausoleum. The tomb underwent numerous renovations. Presently, it is a square chamber supported by twelve pillars and small towers on all the corners. The central mausoleum is octagonal in shape with a domed top. However, the dome on the top is not as explicit as it is on the mausoleum of Nizamuddin Awaliya and Moinuddin Chishti located in Ajmer. The chamber is enclosed with perforated screens through which the grave of the saint can be seen. The Chishti Sufis were the most respected mystics during the medieval centuries and this led to the constant extension of the hospice areas. Later, in the seventeenth century, a *Mahfil Khana* or *Majlis Khana* (symposium hall or assembly hall) was added, and in the eighteenth century a mosque was built by the Mughal emperor Farrukhsiyar. The constant expansion of the premise is indicative of the fact that many people visit the shrine regularly and the extensions were made to accommodate the increasing crowds.

Maai Sahib and Bibi Sahib

Bibi Zuleikha, popularly known as Maai Sahib was mother of Shaikh Nizamuddin Awaliya. Her resting place is located at Adchini, a place near Qutub Minar. Bibi Zuleikha passed away in 1250 which was long before her son came to be known as a great mystic. She was buried in her house. This grave is very different from other contemporary ones as it is one of two graves placed parallel to each other on a raised platform, a deviant feature of the time. The shrine is named 'Maai Sahib aur Bibi Sahib ki mazaar'. Shaikh Awaliya's sister, Bibi Sahib, was buried besides her mother. Out of the two graves in the burial chamber, the smaller grave, is of Bibi Jannat who was the daughter of Bibi Zulekha. Similar to the other shrines, *chiragi, roshni* and *niyaz* are offered along with flowers, mainly red roses. The latticework on the northern and southern side form a curtain around the graves and the two gates in the centre of the northern and the southern *jallis* facilitate the entry and exit to the grave chamber. A concrete wall forms the western side of the burial chamber and the eastern side is made of marble latticework. The outer side of the western wall houses a mosque, which is open to all souls who want to offer *namaz*; mainly men use this area while women flock to the small verandah located on the northern side. The top of the burial chamber is also very different compared to other domes and tops made in those days. Above the four surrounding walls of the burial chamber, there are a number of running arches on all sides. The top is octagonal-shaped, and is placed on a flat roof with small *roshandaans* on each corner. This makes the number of *roshandaans* eight. All the eight elevations of the top are decorated with floral design paintings and the different names of Allah appear on the running base shaft. These names are slightly raised and are painted in gold.

This *dargah* is also different from all the other Sufi centres, as women are allowed to visit the inner chambers. Another deviant practice that is evident at this shrine is about the day that has been prescribed for making the holy visits. The *jummaraat* (Thursday) is considered as an ideal day for visiting Sufi *dargahs*, but this *dargah* is visited on Wednesdays. Dargah Quli Khan, a Persian noble, who recorded the happenings of Delhi during the eighteenth century noted in his diary *Muraqqa-i-Dilli* that visitors came to the holy shrine of Bibi Zuleikha on Thursday. This indicates that the shift in the visit day to Wednesdays came into effect only after the late eighteenth century. It is interesting to note that women were the exclusive visitors to the shrine during those days as well. Surprisingly, a tulsi plant in the centre of the courtyard stands alone to bear the smoke of the *agarbattis* that are lit by the devotees. A large *vazu-kahna* in the outer courtyard is covered with tin sheds and a small door on the left leads to the main road, Sri Aurobindo Marg. The spiritual significance of the Maai Sahib's *dargah* can be accessed from the saying of Nizamuddin Awaliya that whenever he lost hope he used to spend time at the *mazaar* of his mother, sitting there in silence. Thus, it can be said that the Maai Sahib's *dargah* is a place for women to look to the path of spirituality. The historicity of this exclusion from active social and economic life that is marked around the *dargah* of these female saints cannot be proven due to the lack of tangible evidence. As opposed to this, all the shrines of male Sufi saints are shrouded with crowded market areas reflecting active social and economic engagements.

In the thirteenth century, Delhi became a major centre for Sufism due to the activities of Nizamuddin Awaliya which were carried forward by Nasiruddin Chirag Dehlavi. This enhanced the cultural matrix of the imperial capital, and it gradually became the root cause for cultural syncretism. The same continues even today in the form of the *sama, mehfils, majlis, qawaalis, Urs* and the annual festival of *phool walo ki sair*. All the Sufi saints here are of the Chistiya Silsilah, and much of their rituals are inspired from the traditions and customs of the Ajmer shrine.

Knowing the correct history of Delhi and its monuments is a task for anyone, as all places have multiple histories around them. The problem for the listener is to sort out the true version that he or she is able to relate to. As history works in the concentric circles of time, space and knowledge, all these work in the same time. The conscious working and intersecting of the points, facts and reasons helps the person to pick the best acceptable narrative. Therefore, the same event is surrounded with many stories, and each listeners trust the version that is acceptable to them as per the limitations of their knowledge.

Tombs of the City

While some saints were able to earn mausoleums and tombs, many others remained unnoticed. The ruling classes were able to secure most of the resources, and therefore were able to create history and build monuments to mark their remembrances. During medieval times, it was a general understanding that tombs were the most explicit way to be remembered by future generations. Therefore, the tombs became a choice of the elites, so much so that many of them constructed their burial chambers even while alive. The most illustrious examples of this desire are the tombs of Sikandar Lodi and Humayun, present amongst many others. Many tombs were erected in Delhi with marvellous designs. In order to acknowledge their engineering expertise, this section discusses some famous tombs on the basis of their architectural style.

An aerial view of Delhi helps to understand that its landscape is thickly dotted with graves. Various domes and tombs of different sizes and styles are visible throughout the city. During medieval times, Delhi was the prime location for the construction of tombs due to various reasons such as the presence of Sufi saints and the desire to be buried next to them, the significance of the city as an imperial capital, etc. Many scholars have tried to collect details about these tombs, but mainly succeeded only in providing the locations of the tombs. Here, an effort has been made to understand locations along with the surroundings and the depleting condition of the monumental tombs, since many of them are losing their architectural beauty. The greatest threat to these heritage monuments comes from the encroachments and modifications made by the present occupants who lack a sense of attachment towards them. Each of the tombs discussed here are art pieces and have something special to offer. Art historian Savita Kumari's study of the Delhi Sultanate tombs based on their architectural designs is an exclusive work, one of its kind.[103] Her work is a detailed study of the specification of the tombs. It is rich in terms of the plates and the classification of the tombs as per their outer structures such as square, octagonal and pillared tombs. However, an inquiry into the cultural and the social aspects of the tombs and their critical assessments are absent.

Iltutmish's (Altamash) Tomb

A detour to the right of the Quwwat-ul-Islam Masjid leads to the tomb of Shams-ud-din Iltutmish (Altamash), the second Muhammadan king of India. Champbell opines that Iltutmish built his own tomb at one end of a new mosque. He propounded this on the basis of the similarities between the mosque and the tomb. Whereas, Sir Saiyyad Ahmed Khan believes that it was built by Razia Sultana (daughter of Iltutmish), though he didn't provide reasons for this

---

[103]Savita Kumari, *Tombs of Delhi: Sultanate Period*, Bharatiya Kala Prakashan, Delhi, 2006.

contention.[104] While General Cunningham mentions, 'the tomb is of the same age as the Qutub Minar,'[105] Hearn writes, 'There is no other tomb anywhere extant of earlier date. The carving of the interior is exquisite, and in very much the same style as that of the work on the great arches; it was probably carried out by the same artisans, or by their pupils.'[106] As there is no roof on this tomb, Spear notes, 'such a tomb should have no covering; perhaps it had a plain roof made of beams of timber', as it appears to be a tradition for devoted Muslims.[107] The most popular example of the uncovered graves of a ruler is the grave of Aurangzeb at Khuldabad in Aurangabad. In the tomb of Altamash, a triple prayer niche known as a *mihrab* on the western wall is an intricate and beautifully made structure with the *kufi* style of calligraphy. The central *mihrab* has been highlighted with marble, which was not considered great for use in those days. Traces of paintings are still clear on the carvings at the top. As stated earlier, the tomb is roofless, and it cannot be said with certainty if it ever possessed one. Hearns writes:

> But it is doubtful if they could have undertaken a dome of twenty eight feet span in those days. Not the least of the difficulties would have been the centering. Tavernier states that the centering of the tomb of Taj Mahal, at

---

[104]Stephen Carr, *The Archaeology and Monumental Remains of Delhi*, Ludhiana, 1876, p.73.

[105]Ibid., p.73.

[106]Gordon Risley Hearn, *The Seven Cities of Delhi*, W. Thacker & Co., London, 1906, p.56.

[107]Percival Spear, *Delhi: Its Monuments and History*, Oxford University Press, Delhi, 1994, p.57.

Agra, cost as much as the rest of the building.[108] Thus indicating that making of the dome was an expensive and tedious effort which demanded specializations.

Fanshawe adds, 'The chamber [that] was intended to be roofed is clear from the remains of the lowest course of a dome on the top of the south wall.'[109] The burial chamber of the tomb is a square of 29.5 feet, and there are three arched entrances to the grave from the northern, eastern and southern sides. Carr has provided extensive architectural specifications and measures of the *mihrabs* collectively and individually, as well as for the plinth and the casket. The grave itself is a handsome structure of unusual height and size, with a band of text round the plinth, which is also unusual. Fanshawe writes:

[T]hough small, it is one of the richest examples of Hindu art applied to Muhammadan purposes that Old Delhi affords, and is...extremely beautiful... In addition to the beauty of its details, it is interesting as being the oldest tomb known to exist in India.[110]

All these specifications highlight that the second sultan of the Sultanate had a peaceful time, and he was also able to generate loyalty and acceptance amongst his fellow beings who all were members of the *Chihilgani*. A decent burial speaks a lot about the personality of a person and his access to the resources.

The son and successor of Iltutmish, Firuz Shah, became victim to the favour shown by the nobility to accept the

---

[108]Hearn, *The Seven Cities of Delhi*, p.56.

[109]H.C. Fanshawe, *Delhi: Past and Present*, John Murray, London, 1902, p.269.

[110]Ibid., pp.269–70.

accession of his sister Raziya. He was put in jail, where he died. He was buried beside his elder brother, Nasiruddin Muhammud Shah, in the village of Malikpur. Later, Bahram Shah—the younger brother of Firuz Shah—was also buried in the same tomb. The contention regarding the claims of the graves are confusing due to the absence of inscription but some indications regarding the same can be made by looking at the style of the construction. For a popular architect, Tremlett, the domes were more than indication that they are works by Firuz Shah Tughlaq, as noted by Stephen Carr.[111] Interestingly, many modern authors miss these sites as they consider them minor sites. The absence of evidence around these monuments has been a major roadblock in recording and discovering the history around them.

Mazaar (grave) of Razia Sultana

The only empress of India during the Sultanate, Razia Sultana was a descendent of the Mamluk Dynasty. She reigned from 1236 to 1240, and was deposed by her nobles who were unable to take commands from a woman. There are various contentions about the burial site of the queen. Most believe that the site of the burial, which is lying in a neglected state, is near Turkman Gate. The other two suggested sites are at Kaithal and Tonk in Haryana. These varied hypotheses regarding the location of the site are due to the lack of documentary evidences. The only empress of India was accepted by the residents of Old Delhi, as it can be traced from the location and the monumental design of her grave. The description of the grave as provided

---

[111]Carr, *The Archaeology and Monumental Remains of Delhi*, p.76.

by Carr is not sufficient to clear any other doubt except the location of the grave near the Turkman Gate which is based on the information provided by Ibn Battuta.[112] It can be proposed that the royal lady was not accepted by the fellow sultanate managers, and therefore, a burial space was not allotted in the area where other predecessing rulers of the Sultanate rested. During the sultanate times, the area of Old Delhi (Turkman Gate) was a forested area, and a burial in the forest indicates that the fellow beings of Raziya wanted to push her away from memory. Secondly, the grave is an ordinary concrete structure lacking any ornamentation and inscription, as many of her contemporaries did not want her to be recorded and remembered in history. This attempt at erasing the past is a success, as very few visit her grave to say a *fatiha*. The present state machinery too neglects the grave. As for the structure, it is made of lime mortar, rubble stones and ordinary stones. There are two graves parallel to each other and are placed on a little raised platform. The other grave is in the name of Altunia or Yakut. The complete absence of inscription on the grave and its surroundings has allowed greater confusion to creep in, and encourages the creation of legendary tales around this monument. Although her grave did not have a dome or a tomb, as a queen she was still an exception in those times. Today, she continues to haunt the professional historian, indefinitely.

Tomb of Balban

Nasir-ud-din Mahmud, son of Altamash, finally succeeded Raziya Sultana after troubled times, and ruled under the auspices

---

[112]Carr, *The Archaeology and Monumental Remains of Delhi*, pp.77–78.

of his minister and brother-in-law, Balban. Since Sultan Nasir-ud-din did not have a male heir, after his death Balban declared himself the sultan of Delhi. Balban ascended the throne *c.*1266 at the age of sixty with the title of Sultan Ghiyasuddin Balban. He disintegrated the *Chihalgani*—a group of the forty most important nobles—in the court to make sure that everyone stayed loyal to the crown and established an efficient espionage system to execute spies like Umayyad Barid. Secret reporters and news writers were placed in every department, and only the independent spies were answerable to the sultan. Balban was the only ruler of the Sultanate who was popular for his shrewdness and statesmanship. He was able to make his position in the court due to his administrative qualities and because he was an able military general. Besides, his court was also known for pomp and show. The Sufi saint Nizamuddin Awaliya settled in Delhi during the time of the Emperor Balban.[113] The location of Balban's tomb can be confirmed from the statement, 'the Lal Kot on the right, and on the left the red front of the Jamali Mosque and the huge ruin of the tomb of Sultan Balban to the east of it.'[114] Further, Fanshawe adds:

> [N]earer and to the north of the road to Tughlakabad are the large groves of trees which mark the Hauz Rani and Khirki, while south of the road and close to the Kutab are the Jamali Mosque and the lofty ruins of the tomb of the sultan Balban, and under it on the south the Dargah of the Kutab Sahib, and the houses of Mahrauli half hidden in trees.[115]

---

[113]Fanshawe, *Delhi: Past and Present*, p.237.
[114]Ibid., p.256.
[115]Ibid., p.269.

The tomb is a few minutes' walk from Qutub Minar.[116] Another account places it near the tomb of Nizam-ud-din Awaliya, within the fort of Marzgan, which was built by Balban, and was sometimes called Ghiaspur. Balban died in 1287, and his tomb, which is in complete ruins, is near the Jamali Masjid.[117] He was buried at the Dar-ul-Aman, or the House of Refuge. This building is respected in history more as an institution than as an architectural structure. The Dar-ul-Aman was the bed and resting place of great men, the Sultan Balban and his son, the Khan-i-Shahid.[118] Ibn Battuta notes, 'Whenever any debtor entered this place his debt was adjudged, and in like manner every person found justice; even manslayer deliverance from his adversary; and every person in fear protection.'[119] The tomb is a square building, like the tomb of Altamash and the Alai Darwaza, but was larger than either of these. On each side of the tomb is a spacious room, which may have formed the Dar-ul-Aman established by this king. 'Ibn Battuta says he visited his grave in it—where his son Sher Khan, the Khan-i-Shahid, was interred only two years before him.'[120] The description of Balban's tomb by Stephen Carr is related with the Red Palace and he suggests it is twice in size as compared with the tomb of Iltutmish. Further he notes that Firuz Shah Khilji came to the tomb of Balban to pay his obeisance after his coronation at Kasr Safed.[121] The octagonal

---

[116]Carr, *The Archaeology and Monumental Remains of Delhi*, p.80.

[117]Hearn, *The Seven Cities of Delhi*, p.181.

[118]Fanshawe, *Delhi: Past and Present*, p.275.

[119]Kumari, Tombs of Delhi, p.23 and Carr, *The Archaeology and Monumental Remains of Delhi*, p.80.

[120]Fanshawe, *Delhi: Past and Present*, p.278.

[121]Carr, *The Archaeology and Monumental Remains of Delhi*, pp.79–81.

top of the tomb is supported by the four walls and the side chamber is also domeless. The domes have collapsed over time and the uneven traces of the domes can be seen on the top of the four side walls. Traces of paintings are visible on the inner wall of the eastern wall.[122] The tomb has three entrances and the northern wall is closed. The eastern entrance is the main entry gate to the grave chamber, as the other two gates are smaller in size as compared to the arch in the eastern wall. The tomb is lying in ruin due to trespassing by the locals and misuse by alcoholics and drug addicts who use it as a den. The marvels of its architecture and its cultural importance are buried in the past.

Tomb of Alauddin Khilji

According to Carr, 'The Corpse of Alauddin was bought out from the red palace of Siri and was buried in a tomb in front of Jama Masjid.'[123] Firoz Shah claimed to maintain the Tomb of Sultan Alauddin, stating, 'I repaired it, and furnished it with a sandalwood door.'[124] Sir Sayyid Ahmed Khan also accepted this version.

The tomb has two side chambers that are rectangular in shape and the central chamber is square. The length is fifty feet and the width is thirty-two feet. The tomb is located in the *madarssa* complex. The central and western chambers are provided by ambulatories and the eastern chamber accommodates the steps leading to the top of the building. It

---

[122]Carr, *The Archaeology and Monumental Remains of Delhi*, Ibid., p.81.
[123]Ibid., p.88.
[124]Ibid.

can be approached by a passageway at the back of the tombs. Many other authors also confirm the grave of Alauddin Khilji in the same *madarssa* complex. Hearn states:

> Ala-ud-din, who died before he could completely carry out his plans. He was able, however, to add a gateway, which is close to the Kutb Minar, and some colonnades, which extend to the east of it. At one end of the line of arches is the tomb of this king, at the further end that of Altamash, builder of the first additions to the mosque.[125]

The tomb is a specific building as it was the earliest building to use pendentives to support the dome. This feature had gained popularity and was used in the tomb of Ghiyasuddin Tughlaq. Much of the monument is in ruins now and the dome on the top of the building is no more visible as it has attained decline over time. The inscription to claim the grave inside the monument is completely missing, thus most of these claims are based on the literary evidences. The innovative efforts by Khilji, an economist who initiated market reforms, price and weight regulations, and monetary reforms by introducing new coins have been accepted well down in history, but the personality has not been granted his due. The complete absence of inscription, squinch and a cenotaph on the grave is indicative of the spoilt relationship between the deceased and the successor. It is possible that too many regulations and control introduced by the ruler did not go down well with the corrupt administrative machinery. Therefore, after his death, his officials treated him poorly.

---

[125]Hearn, *The Seven Cities of Delhi.*

Tomb of Ghiyassudin Tughlaq

Ghiyassudin displayed the same spirit in building the mosques and the forts as his predecessors, Qutubuddin Aibak, Iltutmish and Alauddin Khilji. Even during his short reign of five years (1321–1325), he undertook the task of building the city and citadel of Tughlaqabad and on the southern side of the citadel city he built his own tomb. Although the city is in ruins today due to a curse by Nizamuddin Awaliya, as believed by the local Gujars who reside here, the tomb still reflects its grandeur.[126] Inscriptional evidence for this tomb is also not available, as it was the case with many of his predecessors. Like the tombs of Khilji, Balban and Razia Sultana have been certified by the notes of Ibn Battuta, the same is true for Ghiyassudin Tughlaq.[127] Carr has challenged Ibn Battuta and says that it was work of Muhammud Shah but was definitely built within a year from the death of the ruler.[128] After the Afghanpur tragedy c.1325, 'he was carried away at night to the tomb which he had himself built near the city, called after him, Tughlaqabad, and there he was buried.'[129] He died after falling from a wooden pavilion.

The architectural style of the tomb is worth mentioning as it is a tomb with fortification walls and enclosing walls which cover the grave and provide an imposing structure. The walls are thicker at the bottom, and gradually reduce in thickness as they rise up; this is a distinct structural specification of the Tughlaq

---

[126]Carr, *The Archaeology and Monumental Remains of Delhi*, p.92.

[127]Kumari, *Tombs of Delhi*, p.26.

[128]Carr, *The Archaeology and Monumental Remains of Delhi*, p.95.

[129]R. Nath, *History of Sultanate Architecture*, Abhinav Publication, New Delhi, 1978, p.54.

buildings, and has acquired significant popularity. The thickness at the bottom was mainly to make the structure stable.[130] This also changed the aesthetic concept of the Tughlaq buildings, and it was followed on a large scale in the later constructions. The specific measurements of the tomb are noted by Stephen Carr.[131] This is a major example that indicates the transfer of Iranian and Central Asian traditions into India. The tomb is located inside the walled citadel. There is an artificial lake around the tomb that separates it from the mainland. The water into the lake comes from many natural drains and flows into the base of the fort. The total height of the tomb with the pinnacle is 80 ft and the marble dome is at 70 ft, which is stripped with the red stone. The intricate design of the tomb is a rare architectural marvel and is in good order, except for the decay that can be seen on the monument. The legends around the tomb are still young and passed on with conviction.

Firoz Shah Tughlaq

Since Muhammad Tughlaq had no male heirs, his generals elected Firoz Shah Tughlaq, a nephew of the founder of the dynasty, and son of a Hindu princess to the throne. He was educated and brought up by his uncle, and had enjoyed the special favours of his cousin, to whom he was grateful.[132]

Firoz Shah Tughlaq was a great patron of the building activities and made many new structures along with Firozabad city and numerous other public works. The other contributions

---

[130]Fanshawe, *Delhi: Past and Present*, pp.289–92.

[131]Carr, *The Archaeology and Monumental Remains of Delhi*, p.95.

[132]Hearn, *The Seven Cities of Delhi*, pp.196–97.

by the ruler were the renovations of various structures.[133] He was the ruler who made multi-dimensional contributions and he didn't require any kind of tomb to be remembered, but the order and the norm of the day asked for a mausoleum, and thus, it was instituted.

The location of the tomb, according to Fanshawe, was 'above Jahanpanah and to the north-west rises the depressed pale dome of the tomb of the Emperor Firoz Shah in Hauz Khas, and beyond it the bright pointed dome of Safdar Jang's tomb.'[134] The location has been highlighted by Hearn as 'at mile nine from Delhi, and two from the Kutub Minar, the tomb of Firoz Shah is still on the left further round of course; a mile behind, and close to the road, there is a group of nameless tombs, near Mujahidpur.'[135] Thus, the surety of the location comes from various authentic records. According to Sir Saiyyad Ahmed Khan, the tomb of Firoz Shah was built in 1389 by Nasiruddin Tughlaq Shah.[136] The tomb emerges from a square, converging into an octagon at the top. At the roof, the curves expand into a sixteen-sided figure, culminating in a honeycombed hive and it finally merges at the inner central top of the roof. Presently, the rich paints in these structures are visible only after investing intense efforts, but the record collected around a century ago clearly confirms its presence.[137] The lofty size of the tomb dims due to the decay of the heritage structures around it.

---

[133]Fanshawe, *Delhi: Past and Present*, pp.273–75.

[134]Ibid., p.268 and p.319.

[135]Hearn, *The Seven Cities of Delhi*, pp.47–48.

[136]Carr, *The Archaeology and Monumental Remains of Delhi*, p.157.

[137]Ibid., p.158.

The Tombs of the Lodis

After the death of Firoz Shah, Delhi went through a lot of turmoil. The most vehement blow was the invasion by Timur who ransacked the city and returned to his native seat of power after collecting much wealth and money. The difficulties to succession were many, and this troubled the generals who had diverse views regarding accession. The Afghans had an upper hand in the polity of the city during the fifteenth century and a contention for equal power amongst the generals led to the collapse of a centralized authority. The struggle and contention between Afghan generals Daulat Khan Lodi and Khizr Khan led to the further decline of the city and its administration. Mubarak Shah and his ambitions could not stand for long, and he had a brief stint as a ruler before he was assassinated. However, during his short-lived reign he was able to contribute a tomb for his own burial. The last Shah Dynasty ruler was Muhammad Shah, the grandson of Khizr Khan.[138] His reign was very short and was shrouded in conspiracies and he was always working, mainly to save his life. The king of Malwa, Alauddin Mahmud Shah, invaded Delhi *c. 1440*. Bahlul Lodi with his army was able to give a tough resistance and the invader was forced to retreat. Mahmud Shah died in 1445 and 'his tomb is one of the finest of the period; it has been noticed near the village of Khairpur.'[139] An interesting and detailed comparative study of the tombs of Mubarak Shah and Muhammad Shah has been carried out by Savita Kumari, and she is able to highlight the specific features of both the tombs

---

[138]Hearn, *The Seven Cities of Delhi*, p.205.
[139]Ibid.

along with their architectonics.[140] Both tombs look alike from the outside and have many similarities such as the presence of *chhajas* (canopies) three consecutive arches on each side of the extended verandah, an extensive pasting of stone on the pillars, and a lotus flower on the top. The transitional shift in the art of architecture is clearly visible inside the tombs. Both the monuments are examples of medieval architectural excellence. To access the health of Muhammud Shah's tomb, a comparison can be made through the pictures that were collected by both the scholars across a gap of nearly a hundred and twenty years.[141] The weak successor of Muhammud Shah was Alam Shah and he was unable to maintain any space for himself. Therefore, another dynasty came to the throne of Delhi.

Delhi fell into the hands of the Lodis and the dynasty was kickstarted by Bahlul Lodi. The dynasty lasted for seventy-five years from 1451 to 1526. The principle of *gaziship* was guiding all succession in medieval India. Bahlul Lodi was unable to continue due to constant internal struggles and external challenges. Therefore, he divided the kingdom amongst his nobles and kept Delhi for his son. But when his son was also denied Delhi, due to internal conspiracies and challenges, the seat of the capital was moved to Agra. Bahlul Lodi died *c.*1488, and was buried in his own garden, opposite the enclosure of Roshan Chirag Delhi.[142] This monument is also not supported by any literary evidence or any of the archaeological evidences.

---

[140]Kumari, *Tombs of Delhi*, pp.53–55.

[141]Hearn, *The Seven Cities of Delhi*, p.205 and Kumari, *Tombs of Delhi*, plate 59.

[142]Hearn, *The Seven Cities of Delhi*, p.207.

Hafiz-al-Din Ahmad was the first to identify this monument on the basis of tradition, and it was later accepted by Sangin Beg and Sayyid Ahmad Khan without any contemporary literature to support their claim.[143] Historian Simon Digby provides well-supported literary evidences to refute this.[144] An inscription found near Roshan Chirag Delhi indicates that the tomb is of a lady who was associated with Bahlul Lodi.[145] The craftsmanship and style of the tomb has been discussed in detail by various intrigued archaeologists.

Percival Spear describes the style of the tomb architecture that was employed by the Sayyids and the Lodis. Through this he has made an effort to distinguish these styles from the architectonics of the sultanate. He termed it as the 'Lodi style' juxtaposing Bishop Heber who called it 'Pathan architecture'.[146] He further brings in the epithets like 'Hindu style' to describe the style of tombs like the Bara Gumbad, which was the first full dome in Delhi.[147] The architectonics of Bara Gumbad have led historians to take varied positions on the utility of the building.[148] The finest example of the full dome is the tomb of Sher Shah at Sasaram in present-day Gaya, Bihar. It is interesting to note that the tombs attributed to the Lodis have outnumbered those of the early and mid-sultanate period. This emergence clearly indicates

---

[143]Kumari, *Tombs of Delhi*, p.40.

[144]Simon Digby, 'The Tomb of Bahlul Lodi', Vol.38, No.3, *Bulletin of the School of Oriental and African Studies*, Cambridge University Press, London, 1975, pp.550–61.

[145]Kumari, *Tombs of Delhi*, p.41.

[146]Spear, *Delhi: Its Monuments and History*, p.44.

[147]Ibid., p.105.

[148]Kumari, *Tombs of Delhi*, p.40.

the changing nature of kingship. The distinction between the Turk and the Afghan (Lodhi) architecture is clearly indicative of the theories of kingship. Complimenting the work of the Afghans, Heber said that 'they built like giants and finished their work like jewellers.'[149] Sikander Lodi transferred his seat of capital to Agra, but chose Delhi for the construction of his tomb. This highlights the political and cultural significance of Delhi as a city.

The architectural significance of Sikander Lodi's tomb is that it marks the first double dome in India. This style is just to add loftiness to the structure and to make it more imposing. This tomb is a shift from the fortified Sultanate tombs, and the verandahs with square pillars are interesting additions. It is also the earliest tomb constructed in a garden enclosure. The tombs have been made to keep remembrances alive and different styles were adopted to make a mark. In a nutshell, it can be put forward that the tombs of the sultanate, the Sayyids and the Lodis are structures of marvel and they still represent the same. The mammoth task of constructing these massive structures was carried out with the coordination of many agencies and a large amount of labour. Huge sums were dedicated for accomplishing these monuments. But, the lifespan of many monuments have been cut short due to the lack of maintenance and various historical and political factors.

Another notable tomb of the sixteenth century was that of Isa Khan, who was a noble in the court of Sher Shah. This tomb is situated near the mausoleum of Humayun. The tomb and the mosque around it were both built by Isa Khan in 1547 during the reign of Salim Shah. The tomb is octagonal

---

[149]Spear, *Delhi: Its Monuments and History*, p.44.

in shape and was built with a combination of marble and red sandstone. The inscription on the tomb is enough to clearly indicate the date and the patron of the structure.[150]

With the coming of the Mughals, new styles also arrived on the Indian landscape and most of these were well accepted. The monuments of the Mughals are massive and much more ornamental as compared with the pre-Mughal Islamic dynasties. The popular and impressive Mughal tombs that are situated in Delhi are Humayun's Tomb and Safdarjung's Tomb. Both tombs mark the structures of different centuries extending from the sixteenth century into the eighteenth century. Other notable tombs of the Mughal reign in Delhi are of Adham Khan and Atgah Khan. The mausoleum of the former is in Mehrauli, and the latter rests at Nizamuddin. The tomb of Adham Khan was built by Maham Anga, the mother of the deceased. She was also a patron of the *madarssa* Khair-ul-Manazil. Carr gives a detailed description of her mausoleum, and credits Akbar for building the tombs over both mother and son's graves.[151]

Humayun's Tomb

Humayun's literary inclinations have been well recorded. Sher Mandal, an elegant octagonal building of Sher Shah, was used by him as a library where precious manuscripts were kept. Later, this library became the death spot of Humayun. On 24 January 1556, after hearing the *azan* of Muezzin from a nearby mosque, the emperor bowed on the second step of the

---

[150]Carr, *The Archaeology and Monumental Remains of Delhi*, p.198.
[151]Ibid., pp.199–202.

library in order to show respect to the call of prayer. While
doing this, his foot was entangled in his robe due to which
he fell down and his temple hit a sharp edge. Three days later,
the emperor died. The tomb for the burial of the emperor
of Hindustan was built by Hamida Banu Begum, widow of
Humayun and mother of Akbar, who was popularly known
as Haji Begum. The architect for the mausoleum was Mirak
Mirza Ghiyas, a Persian, who gave India its first dome in the
Persian style.[152] The work of the tomb began *c.*1564, and was
completed in 1573, 'at a cost of fifteen lac rupees'.[153] Haji
Begum died in 1603 and was buried along with her husband
in the same tomb.[154] The tomb stands the test of time, and
even today the dome of this mausoleum is a landmark for
many researchers and travellers who visit Delhi. The dome is
made of white marble. Fanshawe notes:

> Haji Begam...who built the tomb and Arab Sarai, is buried
> in the north-east corner...of the building. The other
> corner rooms also contain graves, which are nameless,
> but are known to include those of the unfortunate Dara
> Shiekoh, of two of the brothers of Shah Alam Bahadur
> Shah, who fought against him for the Empire, and...
> three sons of these, and of the Emperors Jahandar Shah
> (d.1761) and Alamgir II (d.1712). The Emperor Jehangir
> records in his memoirs that while in pursuit of his son,
> Prince Khusru, he visited the tomb of his grandfather,

---

[152]Bamber Gascoigne, *The Great Moghuls*, B.I. Publications in association
with Jonathan Cape London, New Delhi, 1971, p.99; Spear, *Delhi: Its
Monuments and History*, p.33.
[153]Carr, *The Archaeology and Monumental Remains of Delhi*, p.203.
[154]Spear, *Delhi: Its Monuments and History*, p.33.

and distributed alms at it and at the tomb of Nizam-ud-din-Aulia, to which also he went.[155]

The graves around the burial site of Humayun are also confirmed by Carr and Hearn.[156] Carr, Hearn and Fanshawe agree on the architectural specification and the geographical placing of the tomb. Designed in the Persian style, the *charbagh* around the tomb of Humayun was the first-ever introduced in India, with trees and flowering plants. The channels that ran through the *baghs* carried water which was also used for watering the plants and the fruit trees. It was also a mechanism that was devised to reduce heat in the interiors. This marvellous building and its gardens continue to exist, and are not merely a glory of the past. The source of water for the *baghs* was the river Yamuna but the constant shift of the river has cut off the water supply to the monument today. As compared to many other monuments that remain today, this is the best maintained structure where lakhs of visitors flock throughout the year. It is also a picnic spot for the locals who reside in the Nizamuddin basti. Many couples enjoy a quiet time here, and are commonly spotted in the gardens, staircase, verandahs and the ante-chambers of the monument.

Tomb of Safdarjung

The tomb of Safdarjung is the mausoleum of Nawab Abul Mansur Ali Khan, who was the prime minister of the emperor Ahmad Shah and nephew of Nawab Wazir Sa'adat Ali Khan,

---

[155]Fanshawe, *Delhi: Past and Present*, pp.230–31.
[156]Carr, *The Archaeology and Monumental Remains of Delhi*, p.203 and Hearn, *The Seven Cities of Delhi*, pp.61–64.

the man who founded the House of Oudh.[157] He was also second Nawab of Oudh.[158] The title Safdarjung means, 'the disperser of the battle ranks'. This tomb was patronized by his son Shuja-udaulah, under the supervision of Sidi Balal Muhammad Khan, at a cost of three lakh rupees.[159] As per Hearn, 'the building follows rather the bad principle of "constructing ornament" than of "ornamenting construction" there is a too free use of plaster'.[160] Carr also refers to this tomb as poor and unimpressive.[161] Bishop Heber called it 'the colour of potted meat'.[162] It is 60 sq. ft and 90 ft high, surmounted by a marble dome, which is, unfortunately, bulbous and heavy. It stands on a high terrace in an enclosed garden, and the view of it through the gateway is an effective one. It was the last large mausoleum to be erected near Delhi, and it cost £30,000.[163] Safdarjung's successors were independent of imperial control from Delhi, and preferred to be buried in Lucknow. The choice of the new location was perhaps due to religious reasons as the family was a follower of the Shia sect. Delhi had no cultural base for the Shias due to the political dominance of the Sunnis, who ruled the city for centuries.

Delhi has also been a house of many other monuments such as temples, mosques and gurudwaras. Most of these were built during the medieval centuries. The exclusion of a discussion on ancient monuments in this book is not intentional, but

---

[157]Fanshawe, *Delhi: Past and Present*, p.246.

[158]Spear, *Delhi: Its Monuments and History*, p.50.

[159]Carr, *The Archaeology and Monumental Remains of Delhi*, p.278.

[160]Hearn, *The Seven Cities of Delhi*, pp.46–47.

[161]Carr, *The Archaeology and Monumental Remains of Delhi*, p.278.

[162]Spear, *Delhi: Its Monuments and History*, p.50.

[163]Hearn, *The Seven Cities of Delhi*, pp.46–47.

is limited due to the non-availability of archaeological and literary evidences to prove their existence. What is possible has been attempted in the preceding sections, and whatever information is available on ancient Delhi has been provided. The major mosques studied in this book are Quwwat-ul-Islam, Jami Mosque, Qutala Firuz Shah, Jama Masjid, Sunahari Mosque and Fatehpuri Mosque. The most popular temple that was constructed in the medieval times—and still stands the test of times is the Jain temple located in front of Lal Qila. The Kalkaji temple is another popular site for devotees and the historical roots of the temple have been discussed with regard to the ancient city of Yoginipuram. The Gurudwara of Sisganj and Bangla Sahib (erstwhile Jaisinghpura palace of Kachhwaha Raja Jai Singh) are constructions of the eighteenth century. All the religious institutions will be discussed later in detail, but all these monuments do form part of our shared 'alive past', which stands before us in the form of various monuments. Besides these, there are many other monuments such as the Jantar Mantar and various administrative buildings that were contributed by the colonial masters for different state activities. It can be said that nearly all the buildings in Delhi speak of their past, and have contributed immensely to the making of this sovereign city.

It is undeniable that these monuments whisper to us the past of this city, and allow us to understand the times gone by. It is therefore imperative to conserve them and study them objectively.

5

THE CHARISMA OF THE CITY

This section of the book is more about the way this city has been sensed by its inhabitants and how diverse souls who arrive in this city respond to the changes and interact in the cultural arena of this political capital. Migration and emigration is nothing new to this city. It has been a feature of Delhi for centuries. Many studies have highlighted the significance of certain cities in terms of their economy or history. Most of the studies miss the cultural aspect due to the vastness of the idea or the impossibility to tackle and integrate all the diverse subjects. No doubt it is difficult to weave together a smooth fabric about many centuries of the cultural past of a city which has been dyed in various hues of pleasure, trauma, atrocities and struggles. Interestingly, the city of Delhi is also like many other cities of the globe in terms of its historical glory which has been highlighted in the preceding discussions. The fact of this city lies in its acceptance of its geographical location which has made it a candle for all kind of moths.

In historical terms, the city rose to prominence only after the settlement of the Delhi Sultanate. Prior to the sultanate, it was an ordinary settlement as is proven by archaeological findings. Stories and anecdotes are integral to the formation of any city. Many stories about its founders are circulated by self-appointed guides, which include tales of ghosts and unaccomplished love projects of the city makers. The battles for acquiring various sources that were required for state formation are an integral part of such histories. Delhi is no exception to this, and the battles that took place clearly indicate that they were the mechanisms to ensure a share in the resources that would boost the economy of the state.

The early medieval period has seen a lot of political and economic upheaval. Each episode stands for its own, and has to be approached sympathetically and with critical acumen. Many a time, political dispensations try to erase the past by creating a clout and rewrite the history of a city and its structures. In this process, the state machinery and bureaucracy are involved at various levels to generally elevate the position of the state to a new level, and as a result of this process the past gets crucified for the needs of the present.

The city of Delhi is no exception to this historical and political process, and its history has been told, retold and redone at various diverse levels, many times over. In this, many groups, sects and communities also bring in their versions to assert their historical existence. It is therefore essential for a researcher to be conscious while recording these versions, and apply the necessary filters before bringing these versions into the main historical writing. An innovative approach in writing history is visible in the much-acclaimed work of Sunil Kumar, who has investigated the sites and has been able to notice the very recent changes made around the monuments of his study by relying on Persian documents and intense fieldwork. Following a similar theme, this chapter will deviate a little but will emphasize on the historical events and the glamour that Delhi has been maintaining in different ways over the centuries.

Delhi under Alauddin Khilji

The resources at hand that were accumulated after the popular price regulation and market reforms of Alauddin Khilji allowed the Sultan to defend the city against the Mongol threat. The most terrifying and heinous genocides of the world were carried out by the Mongols who destroyed city after city, not even sparing the lives of animals and children.[164] In this phase, the economically flourishing, culturally effluent and prosperous cities of Samarkand, Bukhara, Nishapur and Baghdad were also targeted by the Mongol armies, and were destroyed in such a manner that not even a single full structure remained behind, that can testify to the event. This barbarous and heinous slaughter forced much of its population to move out and look for safe spaces for survival. In this search, many scholars of literature, religious jurisprudence and artisans came to the threshold of Delhi which was then a flourishing city.

The arrival of people of pen and thought helped the slaves who were on the highway of ruler ship. They were in need of a learned class that could organize their kingdom and govern through an organized system of administration and revenue collection. The sultanate was surviving and sustaining itself only through revenue collection. Therefore, the state required a large section of literates to draft and maintain the revenue records and make periodic entries. The educated shelter seekers were best suited for these clerical jobs. The conversion

---

[164]Jack Weatherford, *The Secret History of the Mongol Queens: How the Daughters of Genghis Khan Rescued His Empire*, Crown Publishing Group, New York, 2010.

of the socially alienated, boycotted and neglected classes also created a section of indigenous Muslim population who were culturally rooted in the Hind. These new converts were also looking forward to the religious leaders who would serve as teachers (*alim/ulama/maulvi*) for guiding and helping them on the path of religion (*din*) where the initial and prime activity was reading the Holy Quran. Reading the religious script was an essential requirement for abiding by the principles of religion. Thus, religious training was carried out by teaching the *hadiths*, *sunnat*, followed by religious literatures. The educated class was also required in the *madarssas* and the mosques for producing copies of the Quran. These demands absorbed nearly all the literates who arrived in the city to make a living. The Sufis were also active in political and religious activities. They continued to maintain a superior position through their spiritual and religious influences. Of course, this was due to their training in religious scriptures, Islamic theology, jurisprudence and constant engagement with varied sections of the society who were coming to them for the fulfilment of their unattained wishes, believing in the mystic power of the saints. The network that was at work was very cohesive and always kept the saints at the centre. The influence of the saints helped him to acquire a significant position in the city as is evident in case of Hazrat Nizamuddin Awaliya (popularly called *Hazrat-i-Dilli*).[165] The influence of a few saints rose to the extent that it became a cause of conflict between the Sufi saints and the sultans, as

---

[165]Raziuddin Aquil, 'Hazrat-i-Delhi: Making of the Chishti Sufi Center and the Stronghold of Islam' *South Asia Research*, Vol. 28, No. 1 (2008), pp.23–48.

both groups attempted to assert the 'claim to authority'. In one of his interesting works, Simon Digby has explored the relationships that have existed between the various sultans of the Delhi Sultanate and the contemporary Sufi Sheikhs during the thirteenth and fourteenth centuries.[166] Anecdotes from the *tazkiras* literature enrich his work and keep the reader engaged with the text. The assertion of authority is evident through the actions employed by the sultans and apparently by the saints. Thus, the city of Delhi during the sultanate times was emerging as an economic centre enshrined with the best features of art, culture and religion. For many, Delhi was *Dur-ul-Islam* (an abode of Islam), which was being built on the principles of Islam. More or less a similar kind of polity and administration continued to guide the Mughal state. Babur was the founder of Mughal rule in India during 1526, but soon he shifted to Agra. A long exile was imposed on Humayun after loss of territories to Sher Shah and it kept the former away from Indian territories. After regaining control over the lost territories, Humayun spent some time in Delhi. Akbar and Jahangir continued to rule from the Mughal capital of Agra. Delhi served as a garrison ground for their armies and the environs of Delhi were used as the imperial hunting grounds. It was only Shah Jahan who paid attention to Delhi and decided to make it his capital. In pursuit of his objective, he laid the foundation of *Qila-i-Mubarak* (Lal Qila) after the death of Mumtaz Begum. The city came into prominence and attained power during the introduction of Islamic rule, and the inauguration of Shajahanbad was unrivalled in its

---

[166]Simon Digby, 'The Sufi Shaykh and the Sultan: A Conflict of Claims to Authority in Medieval India', *Iran*, Vol. 28 (1990), pp.71–81.

reputation as the most looked-forward to metropolis in the world. The death of Aurangzeb seized the fate of the city irreversibly and the period of tragic court struggles, civil wars, rebellions and invasions set in. With the coming of the British in the nineteenth century, it regained its popularity and was expended further, and there it attained the status of the 'Rome of Asia'.[167] This pre-eminent centre of trade and culture was also a 'metropolis of Asia'.[168] The British toned up the falling administration of the city. Until 1809, Delhi was treated as a *Suba*, and it was only *c.*1819 that it was divided into districts. Charles Metcalf was the second Resident, and he developed a 'Delhi System' to improve the administrative management of the city, along with the revenue and the judicial setup. The city continued to lure new rulers and its unobliterated charisma pushed the British to hold three *darbars* in Delhi, even when it was no longer a capital. At the third *darbar* which was staged *c.*1911 under the patronage of King George V, the shift of capital from Calcutta to Delhi was announced. This transfer of the capital re-affirmed the lost glory of the city and once again Delhi was made the capital city. The reasons for transfer of the capital from the initial capital town of the company (Calcutta) were explained by Lord Harding in a letter dated 25 August 1911. It was addressed to the Secretary of the State for India:

> ...political advantages of the transfer...Delhi is still a name to conjure with. It is intimately associated in the

---

[167]H.K. Kaul, *Historic Delhi: An Anthology*, Oxford University Press, Delhi, 1998, Second impression, p. xvii.

[168]Count Han Von Koenigsmarck, *A German Staff Officer in India*, London, 1910, pp.170–71. *Cf.* H.K. Kaul, *Historic Delhi: An Anthology*, pp.6–7.

minds of the Hindus with sacred legends...in the plains of Delhi that the Pandava princes fought...the epic struggle recorded in Mahabharata and celebrated on the banks of the Jumna the famous sacrifice...site of city which they founded and called Indraprastha...to the Mahomedans it would be a source of unbounded gratification to see the ancient capital of the Moguls restored to its proud position as the seat of Empire. Throughout India...every walled town has its 'Delhi Gate' and among the masses of the people it is still revered as the seat of Empire. The imagination of the people of India as nothing else can do, would send...a wave of enthusiasm throughout the country and would be accepted by all as the assertion of an unfaltering determination to maintain British rule in India.[169]

This letter conveyed the charisma of the city, and its acceptance as a capital by the masses of the country. It also reinforced the need for the British to work along the same lines and shift the capital to Delhi, in order to survive in the subcontinent. Here, Lord Harding has tried to see Delhi through the eyes of both the Hindus and Muslims, and subsequently invoked separate connections felt by both the groups. This appropriation cannot be accepted with full consensus as the inhabitants of the city were not yet so divided along religious lines in the early decades of the twentieth century as was highlighted by the official in his letter. There were many other common grounds for the public during the nineteenth century to associate and stand together for their city. This shift of capital from Calcutta

---

[169]Kaul, *Historic Delhi: An Anthology*, p.xxvii.

to Delhi was about to push changes both in the face and fate of the city. Highlighting the same change, Norah Rowan Hamilton wrote in 1915:

> Delhi the magnificent. Delhi the terrible! What orgies of feasting, what horrors of pillage and bloodshed has it not endured. Delhi that has been thrice created capital, to three conquering and conquered races, and to-day has just been declared capital once more.[170]

The foundation stone of the new capital was laid by George V and Queen Mary in the coronation park. The final destination for the capital was Raisina Hill as the sweeping view of the monuments and the old cities was visible from here along with the silver streak of the Yamuna. The hill was flattened to construct the Viceroy's House, which had 340 rooms, 227 columns, 35 loggias, 37 fountains, and 12 acres of garden, a swimming pool, golf course, tennis court and lavish gardens.[171] The garden courts and the Rajpath (Kingsway) separated the North and South secretariat blocks. India Gate was a war memorial and Rajpath connected the Viceroy's house to it. The city continued to grow and expand and soon it became the centre for India's political life. The national movement and the various activities that led India on the path to freedom were centred in Delhi, and the entire nation looked towards the imperial capital to set in the next action for the greater cause of Independence.

The British rule ended on 15 August 1947, and India

[170]Norah Rowan Hamilton, *Through Wonderful India and Beyond*, Holden & Hardingham, 1915, p.138.
[171]Kaul, *Historic Delhi: An Anthology*, p.xxviii.

advanced towards freedom with the Partition of the country under the two-nation theory. The freedom struggle has tested the amity of the Hindus, Muslims, Christians and Sikhs. Partition tore away the belief of the inhabitants and the patience of the migrants and refugees was put to a heinous testing board. It resulted in widespread riots, loots, mass murders, and all this created a traumatic experience for the inhabitants on both the sides of the border. Historically shared communal harmony was raped to the extent that citizens of all the faiths lost hope in each other. The efforts of Mahatma Gandhi to restore communal harmony are well known. But before the attainment of normalcy, Gandhi was shot dead by Nathuram Godse at the Birla House on 30 January 1948. A legend left forever with the words *'Hey Ram'!* on his lips without the hope of ever returning. This closed one phase of India's struggle, and the first prime minister of the country tried to hold together the citizens and calm the political turmoil. He became the architect of the nation which had suffered under colonialism, and was left poor and naked by the colonizers, and was now being pushed through the trauma of Partition. The nation suffered for two centuries under the yoke of foreign rule during which the self-sufficient economy of the nation was destroyed, irreparably.[172] The nation was jolted with the shock of Partition and the challenge ahead was to revive from the dark days of exploitation. The cultural and social fabric of the nation was also destroyed due to communal rifts and economic devastation. The love and the affection of the first Indian prime minister for the city were

---

[172]Shashi Tharoor, *An Era of Darkness: The British Empire in India*, Aleph Book Company, Delhi, 2016.

immense and this did not allow him to move away from it. So, Delhi as capital with its Red Fort became the symbol of free India, and the prime minister delivered his first speech on the eve of Independence from the top of this monument. With the declaration of Independence, India adopted a parliamentary system of governance and the city became a focal point for the members of parliament, ministers and various ministries, government organizations, offices and agencies and their branches. The city was carefully nurtured by the leaders for the betterment of the nation.

As the capital of the Republic of India, Delhi was expanding at a very fast pace, at a rate of one lakh people coming in the capital city each year. The city expanded considerably and changed rapidly to accommodate the influx. Post 1947, New Delhi was becoming more untidy, clumsy, a hostage of slums with innumerable inconveniences such as traffic jams, pollution and the blemishes of redundant junk and piles of garbage. Yet, Delhi retains its role as one of the major cities of the world.

Each conqueror of the city adorned Delhi with the best of their times. This bejewelling set in by the various dynasties tickled Perceval Landon to call Delhi 'The Mistress of every Conqueror'.[173] The city through the centuries was able to gather many titles for its representation. Out of those, the most popular title for Delhi, is 'The city of scents' given by Walter Tibbits.[174] She also puts light on the doves of city along

---

[173]Perceval Landon, *Under the Sun*, Hurst and Blackett, London, 1906, pp.49–52. For details, see Appendix I.

[174]Walter Tibbits, *The Voice of the Orient*, The Theosophical Publication Society, London and Thacker & Co., Bombay, 1909, p.114. For further

with the exquisite perfume shops. Stephen Carr has written extensively on the seven cities of Delhi and has honoured the historicity of the city. While Hearn called Delhi as 'the Rome of India',[175] Frederick Treves went ahead and called the city, 'the Rome of Asia'.[176] Subhan Rai writing in the seventeenth century equated the city of Delhi with the river Ganga. He states:

> Although each of the rulers of Hindustan found a city, and made it the seat of his government, still in all parts of dominions Delhi is famous as the capital of all the rulers of Hindustan. In the year 1048 A.H (A.D. 1638), and in the twelfth year of his reign...built a city near Delhi, which he named Shah-Jahan-abad. Through the building of this great city, all the cities which have been mentioned as having been built by former kings have been eclipsed, and are included under the general name of Shah-Jahan-abad, just as the many rivers which fall into the Ganges are known only by the name of Ganges.[177]

The quality to 'assimilate all that came in', made Rai compare the city with the river Ganga, which has been running as a cultural carriage of India, in which everyone who approaches the river is able to get a share.

The city that housed the politically powerful masses also offered peace and respect to the dead. Ibn Battuta in the fourteenth century recorded:

---

details, see Appendix II.

[175]Gordon Risley Hearn, *The Seven Cities of Delhi*, W. Thacker & Co., London, 1906, p.1.

[176]Frederick Treves, *The Other Side of Lantern*, Cassell & Co., London, 1906, p.90. See Appendix III.

[177]Kaul, *Historic Delhi: An Anthology*, p.20.

This is beautiful place of burial; they build domed pavilions in it and every grave must have a *mihrab* beside it, even if there is no dome over it. They plant in it flowering trees such as the tuberose, the *raibul*, the *nisrin* and others. In that country there are always flowers in bloom at every season of the year.[178]

Many others have also written about the city and its assimilating qualities. Interestingly, the city has shown respect to all the classes, and nearly all sections have tried to contribute to the city in some or the other way. The more you explore this city, you generate more and more respect for it and its inhabitants who have kept its spirit alive, and stayed vibrant to cater to all incoming groups and visitors who wanted to sense the soul of this century-old versatile capital of India.

As mentioned previously, Delhi has witnessed the rise and fall of many empires and several rulers. In this process of rise and fall, its inhabitants have experienced bloodshed and grandeur and have lived with the monuments that were built over the centuries. The remarkable modern Delhi is an assimilation of these lived experiences and today the entire world looks towards it as a premier educational, intellectual and cultural centre. The sprawling markets provide items that have represented India for centuries, such as *itar* (perfume), incense, flowers, clothes, glass works, artefacts, jewellery, and so on. The streets and the markets of Delhi have been defined as:

[...] once more in Delhi...jewels of fabulous price, wrought silver and gold, Kashmiri shawls carved or

---

[178]Kaul, *Historic Delhi: An Anthology*, p.23.

inlaid ivories, stuff woven with gold and silver threads that look as diaphanous as gossamer, and that sell by their weight of metal. Delhi is usually prosperous...and the Durbar has brought prosperity within her gates.[179]

Delhi is a vibrant city, pregnant with the vast opportunities it provides to its many vagrants. No doubt it is a political corner of the world and people look to Delhi to learn from its spirit through which it has survived through the centuries. The starting point for any researcher is the city, the street, the town, the houses and the markets. At times, many families come to the centre of history writing due to their role in the events of the history. Besides these physical survivals, what attracts one to the past of certain cities is their spirit that has never allowed the city to go in ruins. Delhi also represents one of those cities, who even after multiple declines comes back to life with the same vigour.

The charisma of this city lies in its ability to restore its glory even after much destruction. It is something that continues even in the twenty-first century, while maintaining all its dynamics of religion, culture and history. This is the city that conducts itself well with its visuals of the past, its endorsed pride, delight and dignity.

---

[179]Hamilton, *Through Wonderful India and beyond*, pp.164–65.

6

THE CORN-FIT CULTURES

Ya taqt! Ya tabut!
(Either, throne or, coffin!)

This is a popular Persian couplet that shows how strong the desire for the throne was in medieval centuries. In fact, the struggle to gain the *taqt* (throne) has always guided Delhi's destiny. Although the throne was the ultimate desire of many, very few succeeded to attain it. At times, even the *tabut* was chosen over regular service which was offered under the reign of one's own brother—usually as an official or *chakar* of the state. During the Sultanate period, the struggle amongst equals, and in the Mughal Empire, the contest for the throne amongst brothers was a regular feature and the means to secure the top position. It is sad to note that none of the successions were peaceful and nearly all of them were marked with bloodshed, killings and acts of treachery. These struggles also guided the discourse in the past and have shaped history in the way it is visible to us today.

The history of Delhi is more lived than studied, because it is visible in every nook and corner. Many a time, this abundance of history is a reason for people to take it for granted. Present-day historians show more respect for tradition and culture in comparison to previous generations of history writers for whom tradition was merely an old wives' tale. Much of the early history of Delhi—and in fact all the major cities of today—are more like legends which were later penned down. This continued for a while due to the touching faith held by our forefathers and their constant belief in the memory and their confidence in the ability of the early transmitters who passed on everything orally. Digging into such oral histories is more rewarding than simply reading. Many a time, the versions collected from these recordings and transmissions are inspiring, and help understand the different paradigms and aspirations of the populace and the beliefs held by them. With the invention of paper, official recording of histories became the norm. Gradually, written evidences in the form of histories and *tazkiras* became the doyens of information, and later formed an ample source through which histories could be reconstructed. This expansion in the world of writing motivated many others to record the actions of the state from a different perspective, and allowed them to do critical study of the state and its apparatuses. Finally, a joint study of both views enabled the culling out of the true nature of states. Thus, during the twelfth century, with the introduction of paper, there was a shift from the large, oral and customary society to a record-based society, which extended into the present. Further, the vast use of vernaculars led to a substantial increase in the source material. This material appeared in various forms such as informal letters, diaries, poems and the regular recordings of events by the individuals. This also increased the dependence on multiple testimonies against the earlier reliance on single sources of information, such as state records. However, it complicated the situation for the scholars, who were expected to filter all the available sources to reach at facts and the most correct sequence of the happenings. References were also incorporated from other disciplines and this led to an encroachment of the field by many other performers. With this, the task of exploring the past became a multi-disciplinary subject that was expected to be read in coordination with many other disciplines, in order to reach the most acceptable and accurate version of the past. This has contributed immensely to reach the true aspects of the historical past and has helped to understand events relating to the environment, polity, economics, etc. This was the landmark contribution by the Annales school of historical thought. This school has completely revolutionized the way of understanding and writing history. This contribution was significant and timely. The 1960s saw a revolution in historical writings and it has continued to shape the subject in a better way.

As the literary sources of all times hold significant value, a careful scrutiny of all these multiple evidences is required to explore all the possibilities and distortions that come in the works of authors. Archival data was considered secondary to literary evidences, but in recent years, archival records have been gaining prominence over other sources as the former are not subjected to frequent changes. Archives are considered a vast storehouse of facts, free from biases and are thus inconvertible sources. All these developments have completely transformed history writing in the twentieth century. This has also extended the material base for writing and compiling histories. Thus, using records as evidence, we have to subject them to sensitive criticism, which makes it possible to discover the material behind them and the impressions which they were intended to produce. So, it can be said that sources can be extensive and wide-ranging, such as chroniclers' materials, manuscripts, letters, diaries, travelogues, official sermons, archival documents, etc. but the historian has to assess them through a critical approach. They need to understand the approach and objective behind the creation of these sources, and have an eye to explore and locate the forgery as well as authenticity of the material used by them. At every stage in the evolution of historical science, forgery has played an important role. The ugly ring this word carries has to be broken with proper caution and care, without harming the truth and the other aspects of the event that are surrounded by this act. Sporadic forgery of characters and literary works has continued over the ages. The discovery of truth and events is the task of any historian, and he must accomplish it by collating various contemporary evidences.

Delhi's Social Life

Finally, the study of history imposes rigorous rules of the discipline along with self-discipline upon the one who pursues it. Existing political and social institutions retain strong links with the past. The task for the historians is to view the distant past rather than the near present. This chapter aims to show a different side of the city by looking at social life as depicted in memoirs, travelogues and diaries. Many European travellers who came to Delhi were visiting the markets and the countryside, and their narratives were also inspired by the stories and social customs that were appearing alien to them. This unawareness made them record all that they encountered and everything which astonished them.

Niccolao Manucci, the Italian traveller, recorded details about the city, the empire, the ruler, the household, populace, markets and the various norms and rules that appeared amusing or surprising to him. Writing in the seventeenth century, he came across a Delhi that was ruled by the Mughals, and being a man of medicine he got access to the imperial quarters and was enrolled in the service of the state. With this appointment, he became the first-hand information collector and compiler of the happenings in the imperial city. He writes of his enrolment in the following words:

> On my reaching Dihli several nobles took notice of my arrival...the chief of these was the Master of the Ceremonies of Shah Alam, whose wife was very ill and given up by doctors. My treatment to her renewed my reputation, which, during my absence of a year, had been somewhat diminished....the household of Shah Alam did not approve of my continuing at court after having cured the said women...she besought the prince one night to take me into his service, allotting me noble's pay...I was a privileged person, for I agreed to serve on no other condition than that I must be left free, nor must anyone else give me orders...and thus, unwilling as I was to serve Aurangzeb, I was the servant of his son, beginning my service in the year one thousand six hundred and seventy-eight (1678 AD).[180]

During the reign of Emperor Aurangzeb, the ban on music, both instrumental and singing, was introduced in the city. The excessive culture of music in the city made the emperor do this. The love for music in the populace of the city can be sensed by the reaction that spurted at the time of the ban. According to Manucci, both sections of the society,

---

[180]Niccolao Manucci, *Mogul India*, 4 Vols, translated by William Irvine, Low Price Publication, Delhi, 1907–08, reprint 2005, Vol. 2, p.215.

'Moguls and Hindus [were] very fond of listening to songs and instrumental music.'[181] This ban entitled an officer to arrest people who were practising music and break their instruments. 'Thus was caused a great destruction of musical instruments.'[182] The collective spirit of the city was visible after the ban when about one thousand affected souls came out and assembled on a Friday when the emperor was going to the mosque to offer the *namaz-i-jumma*. The demonstration with twenty highly ornamented biers crying aloud seemed as if they were grieving a death.[183] This protest did not help them get any relief but the event is indicative of the spirit which united the people of this city against atrocities and bans. In spite of the emperor's order, the nobles did not cease to listen to music, although they did it in secret. Delhi has also seen many of Aurangzeb's other experiments, such as measures against miracle-making saints and the murder of Dara Shikoh, who was declared a *kafir* by Aurangzeb due to the former's appreciation of different religious tenets.[184]

Delhi assimilated appreciations, criticisms, bans, and finally emerged through it all. The social life of Delhi was marked by different aspects of life and systems. To broadly mark the features of its social life one can say it was a city of beauty as defined by Amir Khusro.[185] It is a city that witnessed a great deal—the riots of the fourteenth century which threw the city

---

[181]Ibid., pp.7–8, *Cf.* H.K. Kaul, *Historic Delhi: An Anthology*, Oxford University Press, Delhi, 1998, Second impression p.63.

[182]Manucci, *Mogul India*, pp.7–8, Cf. Kaul, *Historic Delhi*, p.63.

[183]Ibid.

[184]Kaul, *Historic Delhi*, p.65.

[185]'O Delhi and its young beauties with turbans placed roguishly awry on their heads!'; Ibid.

out of gear, the *jogis* of Delhi who were a great allurement for the onlookers due to their appearances, the bans introduced in the city which made people come together to oppose the whims of the state, the massacre of Sikhs in the eighteenth century which was strongly criticized by the inhabitants, and so on. The robbers, too, had their areas of action. The crowds of the city were whimsical men of resources who bribed their way to secure their fortunes in government tenders, the Christians of the city were mainly converts from the Chamar caste, the Delhi Gujars were more popular than the Jats of the city and cattle-lifting was their favourite avocation. The caste system in Delhi was strong in the nineteenth century as it was in the other parts of India and even *firangis* had a tough time dealing with it. The admiration for the Englishmen amongst the locals was immense. While English missionaries were hard at work to convert the natives, but they rarely attained success. Various means of entertainment that show continuity and change, such as nautch girls, theatre performance and the *ukhbar*, were available in the city.[186] These events had many dimensions of cruelty, guilt, kindness and struggle.

The work of Stephen P. Blake was a timely intervention that provides a vivid portrayal of the Mughal city of Delhi. The detailed study of the city plan, its popular culture and many other dimensions help to get a live glimpse of Shahjahanabad.[187] The work of Shama Mitra Chenoy also explores the city of

---

[186]Ibid., pp.59–83.

[187]S.P. Blake, *Shahjahanabad: The Sovereign City in Mughal India 1639–1739*, South Asian Studies 49, Cambridge University Press, Delhi, reprint 2017.

Shahjahanabad but it is very limited in its approach.[188] *Delhi: Unknown Tales of a City* by R.V. Smith[189] is another handiwork about the imperial city, but its content reflects that it is more of a non-academic reading, best meant for the novice visitor to understand the present city. The work of William Dalrymple is well-known to the scholars of medieval and modern history and highlights different events and monuments of the city, but often independently—a continuing history is missing in his works as well. Safvi has been writing on the city for quite some time but her works are limited to the monuments, and the link between the city culture and its buildings is a great miss. The culture of the city is multi-layered and each pocket of the city is a cultural bowl, containing and nurturing the multiplicity of its emergence. The city has a wide population and different sections dominate certain pockets. The city has expanded immensely since the time of its inception during the eight century. The many changes of dynasties have certainly contributed to it but the destructions by the new reigns cannot be denied. Much of its political history was recorded along with some social happenings. The cultural developments around the celebrations of the state have been treated well by the chroniclers. The inputs of general popular culture of any regional space shapes the overall culture of a locality and indicated towards the acceptances and rejections. Various free souls were noting and maintaining diaries, and many a time festivals, gatherings, events and the details of the markets

---

[188]S.M. Chenoy, *Shahjahanabad: A City of Delhi 1638–1857*, Munshiram Manoharlal Publishers, New Delhi, reprint 2015.

[189]R.V. Smith, *Delhi: Unknown Tales of a City*, Roli Books, New Delhi, Second impression, 2016.

and the places visited by the recorder do appear. These notes indicate towards the language of the writer and its intricacies. Linking to various other contemporary surroundings, many other features of the age can also be highlighted. Thus, the general popular culture of the city does not appear clearly in any of their works, but any interested historian has to string together many events by pulling in vivid strands from different collections to explore the cultural cantors of a city.

Marriages in Delhi

The institution of marriage is central to every culture. Delhi, too, has seen extensive and grand marriage processions loaded with resources, as marriage was strongly associated with family systems and society. Grand marriage processions were taken out for royal families, nobles and wealthy subjects. Or, to put it more aptly, only the wealthy had the resources to hold processions, as these were lavish affairs meant to display the power and grandeur of the self and at times families. A share in the wealth mainly came through participation in the state activities, and the surplus available to the elites encouraged them to enter into different social stratas of the city. Detailed notes on weddings, marriage processions and betrothals by some officials in the nineteenth century indicate their wealth and the social norms they followed. As people were settling down in the cultural ambit of the city, the social celebrations and rituals were also settling down gradually as integral ingredients of the day-to-day life. The classification of Islamic and Hindu rituals around marriages came up only around the twentieth century. Prior to this, marriage processions were also a part of Muslim weddings, and glamour of weddings was not at all guided by religion. Prohibitions on cultural acts as per religious principles were introduced only during the twentieth century. Earlier, marriages were celebrated as events to maximize participation of society.

A decade before the Great Uprising of 1857, Colin Mackenzie notes:

> to see the marriage procession...we drove to a house in Chandi Chouk, belonging to one of a native sub-collectors, a Mussalman...it was a mile long! The balconies and flat roofs of the house, which were generally low, were covered by people; here was a variegated group of men and children...just as we had seated...number of palkis were passing...many of these were gorgeously dressed in brocade or velvet with Greek caps of gold and silver...the ladies of the king's harem were there in bullock carts, with scarlet hangings, to see the show... eastern processions are like eastern life, they comprise the greatest contrast of poverty and magnificence...after this appeared many nauch girls, splendidly dressed in red and gold...the blaze of torches opposite the bride's house was very pretty.[190]

A report of another procession appears nearly after a decade in 1866. The grandeur of the wedding is defined in the following words by E.F. Wyman:

> ...the latter gaily decorated with scarlet cloth, hung with jingling bells, and packed with white-robed Mussulmen,

---

[190]Colin Mackenzie, *Life in the Mission, the Camp, and the Zenana or Six years in India*, Richard Bentley, London, 1853, pp.179–82.

gaily sporting the brightest of scarfs...a score of mounted gentry brought up the rear, dressed in all the colours of the rainbow, their steeds, no less gaily arrayed, proudly arching their neck with all the grace of the Arab, curvetting and prancing the while...about the cavalcade marched musicians in groups of two and four...imagine all this—the finery, the wealth, the dirt, the poverty, the crowd, the noise...and you will have some idea, though even then an imperfect one, of the procession of a 'rich' native wedding.[191]

Prior to the wedding, the betrothal was arranged and it was considered the next most important ceremony after the birth of a person. In the late nineteenth century, Oswall Wood writes:

the proceedings are much the same for Jats and Gujars, the Muhammadans following the Hindus with striking similarity. Matters are thus managed...on the search of suitable match...amount of fee slightly varies in different tribes; it is given at the time of dismissal and is called 'bidai' or 'rukhsatana'...the shaikhs say they have only a verbal agreement without any particular ceremony. Meos have slight variation...a rich man will not seldom take a wife, while the Meos and probably all Muhammadans take two or even three, commonly, if they have the means.[192]

---

[191]E.F. Wyman, *From Calcutta to the Snowy Range*, Tinsley Brothers, London, 1866, pp.179–82.

[192]Oswald Wood, *Final Report on the Settlement of Land Revenue in the Delhi District Carried on 1872–77 by Oswald Wood and Completed 1878–80* by R. Maconachie, Victoria Press, Lahore, 1882, pp.2–5.

All these cases indicate that cultural distinction did not exist on the basis of the religious affiliation, and much of the systems worked on the basis of social utility.

The Turkish baths and the massage centres were also a part of the city's culture, and many prominent people accessed these services. J. Bowles Daly wrote:

> I began to feel, on strength of this bath, popular with myself on the assurance of my soundness. The Royal Turkish Bath on the Hamilton-road I strongly recommend...the Perman brothers, in their maddest gyration, can give but a faint idea of how the son of Karim Baksh performs his work.[193]

Merewether also had a similar kind of experience in terms of massages.[194] All these made the city a place of luxury where citizens enjoyed all the intricacies of the age. The continuation of these to the twentieth century indicates the acceptance of the same luxuries by the European masters.

The royalty of the Delhi *darbars* was also a means to highlight the significance of the city and its reign. Ibn Battuta is an authority for reconstructing the history of the fourteenth century. During this time, the seat of the Sultanate was at Delhi. The description of the presentation ceremony and hospitality highlights the grandeur, etiquette, mannerism and wealth of the Sultanate. The extensive processes that were followed while receiving gifts in the chamberlains and

---

[193]J. Bowles Daly, *Indian Sketches and Rambles*, Patrick Press, Calcutta, 1896, pp.108–09.
[194]F.H.S Merewether, *A Tour through Famine Districts of India*, A.D. Innes, London, 1898, pp.229–30.

from the provincial officials were different, and accordingly the gesture in reciprocation also varied as per the status of the individual.[195] The hospitality extended to the author was arranged by the mother of the sultan.[196] It is significant to highlight here that women in those times had the means and resources to entertain guests and had the freedom to extend the reception as per their will. It is certain that the mother of the sultan held a significant position in the empire. Similar kinds of descriptions, such as royal processions during the reign of Muhammad Tughlaq, the public audience of Firuz Shah, the court ceremonies of the Mughals, the public audience where the omrah, raja and the ambassadors all stood, followed by the *mansabdars*, the visit to the emperor, royalty of the *Tasbeeh Khana* of Shah Alam, a description of a visit to the princess, an encounter with Begum Sahiba Zeenat Mahal and the ball of the Viceroy, all indicate to the royalty that the city has witnessed over six hundred years. The glamour of the reigns was highlighted through military activities that continued from the slave dynasty down to the colonial rulers. The details of the viceroy's ball highlight the following:

> the reception room has been converted into ballroom where, between a military band and two gilded platforms...the Englishwomen, for the most part wives of officers living on their pay, added nothing to the general effect; but the magnificence of the men's uniforms, the sheen of golden veils...[197]

---

[195]Kaul, *Historic Delhi*, p.92.
[196]Ibid., p.92.
[197]Ibid., pp.109–10.

The royalty as it started with the grandeur of the Sultanate courts through the display of the military skills and warrior-ship was very much at work even during the twentieth century. All these displays made the city of Delhi a stage for the performance of various royalties that were working constantly to attain loyalties, and were also the means to seek legitimacy from the populace. Processions and public audiences were mechanisms to ensure the participation of the subject populace in the working of the state which, in the long run, secured legitimacy for the apparatuses and the limbs of the state. The secular entity of the city is reflected in the Pankha Mela, in which *pankhas* are carried in a procession on Wednesday to the temple of Jog Maya and later on Thursday to the shrine of Bakhtiyar Kaki.[198] The festival first took place *c.*1812, and is famously known as the *phool walon ki sair* or procession of the florists. An annual three-day celebration by the flower sellers of Delhi is generally held in August or September. Mehrauli was the capital of the Delhi Sultanate rulers, and is an example of the composite culture that has bolstered an environment of communal harmony. Even today, the festival is celebrated by Hindus and Muslims alike. It is also an event for political parties to display their cultural ideas. In this secular festival, the procession is led by *shehnai* players and dancers, bearing large floral fans, called *pankhas*, which are taken to the Jogmaya Temple before they are finally submitted at the *dargah* of Bakhtiyar Kaki. After the interim visit to Jogmaya temple, the procession passes through the

---

[198]Wood, *Final Report on the Settlement of Land Revenue in the Delhi District Carried on 1872–77 by Oswald Wood and Completed 1878–80*, p.132.

bazaars of Mehrauli, in order to reach the *dargah* of the popular Sufi saint of the thirteenth century, Khwaja Bakhtiyar Kaki, where the fans are finally surrendered.

The commercial success of the festival usually helps the state to bring in more and more people. The opportunities provided by any commercial frame of any given region mostly act as a permanent attraction, and they help the state to generate resources for the betterment of economy and expansion of the state's reach. In terms of commercial activities, Delhi was a great centre since the thirteenth century as is evident so far. The price regulations, weights and measures regulations, and the market reforms introduced by Alauddin Khilji further helped to make the city and its markets an organized profit-making zone. The introduction of taxes along with the currency system further enhanced commercial vitality. The effect of these regulations led Al-Biruni to call it 'the wonder of the age'.[199] The taxes that were introduced in the city of Delhi during the fourteenth century were *mustaghall/kira-zamin* (a tax on houses and shops), *jazari* (levied from butchers), *rozi* (imposed on traders) and the service from the animals of the traders (*banjaras* who employed bullocks) as well as three kinds of *jaziya*.[200] The reactions to these taxes of the city inhabitants and the traders were interesting and indicate towards the unity that brought the citizens together. The foundation of the Delhi Sultanate and the establishment of markets revolutionized the city as a commercial hub that accommodated royal workshops, craftsmen, manufacturers, brokers, shopkeepers, artisans, hawkers, jewellers and cloth

---

[199]Kaul, *Historic Delhi*, p.138.
[200]Ibid., pp.139–41.

merchants. A large numbers of skilled weavers were employed to weave and embroider different kinds of robes during the reign of Muhammad Tughlaq. All these initiatives helped the city to emerge as an economic hub whose trade activities were loaded with vibrancy.

Popular Accounts of Shahjahanabad

The most important source as evidence for the popular history of Shahjahanabad is Dargah Quli Khan's diary, which was titled *Muraqqa-i Dilli*. The word *muraqqa* is a Persian word which means 'album', and it was compiled at the beginning of the eighteenth century.[201] So, technically, the work of Dargah Quli Khan is an album of Delhi. It is an extensive work on the culture of the city, as well as its geographical layout, markets, residential quarters, mosques and the specialties of the city. Another important source of eighteenth century Delhi is *Sair-ul-Maazil*.[202] Both sources were written with a time gap of nearly a century; yet, both complement each other. Researchers can use both the sources than depending solely on the *Asar-us-Sanadid* compiled by Sir Saiyyad Ahmed Khan. Historian Nurul Hasan mentions that in principal value, Dargah Quli Khan's work is a description of the city's social life, monuments, its suburbs, its layout and functional features.[203] The description of the market at

---

[201]Saleem Kidwai, 'Dragah Quli Khan: Portrait of a City (Persian)' in R. Vanita R and S. Kidwai (eds), *Same-Sex Love in India*, Palgrave Macmillan, New York, 2000, pp.175–183.

[202]Sangin Beg, *Sair-ul-Maazil*, Sharif Hussain Qasimi (ed.), Ghalib Insitute, New Delhi, 1982.

[203]S. Nurul Hasan, 'The Morphology of a Medieval Indian City: A Case

Chandni Chowk and the articles available therein is extensive, and highlights the metropolitan nature of the market, where even Chinaware was made available. Along with it, the coffee houses (*qahwa khanas*), *karkhanas, majlis khanas, chauki khana, aza khana, tazia khana and ashur khanas* were the spaces meant for the exchange of ideas and cultural significance and understandings. The *madarssa* and the *darush-shafa* (hospital) depicted the charitable side of the city. The streets were known as *kuchas* and the common parlance for it was *gali*. Some streets were named after persons and their popular examples are Kucha-i Balaqi, Kucha-i Pattiram, Kucha-i Ballimaran, Kucha-i jaogiwara, and so on. The use of new parlance (i.e. *gali*) has transformed the Kucha Samosa to Samose Wali Gali and Kucha Batasha Wala is now called Batashe Wali Gali. Interestingly, the Gandhi Gali of present-day Delhi sells perfumes. Collectively, the shops were called *dakakin*. The popular ones in Delhi were *dakakin bastiyan* (general merchants), *dakakin chirimaran* (bird-catchers) and *dakakin halwaiyan* (sweetmeat sellers). Individual shops were called *dukan* and were mostly named after individuals such as Dukan Tek Chand, Dukan Kishan Chand Sharraf, and so on. There were *mandis* to cater to the supplies of the city and these were the wholesale markets. *Chhatta* was another category of markets which literally means a covered lane or covered market. Usually, the *chhattas* were living spaces for the artisans, such as Chhatta Mimaran (masons) and Chhatta Mom-garan (wax-makers). There are also *chattas* named after some people and places, such as Chhatta Jan Nisar Khan,

Study of Shahjahanabad', in Indu Banga (ed.) *The City in Indian History*, Manohar, Delhi, 1991, pp.87–97.

Chhatta Nigambodh Ghat and Chhatta Lahori Darwaza, as
per their associations with the place or the surroundings.
The *katras* were the small square markets, but usually these
were wholesale markets for keeping stocks. Some of these
are also named after the particular commodities they stored.
Some popular examples are Katra (cloth) Bazzazan, Katra
Roghan Zard or Ghi (clarified butter) ka Katra, and Katra Nil
(indigo). Some *katras* were also named after people, such as
Katra Adina Beg Khan and Katra Munshi Kanwal Nain. The
manzils, banglas, havelis and *kothis* were the different types
of residential properties of the city.[204] The distinction of these
city spaces were mainly based on the nature of engagement
and participation of these zones in the economic activities of
the city.

Many other craftsmen were engaged to weave and sew
borders. Shawl-weaving and needle work in Delhi were of
high standard. Other manufacturers were making ornaments,
pictures of buildings, jewellery, shields, swords, ivory
chessboards, miniature paintings and many other specialties,
which were held in high esteem. All these specialties still
survive in Delhi, and the city is known for making such items
that are not available in other parts of the country. Even today
many artists, workers and craftsmen work in the narrow lanes
of Chandni Chowk to make these unattainable goods available.
Antique shops in the deep inside the market still offer many
wonders of the past. Although the market has changed in its
layout to cater to new demands, one can still see elements
that point to continuity from the old city of Shahjahanabad
that flourished in the twelfth century. The vibrancy of the

---

[204]Hasan, 'The Morphology of a Medieval Indian City', pp.92–94.

market can be highlighted and sensed through the day-to-day working of Chandni Chowk market, where non-resident Indians fly in from distant parts of world to shop for their big fat Indian weddings. The purpose of shopping in Chandni Chowk is to get authentic and antique-looking apparels that are custom-designed as per the demands of the buyers. Similar is the story of the jewellery industry and the *chandi* (silver) bazaar of Chandni Chowk, which provides the most authentic designs and metals to the shoppers. The specialized and skilled silversmiths are also ready to create specific designs that are desired by the customers. Other small lanes with different clothing and jewellery items also maintain the supply of a wide variety of items, as required by the customer. All these are made available by skilled craftsmen who work in some dark and dingy corners of this market. It is sad that fame never comes their way. Here, custom-made is the norm of the day.

Kinari Bazaar is the lane to visit if one wants to scroll through a large variety of laces which are used on dresses. Katar Bazaar is known for its vast variety of fabrics. Nai Sadak takes us into a world of paper. Recently, it has also become a huge centre for the sale of stationary items. Inexpensive books can also be found in this market. At times the rates are as low as fifty paise or one rupee. Ballimaran and Dariba are other business hubs of the city. Ballimaran is named after the boatsmen of the Mughal era, where *balli* means oars of a boat and *maran*, the structures that are used to support the oars, thus making it the market for locating boat oars. Today, this market has a long-winding street, throbbing with history, and a litany of shops for fancy footwear, eyewear, bangles and Ayurvedic medicines. The other end of the street houses mouth-watering and probably the cheapest *biryanis, kebabs,*

kachoris, samosas, jalebis, and many other items of daily use
known as *sauda* which were brought by the people living above
these shops. In the evenings, the fragrance of the *gajras* and
paan corners takes over the streets and creates a romantic
setting. So far no study has attempted to explore these streets
and their popular cultures. Thus these lanes are awaiting the
crack of dawn to get their traditions recorded, while striving
against death.

Another medieval city (Siri) houses a posh residential area
that is popularly known as Shahpur Jat. The demographic layout
helps it to gain its name, as the major section of population in
this area is of the Jat community. The medieval remnants of the
area are still in a better position as compared to other structures
and locations of the city. While the locals may not be as aware
of the past that they inhabit, they maintain the heritage sites in
the name of history. After the first demolition drive was carried
out in Delhi—in line with the Master Plan 2021—mostly fashion
designers have occupied this area. The co-existence of both
locals, who have been living here for decades, and designers
is an interesting phenomenon. South Delhi, which houses the
oldest city of Medieval Delhi, that is Mehrauli, has also seen
something similar. Some of the most acclaimed institutions of
the city—IIT Delhi, Soil Testing Institute and Jawaharlal Nehru
University—along with the grand roads in this area, especially
around Qutub Minar, add to its beauty. The posh residential
colony of Vasant Kunj is also about one kilometre from Qutub
Minar. The areas around the monuments are evolving in such
a style that most of these heritage sites, their extensions and
grandeur, are either getting hidden or, buried forever under the
infrastructural developments.

Since medieval times the city of Delhi was also a centre

of education, and many personalities have contributed to its literary culture. The credit for initiating this culture of literacy and education amongst the masses must go to the historians of the Sultanate such as Amir Khusro and others who, along with writing of poetry and prose, were engaged in the *madarssa* education, which helped in the dissemination of knowledge. The Nasiriah College was a contribution made by Razia Sultana, and Minhaj-al Siraj Juzjani was appointed as the caretaker of this institute along with the *kazi*-ship of Gwaliyur.[205] Writing in the fourteenth century, Shihab Al-Din Al-Umari notes:

> People of Delhi are intelligent and sagacious, they speak Persian, Hindi eloquently. Some of the learned men compose good verses in Arabic also. Many of the poets...are not attached to the royal court but compose eulogies...[206]

This clearly indicates the vibrancy of the literary culture that was flourishing in Delhi during the heyday of the Sultanate. The literary culture of Balban's reign can be accessed from the writings of Firishta, who notes:

> In the days of Balban...all the philosophers, poets, and divines, formed a society every night, at the house of the prince Shehid, the heir apparent to the empire; and the noble Chusero the poet presided at those meetings. Another society of musicians, dancers, mimics, players, buffoons and storytellers was constantly convened at the

---

[205]Kaul, *Historic Delhi*, p.112.
[206]Ibid., p.114.

house of the emperor's second son Kera...the Omrahs
followed the example of their superiors, so that various
societies and clubs were formed in every quarter of the
city. The emperor himself, having a great passion for
splendor and magnificence in his palaces, equipages and
liveries, therefore the court became the center for the
initiation of the literary activities. A new city seemed
to lift up its head, and arts arose from the bosoms of
luxury and expense.[207]

Abdu-l Hakk Dehlawi mentions:

[D]uring the time of Alauddin, Delhi was the great
rendezvous for all the most learned and erudite
personages; for, notwithstanding the pride and hauteur,
the neglect and superciliousness, and the want of kindness
and cordiality, with which that monarch treated this
class of people, the spirit of age remained same. Among
the philosophers and poets of those times, the cleverest
and most renowned were Mir Hasan and Mir Khusru...
Mir Khusru...is the Prince of Poets and first amongst
Philosophers...and such skill as he possessed in every
kind and manner of literary composition, both in the
use of ordinary or unusual phraseology, and of plain or
dubious terms, had seldom been allotted to anyone. He
wrote many verses...and compiled and arranged several
diwans...As for Mir Hasan, although he has written
but little poetry, yet what he has written is musical
and pleasing. The illustrious Shaikh's opinion, however,
respecting the difference between their two styles, is

---

[207]Kaul, *Historic Delhi*, p.119.

sufficient; for he declared that our Khusru is the salt of ocean, and Hasan a sweet stream...Muhammad Tughlaq fully appreciated all sort of learning...in the reign of Sultan Firoz also, there were many sages, philosophers and lawyers, who held a place on the throne of study and erudition...[208]

He mentions many other scholars who served at different courts in those times. Kazi Shahbudin Zawali Daulatabadi, Maulana Shaikhu-l Hadad, Mianu-l Hadad, Muttahar Kurrah, Mughis Hansavi, Zahir Dehlawi, Shaikh Saifuddin and Amir Khusro were some of the luminaries of the medieval times.

The appreciation of the literary effluence motivated many to write well. Humayun's inclination to and appreciation for education and books is well-documented. He was himself a prose writer and regularly interacted with poets. Once Reis wanted his petition of leave to be accepted and this was granted by Humayun when he found two ghazals enclosed with the letter.[209] This reflects the emperor's admiration for literary activities and the importance of education in sixteenth-century Delhi. The literary contributions made during Shah Jahan's reign were also immense. Benefits from literature were diverse and profitable, and this inspired many to try their hand at it. The literary culture was dominated by Persian, which was the court language of the time. '[A] tolerable acquaintance with the Persian is now found, by intelligent natives, to be at least as sure a path to rank and emolument...'[210] Besides this, many other languages were also at work in different pockets.

---

[208] Kaul, *Historic Delhi*, pp.115–18.
[209] Ibid., p. 115.
[210] Ibid., p.120.

The *majlis, mehfils, mushairas and gazal mehfils* dominated the city. These cultural activities were not only limited to the court and the living spaces of the Mughal royalty, but also extended to the households of the nobles and the other state officials. Even the inhabitants of the city participated in music and dance assemblies, and were able to access these luxuries during special festivities at their homes and living spaces. While the ban on the music imposed by Aurangzeb disrupted this culture for a bit, it did not fade away entirely. Secretly, the officials and inhabitants practised it, and this helped to keep the soul of the city intact:

> The dying art of distanai-gui is witness to the long journey of literature and its practices in the city.

With the coming of the colonial masters to Delhi, English language was introduced in the city during the third decade of the nineteenth century. The need for an English-educated class was felt by native chiefs and princes with the demand for English teachers and secretaries as per Regulation V of 1831 and Regulations IX and XII of 1833. This led to the successful plantation of the English language, and the growing taste for new literature made the populace buy fifty copies of English grammar in Persian in one single day from the Calcutta School Book Society. The contribution of Ghiyasuddin *madarssa* to the educated circle and the history of Delhi has been well explored. Even today this *madarssa* continues to serve the purpose of education. Presently, it stands as the Zakir Hussain Delhi College, affiliated to the University of Delhi. Many other colleges came up in the city during the twentieth century. The popular ones are Hindu College, St Stephen's College, Miranda House and Lady Shri

Ram, to name a few. These colleges still attract many young ambitious minds from the entire subcontinent. The academic calibre and extra circular excellence of these colleges is reflected through the many political leaders, actors, literary figures, scientists, social scientists and diplomats who have emerged from these institutions. Their far-sighted actions are a reflection of the education they attained here. The University of Delhi was established in 1922, and since the last nine decades the university has constantly left its mark in the field of education and other extra-curricular activities with outstanding performances. This is why it continues to attract the best of students even today.

The uprising of 1857 completely shocked the imperial masters and they desperately wanted to curb the revolutionary tendency with a strong hand. The extra amount of emotions, movements and activities in the British camp led to the besiege of Delhi by the British between June and September 1857. The life in the city during the uprising has been explored marvellously by Mahmood Farooqui.[211] His work provides a unique view of the daily life of the embattled city which was constructed on petitions, applications from ordinary citizens, directives, commands and orders of the officials. The uprising made the soldiers enter the city and declare Bahadur Shah Zafar as their king. The old and ailing king became a symbol of revolt for the people of the city and the country. The acceptance of the Mughal king as their leader further boosted the soldiers emotionally and they took control of many important posts in the city. Later, with much effort,

---

[211]Mahmood Farooqui, *Besieged Voices From Delhi 1857,* Penguin Viking, New Delhi, 2010.

the British forces were able to reclaim the city, and they decided to dismantle various structures of the Red Fort. The anger of the British officials came down heavily on the city, its inhabitants, the soldiers and finally, the royal family. The emperor Bahadur Shah Zafar was arrested under charges of sedition, rebellion, treason and murder. Hodson arrested the king while he was attempting to escape along with troops of hundreds of soldiers.[212] The Military Commission assembled in Delhi on 27 January 1858, and following the trial, the king was exiled to Rangoon under British occupancy. The sons of the emperor were brutally murdered by Hodson. Earl Roberts notes, 'On enquiry I learnt that Hodson had gone a second time to Humayun's tomb that morning with the object of capturing these princes, and on way back to Delhi, had shot them with his own hands...'[213] On inquiry by an officer about the atrocities that were committed in Delhi, the old Zafar replied, 'I don't know; I suppose my people gave themselves up to the devil.'[214] The unity of the people for the cause of Independence pushed the titular majesty to pay heavily in many ways.

The imperial masters demolished some sections of the city after suppressing the uprising of 1857. The city was turned and expanded to house the military. The shift of the capital in 1911 further pushed the geographical extent of the city for accommodating the officials and the administrators. Thus,

---

[212]Kaul, *Historic Delhi*, p.405.

[213]Earl Roberts, *Forty One Years in India*, Macmillan, London, 1911, pp.136–37.

[214]Edward Vibart, *The Sepoy Mutiny as Seen by a Subaltern from Delhi to Lucknow*, Smith Elder, London, 1898, p.149.

new residential colonies and areas like Civil Lines, Outram Lane, Kingsway Camp, Hudson Lane, and others were carved out. These new colonies were meant exclusively for the imperial administrators and their staff. The Partition of India on the eve of Independence in 1947 led to mass migration of Punjabi refugees. Many of the migrants who came from the newly-formed Pakistan were businessmen and to them Delhi appeared a safe zone for business. Thus, the capital city became a huge refugee area where people kept pouring in till the end of the 1950s. The newly formed government made many efforts and established a ministry to cater to the needs of the refugee population. Many refugee colonies were set up in the south and the north of the city to facilitate the immigrants. Lajpat Nagar and Vijay Nagar became prominent refugee colonies. With this, Delhi got one more section added to its already cosmopolitan nature.

After thirty years of Independence, Delhi became a centre for commercial vitality and it also evolved as an education hub, with many colleges being set up. With these introductions, the inflow of population into the city has diverted a bit. Further, with the expanding city and the push and pulls of its struggles, there came another large section of people who formed a large unorganized sector and settled in gigantic unorganized slums scattered across the city. These were uneducated people who formed a service sector, and are an important part of the city's population. The vote bank politics of the newly born democracy never permitted the lawmakers to take strong steps in order to regulate these colonies. Even today, these slums are doing without regular electricity connections, which is a basic amenity of the twenty-first century. The slums are also not supported by sewerage systems, and there are no toilets at all, let alone toilets in every house. The people who reside in these slums are guilty of defecation in the open. As of now, the Swachh Bharat Abhiyan is very much a failure in Delhi.

Thus, with the above narration, it can be said that the city of Delhi is assimilating many cultures and civilizations and is holding all of them intact, like a *bhutta* (corn)! All are rubbing shoulders against each other but none can stand without the other. This is the city that doesn't know how to deny nor does it know how to clean its own backyard. This city appears on the canvas of international shopping markets but also holds a special status as a city of heritage. Much of its tangible history is well explored and its monuments help to hold and travel down in the memories of its past and get their sense in the present. Thus, this city is holding its past in its present and the constantly shifting and changing population of the city is able to relate to its history as they don't want to live in a disconnected world. So, to my understanding, it is the only city which allows its inhabitants to find out its past and relate with the same in the ever-changing present.

7

THE ACHING STRUGGLES

The desire to possess the city led dynasties to rule from this city, and they also made it an imperial capital for centuries in continuity. Many dynasties also contributed to the city in different ways. The most popular way of securing a page in history was through the construction of massive monuments, and even building cities anew. In the process of reaching the zenith, rulers often exploited their subjects, and this finally led to internal disturbances followed by a gradual fall of the kingdom.

Although many cities of Delhi witnessed the decline of dynasties and the assassination of sultans, none of the internal rivalries disturbed the fibre of the city. During all these shifts and changes from the twelfth to the twentieth century, the city and its populace, along with its economy, continued to flourish. In essence, the purpose of all the rulers was to make it a zone of economic prosperity and political stability.

Each city and its civilization acquires prosperity and wealth, before it is eventually pushes into decline. This is a natural process, and the fate of Delhi was no deviation from this trend. The struggles faced by this city have been immense. During the medieval times, plunders and mass massacres were the order of the day as invading armies were supposed to collect the spoils of their raid in order to ensure larger shares. Besides this, war captives were another source of wealth, as they were either recruited as slaves or sold in markets at good prices. The captives were also sold in the market as slaves, and could be bought by any person who had the means to do so.

The people of the city had a very rich repository of tales and they narrated stories of brutality to their younger generations to teach them of the spirit, scars and lessons that history unkindly showered upon them.

Timur's Invasion in 1398

It is important to note that Timur's invasion was not the first instance of destruction that was faced by this city. Before this, Delhi had seen other invasions, but none were against the general population, and never before had there been such a brutal massacre. The earlier wars were mainly assertions to gain control over resources and territory.

After the foundation of the Delhi Sultanate c.1192, Delhi received its first jolt in the fourteenth century when Timur invaded the city. It was the end of Muhammud Shah Tughlaq's reign, and the lengthy notes written by Timur himself indicate much of the barbarism of the invading army. The description of the massacre can best be understood through the words of A.L. Srivastava, who notes:

> ...Timur ascended the throne of Samarqand in 1369... being ambitious and enterprising prince, he undertook aggressive conquests of Persia, Afganistan, Mesopotamia... the fabulous wealth of Hindustan attracted his attention... being a clever diplomat, he pretended that his main object in undertaking an expedition to India was to put down idolatry, which was tolerated by the sultans of Delhi...he

reached the vicinity of Delhi in the first week of December 1398... Before fighting the Tughlaq army, Timur, who wanted to get rid of the embarrassing presence of the prisoners he had made on his way to Delhi, butchered one lakh Hindu captives (looks like exaggeration) in cold blood. Then he fought and defeated Mahmud on 17 December 1398... Timur occupied Delhi on 18 December 1398. The citizens of the capital, headed by the *ulema*, waited on the conqueror and begged to spare his life. Timur agreed to spare the citizens; but owning to the oppressive conduct of the soldiers of the invading force, the people of the city were obliged to offer resistance. Timur now ordered a general plunder and massacre which lasted for several days. Thousands of citizens of Delhi were murdered and thousands were made prisoners. A historian writes: 'High towers were built with the heads of the Hindus, and their bodies became food of ravenous beasts and birds.' The conqueror acquired immediate riches. Every soldier in his army became rich overnight and 'there was none so humble but he had at least twenty slaves'...the conquerors lived in Delhi for fifteen days...he quitted Delhi on January 1, 1399 on a return march to Samarkand... 'After inflicting on India more misery than had ever before been inflicted by any conqueror in a single campaign'...country prostrate and bleeding. There was utter confusion and misery...Rajasthan and Delhi, were so thoroughly ravaged, plundered and even burnt that it took these parts many years, indeed, to recover...lakhs of men, and in some cases, many women and children, too, were butchered in cold blood. The rabi crop standing in fields were completely destroyed...stores of grains were looted...

the city was depopulated and ruined...in the words of the historian Badauni, 'Those of the inhabitants who were left died (of famine and pestilence), while for two months not a bird moved wing in Delhi'.[215]

The Mongol invasion was averted by the polity of Iltutmish and he was also able to convince Genghis Khan to return to his capital of Karakoram through Hindukush *c.*1222. Both the Sultanate and the city were saved from the great catastrophe of the Mongol raids! Thus, the invasion and massacre carried out by Timur was the first great tribulation in the history of Delhi.

The city also went through many other misfortunes such as famines and droughts. While these events were mainly caused by environmental factors, a distant human connection is also visible. While there is no doubt that these tumults disturbed the city, none were so brutal in nature as the invasions from the north-western frontier. All these events and experiences have made Delhi the city it is today.

Invasion by Nader Shah

Another major manmade setback to the city was the invasion of Nader Shah, a Persian ruler whose rise to power has few parallels in history. He was born in a poor Turkmen family of Khurasan in 1688 and passed his boyhood in extreme penury and privation and later turned into a robber. During this time, Central Asia was going through a period of dissolution. The

---

[215]A.L. Srivastava, *The Sultanate of Delhi 711–1526 AD*, 5th edition, Shiva Lal Agarwala & Company: Agra, 1966, pp.222–25.

Shah of Iran was captured by the Afghans and they ruled it
for seven years. These seven years were a period of horror and
atrocities. J. Malcolm writes in the *History of Persia*:

> [N]early a million of her inhabitants had perished, her
> finest provinces had been rendered desert, and her
> proudest edifices levelled with the dust, and this by
> enemies who had neither the force nor the wisdom to
> maintain the conquest.[216]

Iran was surrounded by many political rivals—Russia and
the Sultan of Turkey—and the Afghans were not able to
provide stability. Nader, through his military capabilities
and administrative understanding, was able to alienate all
and secured peace for himself. After derailing the Turks, he
defeated the Afghan ruler of Khurasan and regained Kandahar.
This shows that he was fired with national enthusiasm and
unbounded ambition. Showing respect for the older dynasty
of Iran, he restored the Persian king Shah Tahmasp on the
throne. Expressing his gratitude, the king gave Nader half
of his domain with many riches of the land. Living a life
of a band robber, Nader went to the eastern province. His
absence gave Afghans the opportunity to rise, back and after
defeating the Shah, they forced him to sign a humiliating treaty.
Shah Tahmasp was deposed in 1732, and the people rose in
enthusiasm, urging Nader Shah to take the crown for himself.
Nader declined the throne and installed the eight-month-old
son of Shah as the emperor. He himself acted as regent with
full authority. The baby died and Nader Shah succeeded him,

---

[216]J. Malcolm, *The History of Persia*, 2 Vols, John Murray, London, 1829,
Vol. II, pp.2–5.

with the title of 'Shahanshah' on 26 February 1736. Nader Shah launched expeditions in all directions and rose as the greatest general of the time. In May 1738, he crossed into the Mughal frontier and captured Ghazni in Afghanistan and looking at the might of this invader, the Mughal governor posted at Kabul fled. Kabul was also captured and the imperial treasury, along with forces and stores, was confiscated. Through Peshawar he reached Lahore. The governor of Lahore offered resistance but could not resist the Persian forces for long, and finally submitted to the invader. After taking hostages and fixing the war indemnity of twenty lakh rupees, he started towards Delhi. Passing through Sirhind, Raja Sarai, Ambala and Shahbad, he reached Thaneshwar (in present-day Haryana), and the next day set off to Karnal, which was just twelve miles away from the imperial encampment of the Mughals. The entire region of Punjab was plundered and ravaged.

During all of this, Muhammud Shah was surprisingly inactive and only listening to the developments of Nader Shah. Since the capture of Kabul, no energetic step was taken by the imperial court. It was only on the arrival of the invader at Karnal that the emperor Muhammud Shah called his three top-ranked nobles, Itima-ud-daulah Qamr-ud-din Khan (the Wazir), Nizam-ul-Mulk Asaf Jah (the Regent) and Samsam-ud-daulah Khan Duran (Mir Bakshi), to resist against the invader. The Rajput rulers were also called to aid the resistance and an invite to join the resisting army was also forwarded to the Peshwa (Baji Rao). The army of the Mughals kept waiting outside the city for one month. On hearing of the fall of Lahore, the imperial forces moved to Karnal and waited for the enemy. The emperor also joined his generals. The army of the Mughals had many advantages against the forces of the invader as they were superior in position, number, artillery and cavalry. The total fighting army on the side of the Mughals was 75,000 and the force on the opposite side had 55,000 horses. The total strength of Nader Shah's camp was 1,60,000 soldiers, mounted and armed, who took part in defending their camp and plundering the enemy. Under intelligent military planning, Nader Shah shifted his camp from Sarai Azimabad to a level plain on the north of Kunjpura within the sight of the Jamuna. This shift ensured the supply of water was in plenty for his camp, and from here he was also able to cut off the supplies and the communication lines of the imperial camp. The larger planning in this shift was to have a battle on a ground of his own choice or to invade the city while the forces were busy at the battlefield.

While the troops of the Mughal governor Sa'adat Khan were coming to the battleground, the advance guard of the Shah's army looted the baggage trains of the soldiers and drove away with five hundred camels. After looking at all the developments of the imperial army, the invader quickly divided his army into three guards, prepared three sections of ambush and kept two contingents of five hundred swift riders ready, and finally, under the security of one thousand chosen bodyguards, Nader Shah moved to the field to participate in the battle. To frighten the elephants of the Mughal army he adopted a peculiar device, in which 'a wooden platform was fastened between two camels and naphtha and combustibles were placed on it to be set fire to; the camels were then driven towards the elephants.'[217] The Mughal forces that were under

---

[217]A.C. Banerjee and D.K. Ghose, *A Comprehensive History of India*, People's Publishing House, New Delhi, 1978, p.71.

the leadership of Sa'adat Khan and Khan Durran were not helped by the Nizam due to a personal rivalry, as the latter wished the fall of both. When both the leaders fell, the fighting from the Mughal side ceased. Emperor Muhammud Shah was expecting an attack from the invading force but Nader Shah avoided this and ordered the indiscriminate slaughter of Indians. Nearly eight thousand men were killed and around twelve thousand were wounded on the Mughal side; on the Persian side, the figures were twenty-five hundred dead and five thousand wounded. The camps were looted and the victorious army was able to collect a large booty.

The main cause of defeat of the Mughals was the inability of the ruler and internal rivalries. At the end of the battle, the victor called Sa'adat Khan to his camp at night to enquire about the means by which a large ransom could be collected in a short time, and he could return to his country immediately. Sa'adat Khan informed him that the Nizam was the only person who could settle the terms of peace on behalf of the emperor. Immediately, the Nizam was summoned and Nader Shah agreed to return to his homeland on receiving a sum of fifty lakh. The death of Khan Durran was another setback for the empire. The high office of Mir Bakshi which was occupied by Khan Durran fell vacant. Both the Nizam and Sa'adat Khan coveted this office. The Nizam made his claim to the office and requested the same from the emperor as a reward for the diplomatic service rendered by him. This acceded to, but it infuriated Sa'adat Khan, who decided to take revenge. In his fury, he reached Nader Shah and told him that he had accepted an insignificant amount of indemnity and by reaching the capital alone he would be able to realize twenty crores in cash, jewels and other precious and luxury items.

After waiting for some time Nader Shah called the Nizam and informed him that he couldn't wait any further, and as the Mughals had failed to fulfil the terms of the settlement, the war indemnity would not be anything less than twenty crore. The pleadings and the requests made by the Nizam had no effect and the emperor was called to the camp of Nader Shah. Most of the Mughal camp was deserted and the rest were taken prisoners by the Iranian forces.

Luftullah Khan, the *kotwal* of the city who surrendered the keys to the fort and treasury to the Persian representative, was appointed by Nader Shah. All the roads to the city were closed and guarded by Persian soldiers. Nader Shah left from Karnal along with Muhammud Shah and reached Shalimar Garden after a march of seven days. The welcome and hospitality of the Mughals started from Shalimar Garden. The best clothes with gold work and Turkish carpets were spread out to welcome the invader. The Persian soldiers were accommodated near the Red Fort; some were stationed on the banks of the Yamuna while many others lived in private houses throughout the city. After enjoying the hospitality and reception extended by the Mughal ruler for three days, Nader Shah decided to devise a way to collect the twenty crores. It was the day of Id-ul Zuha, when the invader was thinking of the means to accumulate the wealth. At four in the afternoon, someone spread the news that Nader Shah was murdered on the orders of Muhammud Shah. Without finding the truth of this statement, men on the streets of Delhi rose in fury and opened the doors of the fort and murdered some of the Persian soldiers who were leisurely walking on the streets. This slaughter continued all night, and nearly three thousand Persian soldiers were killed. The news of this slaughter infuriated Nader Shah, and he resolved to take revenge upon the inhabitants of Delhi. The disaster was set free soon to infold.

The next day he reached the Sunhari Masjid to find out in which quarter of the city his men were murdered. Later, he ordered a general massacre of the people. His order was carried out with the greatest alacrity. The soldiers rushed into the wards of the city, plundered all the houses indiscriminately and killed all men, young and old, captured women and set houses on fire. The massacre continued for nearly five hours. On hearing the sad state of affairs, the Mughal emperor pleaded for mercy to save his people. The request of the emperor was acceded to, and the *kotwal* was sent with a Persian soldier to stop the men of Nader Shah. The city was seized, and no one was allowed to enter or exit. The granaries were sealed and all localities within a radius of thirty or forty kilometres were desolated. A systematic exaction began with Muhammud Shah, when he was asked to surrender the treasury, all crown jewels and the famous Koh-i-Noor, as well as the Peacock Throne which was the most celebrated throne of the world.[218] Jean Baptiste Tavernier, who himself was a jeweller, valued the throne at £16 million Pound Sterling. Cash from the public treasuries was seized and the hidden stores were confiscated. All the nobles were asked to surrender their accumulated wealth. Many officials of the state committed suicide to save themselves from humiliation. An order was issued to the general public that each person should pay half the amount of his property as indemnity. A large retinue of accountants and clerks, along with the footmen of the *kotwal* and the Persian military police, reached each house and prepared a list of the

---

[218]See Appendix IV: *The Peacock Throne*.

available property. The owners were called to the court to pay their shares and many were kept waiting in queue to pay their shares. Verandahs of the houses were dug to look for hidden wealth. All the tricks of the trade were applied to this systematic daylight loot!

Nader Shah stayed for two months in the city of Delhi. During this time, coins were made in his name and a *khutba* was also read in his name at the Friday prayers. After returning the capital to Muhammud Shah on 1 May 1739, Nader Shah enlisted 130 accountants and expert financers, 300 masons, 200 blacksmiths, 200 carpenters and 100 stone cutters in his service to build a city like Delhi in his country. This highlights that the desire for a city like Delhi was something irresistible. The charisma of the city and its charm made many aspire for a city like Delhi, and Nader Shah was no exception to it; neither was Timur.

The estimation of wealth carried away by Nader Shah has been provided by many contemporary personalities. Banerjee and Ghose write:

> The total amount of exaction from Delhi was estimated by Nader's secretary at 15 crores in cash, besides a vast quantity of diamonds, jewels, ornaments, cloths, carpets and other costly material. Frazer puts the grand total at 70 crores. Anandram, secretary to the Indian *wazir*, computed the whole lot at 60 lakhs of rupees and several thousand gold coins, gold to the value of one crore of rupees, jewels and diamonds including the Koh-i-Noor, as also the Peacock Throne, all worth 50 crores. In addition, the invader carried away 800 elephants, 10,000 horses and 10,000 camels. The human tribute included

a princess, a daughter of Dawar Baksh, the grandson of Murad and the great-grandson of Shah Jahan...the whole population of the Persian Empire was benefitted of the Indian loot, as the revenue for three years was completely remitted. The army chiefs were liberally rewarded and the soldiers received 18 months' wages, six months' salary as their arrears, the same amount in advance, and six months' salary as a free gift. Each camp follower was paid 60 rupees as wages and 100 rupees as reward.[219]

The wealth of the city fell into the hands of the invader due to the inability of the ruler and the mutual rivalries that were at work in the Mughal court. The city was pushed back into hunger and darkness. The killings affected the city the most, and much human resource was lost. This barbarous event made the city cease functioning in shock, and it took a while for Delhi to come back to its older mode of functioning. The immense market of the city was completely looted and destroyed. The merchants were left with no more resources to invest or start over. The state also had nothing left in its treasury, so there was no scope of taking loans. It was surviving on the bare minimum and the Red Fort became a howling ground for hungry princes and princesses. The city had never faced such systematic loot and plunder. The invader attacked and wanted to carry away booty, but when the secrets of the state were spilled because of internal rivalry, the invader was able to take back more than ever. The weakness of the state further emboldened the Shah to decide all the terms of

---

[219]Banerjee and Ghose, *Comprehensive History of India*, pp.75–76.

settlement and carry them out, as per his own wishes. By the beginning of the eighteenth century, the decline of the Mughal Empire had already set in and the power of the Turko–Mongol dynasty was withering away. This invasion fastened the pace of its decline, and the loot and the payment of war indemnity pushed the Mughals into hunger and poverty for a while, until they regained some share in the resources for their daily expenses.

Invasion by Ahmed Shah Abdali

The destruction set in by the attack of Nader Shah was not yet out from the life and memory of people, when another attack took place. This time also it was from the north-western frontier, and the invader was Ahmed Shah Abdali.

Nader Shah was murdered on 9 June 1747. His mantle fell on an Afghan, Ahmed Shah Abdali. He repeated his master's exploits with equal zeal and violence and invaded Hindustan as many as ten times! He belonged to the Sadozai branch of the Abdali tribe (of Afghans), but he was known as Durrani on his coming to power. He served in the army of Nader Shah as an orderly, and was later promoted to the post of a treasury officer due to his intelligence and loyalty. During Nader Shah's invasion, he was in charge of a contingent. This was his first exchange with the territory of Hindustan, and this interaction gave him the impression that this was a rich country and its political power was in its twilight. The weakening political power and declining military might of the Mughals was becoming known due to the constant raids and internal disturbances that were popping up every now and then. There can be no reason besides the accumulation of wealth that could have motivated Abdali to come to the Indian territory. The element of the Afghan tribes who were serving as a major section in different dynastic military troops during the pre-modern times can best best understood from the words of J.P. Ferrier, 'Gold in Afghanistan is, more than anyone else, the gold of the human race...it is impossible to rely on their promises, their friendship, or their fidelity.'[220] Hence, it can be said that the Afghan tribes survived on wars, as it was a necessity for them to sustain themselves.

Conflicts between tribes have been a tradition in the region of Afghanistan and the tradition of conflict has nurtured the above-mentioned traits amongst the tribes over many centuries. Further, Elphinstone highlights the comprehensive role of the Afghans. He notes:

> For the consolidation of his power...victories would raise his reputation, and his conquests would supply him with the means of maintaining an army, and of attaching the Afghan chiefs by favour and rewards: the hope of plunder would induce many tribes to join him, whom he could not have easily compelled to submit...the troops also, having the king constantly before their eyes, and witnessing the submission of their hereditary chiefs, would learn to regard him as the head of the nation: and he might hope, as the event proved, that his popular manners, and the courage, activity, vigilance, and other military virtues which he possessed, would impress all ranks with respect, and strongly attach his soldiers to his person.[221]

---

[220]J.P. Ferrier, *A History of the Afghans*, John Murray, London, 1858, p.286.

[221]Mountstuart Elphinstone, *An Account of the Kingdom of Cabul and*

The territories of Afghanistan were no more a part of Mughal India. The turbulence caused by the Afghans during the reign of Akbar and the other Mughal rulers are well explored by historians. The rowdiness and the spirit of fighting continued to dominate the tribes in Afghanistan. Ahmed Shah Abdali came to India on the invitation of Shah Nawaz Khan, a Mughal noble with an army of eighteen thousand soldiers. He was called due to an internal dispute of father's property distribution amongst the brothers. The same matter was also reported to the Mughal court, and to avert a catastrophe from the Afghans. The wazir of the empire conferred the governorship of Lahore on Shah Nawaz Khan. However, before the execution of the Mughal court order, the army of Abdali marched in, and this proved to be a late action. Shah Nawaz Khan wanted to divert this advancing army and so sought an interview with the invader, during which he felt offended by the remarks of Abdali. He ordered for Abdali to be put to death by pouring molten lead into his nostrils. This outraged the invader and the opportunities to reconcile were completely lost. In January 1748, Abdali camped near Lahore after crossing river the Ravi. On the next day (11 January 1748), a battle took place between the troops of Abdali and Shah Nawaz Khan, and by evening the results were clear, with great losses incurred on the Mughal side. His approaching defeat led Shah Nawaz to escape to Delhi. While travelling through his route, the troops of Abdali plundered and burned villages. The city of Mughalpura was spared for a ransom of thirty lakh. Securing his position around Lahore, the invader was fully

---

Its Dependencies in Persia, Tartary and India, Richard Bentley, London, 1842, pp.283–84.

prepared to march into Delhi, after crossing Ludhiana and Sirhind. The invader made his position strong by collecting artillery, cash and seizing war material, treasury and stores. The imperial armies faced the invader at Manupur. The bravehearts from the Mughal side were Muin-ul-Mulk and Safdarjung. An accidental fire broke out in the rocket stores of Abdali, burning the gunpowder kept for the field artillery. This fire killed thousands of Afghans on the spot. During the same time, Abdali received the news of his nephew's rise in rebellion at qandahar. And, so, without wasting time and opening his army to the killing in the absence of ammunition, he returned to Afghanistan. As a result, the destruction did not reach Delhi and was averted without any effort from the Mughals who were sitting in the Red Fort.

The second invasion on the territories of Hindustan was inflicted in *c*.1749–50. This was mainly an effort by Ahmed Shah Abdali to restore his political reputation and military prestige that had evaporated during the first invasion due to the irreversible and sudden accident. A short while after the Manupur battle, Muhammud Shah died and was succeeded by his twenty-two-year-old son, Ahmad Shah, who was born of a dancing girl. Mutual rivalries meant that the nobles did not support each other. Many did worse by instigating the central government against their rivals. Muin-ul-Mulk did not get support from Delhi and in return received orders to surrender the revenues. So, this capable governor decided not to oppose Abdali in future. Apparently, the Afghan invader got a share in the revenue of the state, and an agreement was carried out that the revenues from the Chahar Mahal would be paid to him. The non-payment of the revenue as per the settlement terms of the 1750 treaty became a cause of the third invasion in 1751–52. This invasion was significant, and after this the Mughals lost the most important territory of their empire (Punjab), through a formal treaty. Delhi, being the seat of imperial control, fixed a seal to the treaty without any objection. During this invasion, Muin-ul-Mulk was able to reconcile with Abdali due to his clever replies as a captive. Abdali was so impressed by him that he called him Farzand Khan Bahadur (brave son) and bestowed a robe of honour on him.[222]

The fourth invasion was executed by Abdali's forces in 1756–57, that too, after the death of Muin-ul-Mulk. Mughliani Begum was a widow of Muin-ul-Mulk and she was acting as a representative of Abdali in the province of Punjab. In 1756, she was made captive by the Delhi wazir, Imad-ul-Mulk, who coveted the province. The begum complained to Abdali about the behaviour of the Mughal government and the invader once again set out to ruin Delhi. The reports about the advancement of Abdali were reaching Delhi on a daily basis, but the wazir was indifferent and did not take precautionary measures. The roads to the city were also not protected. Marching constantly, Abdali's forces reached the banks of Jamuna and sacked Kairana, Jhanjhana, Shamli and Kandhla and finally encamped at Luni after expelling the Marathas. The Marathas were also troubling the city constantly during these decades and there was utter anarchy in the erstwhile Mughal Empire.

Abdali's forces consisted of thirty-five hardy Afghan warriors. In India, five thousand Afghans of Kasur, twelve thousand Central Asian troops who were formally in the service of the Mughal emperor and eleven thousand musketeers (who

---

[222]Banerjee and Ghose, *Comprehensive History of India*, p.86.

were in mutiny due to non-payment of arrears) and the large army of Najib Khan joined the invader. Therefore, Abdali was able to collect a huge army without initiating any efforts on his own. The way to Delhi was clear as the wazir expressed his inability to fight back. Many people fled to Mathura under the guard of Maharaja Suraj Mal, who had carved out a powerful kingdom in the region of Braj, with a well-protected capital at Bharatpur. On 21 January 1757, Abdali was in the environs of the old city of Mehrauli and a *khutba* was read in his name at two mosques, including the Jami Masjid. The emperor of the kingdom was not expelled, but he decided to stay in the citadel. After two days he came to the city of Shahjahanabad and took residence in the rooms which were previously occupied by the Mughal emperor Alamgir II. The next day, the city was thrown to the atrocities, and loot, sacking, killing and raping became the norm of the day. People were dragged to the streets and slaughtered mercilessly. After a systematic search of houses, an instant demand for one crore was made. Abdali stayed on in the capital for a month. During this period, thousands were killed, and the nobles, queens, women of the harem and all the citizens of the city were reduced to beggary. Many contemporary writers have noted the slaughter conducted by the Afghan forces, and all these uniformly indicate that the merciless killings took place in cold blood. This invasion was not only limited to plunder and killings; it was also an intrusion into the family of the Mughals. Banerjee and Ghose write:

> He stayed in the capital, secured a tribe of girls from the imperial palace, and ransacked the city again. The Abdali married his son Timur Shah to the emperor's

daughter Gauhar-un-nisa. He himself forcibly took into wedlock Hazarat Begum, a sixteen-year-old daughter of the late emperor Muhammaud Shah. This tender lamb was pounced upon by a fierce Afghan of grandfatherly age, whose two ears had been docked and nose was rotting from a leprous carbuncle. The weeping bride was accompanied in exile by Malika-i-Zamani and Sahiba Mahal, the widow of Muhammud Shah, sixteen other ladies of the imperial harem and four hundred maid servants.[223]

The booty looted was immense and the invaders' own goods were loaded on twenty-eight thousand camels, along with many other draught animals such as elephants, mules and bullocks. Many carts were also made into booty carriages. Timur Shah was appointed governor of Punjab, and with this, Abdali left for Afghanistan.

Abdali Invades at the Behest of Najib Khan

An invasion for the fifth time was mainly at the invitation of Najib Khan, who was driven out of Delhi and was hard-pressed by the Marathas. At his invitation, Abdali came again in 1759 with a cavalry of sixty thousand. As his forces reached the banks of Jamuna, they were joined by Afghan governors, namely, Hafiz Rahmat Khan, Dundi Khan, Sadulla Khan and Mulla Sadar, along with their troops. This invasion concluded with the Battle of Panipat in 1761, where the Marathas were fighting against the joint forces of all the Afghan governors of

---

[223]Banerjee and Ghose, *Comprehensive History of India*, p.92.

India, who, in turn, joined hand with Najib Khan under written treaties and Abdali's cavalry. The battle ended disastrously for the Marathas, and the famous Maratha *sardars* Vishwas Rao and Bhau died on the field. With this, Abdali was able to secure his greatest victory. After securing his success in the battle, he went to the tomb of Bu Ali Shah Qalander to offer his obeisance and thank the Almighty. Subsequently, he left Panipat and started for Delhi. He stayed in the capital for two months and repeated the same killings and exploitations. Alamgir II was murdered by Imad-ul-Mulk. Jean Law remarked that Shahjahanabad was a desert as compared to what it had been before, and that the destruction since the time of Nader Shah had left it in a pitiful state.[224]

The destruction of the city has inspired the finest poets to write about the pain felt by the city. The two greatest poets of the times were Mirza Muhammad Rafi (pen name Sauda) and Muhammud Taqi Mir (who wrote under the pen name Mir). Such was the destruction that a new genre of Urdu poetry was made, that lamented on the fate of a city, and called Delhi a *shahr ashob* (ruined city). The inspiration for the same was derived from Persian poetry. Sauda wrote *Qasida-i Shahr Ashob* and *Mukhammas-i Shahr Ashob*—both collections mourned the decline and decay of Shahjahanabad which took place in the decades of the 1740s and 1750s. He also composed a satire on Shidi Faulad Khan, the *kotwal* of the city, who, instead of protecting its inhabitants, joined the forces of the thieves and murderers and shared profits

---

[224]Jean de Lauriston Law, *Memoiressur quelques Affaires del'Empire Mogol, 1756–61*, Alferd Martineau, Paris, 1913, p.354 and p.509.

with them.[225]

For the desolated city of Delhi, Sauda wrote:

Dilli jo ek shahr tha, alam men intikhab,
Rehte the muntakhab hi jahan rozgar ke.
Usko falak ne loot ke barbad kar diya,
Ham rehne wale hai usi ujre diyar ke.

(Delhi, which was a city select of the world where the elite of the time lived, it has been robbed and destroyed by circumstances; I belong to that very desolate city.)[226]

In another composition *Kulliyat* Sauda wrote:

How can I describe the desolation of Delhi? There is no house from where the jackal's cry cannot be heard. The mosques in the evening are unlit and deserted, and only in one house in a hundred will you see a light burning. Its citizens do not possess even the essential cooking pots, and vermin crawl in the place where in former days men used to welcome the coming of spring with music and rejoicing. The lovely buildings which once made the famished man forget his hunger are in ruin now. In the once-beautiful gardens where the nightingales sang his love songs to the rose, the grass grows waist high around the fallen pillars and the ruined arches. In the villages round about, the young women no longer come

---

[225]Mirza Muhammad Rafi Sauda, 'Masnavi Dar Shidi Faulad Khan, Kotwal, Shahjahanabad', *Kulliyat-i Sauda*, 2 Vols, Introduction by Imrat Ashrat, Ram Narain Lal Bini Madhu, Allahabad, 1971, pp.279–82.
[226]S. Nurul Hasan, 'The Morphology of a Medieval Indian City: A Case Study of Shahjahanabad', in Indu Banga (ed.) *The City in Indian History*, Manohar, Delhi, 1991, p.96.

to draw water at the wells and stand talking in the leafy shades of the trees. The villages are deserted, the trees themselves are gone, and the wells are full of corpses. Jahanabad (Delhi), you never deserved this terrible fate, you who were once vibrant with life and love and hope, like the heart of a young lover, you for whom men afloat upon the ocean of the world once set their course as to the promised shore, you from whose dust men came to gather pearls. Not even a lamp of clay now burns where once the chandelier blazed with light. Those who once lived in great mansions now eke out their lives among the ruins. Thousand of hearts once full of hope are sunk in despair. Women of noble birth, veiled from head to toe, stand in the streets carrying in their arms their little children, lovely as fresh flowers; they are ashamed to beg outright, and offer for sale rosaries made from the holy clay of Karbala. But Sauda, still your voice, for your strength fails you now. Every heart is aflame with grief, every eye brimming with tears. There is nothing to be said but this: we are living in a special kind of age. So say no more.[227]

Mir wrote an account of his life, and in a prominent *ghazal*, he rendered the despair and sense of loss that he felt at the destruction of the beautiful city of Delhi.[228] In another,

---

[227]H.K. Kaul, *Historic Delhi: An Anthology*, Oxford University Press, Delhi, 1998, Second impression, pp. 374–75.

[228]The *ghazal* is as follows:

Why do you mock at me and ask yourselves
Where in the world I come from, easterners?
There was a city, famed throughout the world,
Where dwelt the chosen spirits of the age:

composition he wrote affectionately about the beauty of the city, 'The city was aesthetically pleasing. The streets of Delhi are not mere streets. They are like album of a painter.'[229] Both the writings help us to compare the reverence and love that these poet had for the city and how lost and jolted they must have been at the decline of it. In another context Siraj, a noted thirteenth century historian and poet, wrote about the 'beautiful Delhi' in his *qasida*.[230]

After the Battle of Panipat, Delhi was virtually ruled by Najib Khan, and the 1760s was uneventful for the city as the Afghan invader placed him as the master of the empire. During this time Shah Alam, the Mughal emperor, lived mostly at Oudh. Najib Khan died in 1710, and seizing this opportunity, Shah Alam returned to the capital with the help of the Marathas. But, now the capital was a small kingdom limited to the vicinity of Palam. In 1782, the monsoon failed and it brought with it famine, disease and death. In 1784, thieves looted the merchants of the city and collected ransom.[231] In 1787, the Rohilla Afghans under Ghulam Qadir further destabilized the declining city. The Marathas recaptured the city later in 1788. Mahadji Sindhia was able to hold it for

---

Delhi its name, fairest among the fair.

Fate looted it and laid it desolated. And to that ravaged city I belong. Cf. Kaul, *Historic Delhi*, p.375.

[229]Mir Taqi Mir, quoted in M. Sadique, *History of Urdu Literature*, Oxford University Press, Bombay, 1964, p.100.

[230]Iqtidar H. Siddiqui, *Perso-Arabic Sources of Information on the Life and Conditions in the Sultanate of Delhi*, Munshiram Manoharlal Publishers, New Delhi, 1992, p.63

[231]Stephen P. Blake, *Shahjahanabad: The Sovereign City in Mughal India 1639–1739*, p.168.

fifteen years. This was a period of tranquility in the city. Many European officers and travellers who visited the city in the latter part of the eighteenth century wrote about the destroyed buildings, rubble, dirt, poverty, commercial trifling, polluted canals and demolished *havelis*. The beautiful and extraordinary city could not stand against the constant attacks and had lost its glory and glamour.

The last decade of the eighteenth century was marked by constant engagement of the British forces in Delhi. During the same time, the John Company took note of certain things, especially monuments and started to maintain the same. In 1803, the British were able to secure success in southern and eastern India. The success in the Anglo-Maratha wars made them more confident of securing Delhi. After defeating the French commander Louis Bourquien, the British established supremacy in north India. The territory of Shahjahanabad was acquired by the John Company stationed at Madras after the Treaty of Surji Arjungaon was signed *c*.1803. The territories of Delhi as per the treaty comprised Delhi and Hissar division, which were subdivided in 1819 into the districts of Haryana, Rohtak, Panipat, Gurgaon and Delhi. In 1848 and 1853, one hundred and ninety-three square miles from Meerut and Bulandshahar were added to the territory on the eastern side of the river. Lord Lake was decorated for the victory, which he secured in the War of 1803. The ascendancy of the British brought back peace and security to Shahjahanabad and gradually the city was regaining its health. Through the Treaty of 1803, the Britishers didn't make any significant introductions but restricted the domain, revenues and jurisdiction of the Mughal emperor. After the treaty, the emperor was only entitled to receive regular pocket money and *nazar* on festivals and this continued for two years until the terms of the treaty were designed formally. In 1805, the company set the terms of the protection through an order. The terms agreed upon by both the sides were the following:

1. Revenue from lands near the city would be set aside for the emperor.
2. Shah Alam, however, was to have no authority over these lands, collection of revenue and administration of justice being the responsibility of the British.
3. Two courts of justice under British jurisdiction were established, one for the city and the other for the territory surrounding, and the emperor's only right was to confirm a sentence of death.
4. Within the palace-fortress itself, would Shah Alam administer criminal and civil laws.[232]

The situation of Delhi under the Marathas and the English continued to be the same. During the takeover, the British found the city exhausted. The British administrator Charles Metcalfe wrote: 'Robbing in the city of Dihlee was organized in a systematic manner...the city was shared in districts among the villagers of the environs, and the plunder of a particular district was the property of particular villages.'[233] The British army occupied the lands on the northern and the southern side of the palace. The battalions were given the task to build the bazaars, set up the hospital and build accommodations,

---

[232]J.N. Sarkar, *Fall of the Mughal Empire*, 4 Vols, M.C. Sarkar & Sons, Calcutta, 1950, Vol. IV, pp.334–37.
[233]C.T. Metcalf, 'Delhi 1815', *Home Miscellaneous Series*, Vol. 776, Indian Office Library, London, p.1587. *Cf.* Blake, *Shahjahanabad*, p.170.

and the stables were made near Kashmiri Gate. Two battalions were quartered in the Daryaganj area east of Faiz Bazaar. In this area, a bazaar was constructed along with the stables for camels, bullocks and horses. Soon after ascending the city, the British began the work of construction. Many repair works were also carried out, under which the monuments of the city were restored. The rejuvenating city was visible by *c.*1811, and in 1828 a cantonment was built and it was two miles north of the Kashmiri gate. The required infrastructures of the cantonment were also constructed, such as barracks, offices, storerooms and parade-grounds. A space was formed between the ridge, the river and the north wall of the city and people started to live in this area. Thomas Metcalf, brother of Charles Metcalfe and civil servant, also made a great house on the ridge, and soon it became the seat of many official activities. In between 1830 and 1857, the British laid out a cemetery, built a church near Kashmiri Gate, established a college, constructed a club and laid the foundations of a bank, post office, printing press and photographic studio. Many other public works were also carried out by the British.

In the nineteenth century, the city grew, and this expansion created a new class of merchants. The constant growth of population pushed the urgent requirement of organizing the residential colonies. During the 1840s, the city population was on the rise along with many other cultural activities that were financed by Hindu merchants, traders, bankers, artisans, landowners, lawyers, teachers and administrators. While walking in the city in the 1840s, R.R. Heber said the houses at Delhi 'far exceed in grandeur anything seen in

Moscow'.[234] The flowering of cultural, artistic and intellectual activities in the city during the 1830s and 1840s was called 'Delhi Renaissance' by C.F. Andrews.[235] The Delhi College was its locus ailment.[236] The city was recovering from the aliment that was set in by the constant plunders and loots of the Afghans. The economy of the city was also reviving. The census report of 1833 indicates that the total population of the city, excluding the palace, was 119,860. The census of 1843, 1845 and 1853 show a constant rise in the population of the city from 131,000, 137,000 and 151,000, respectively. The constant pressure of the demography was pushing the city to expand outside the walls of the old city, which was the hub of all activities for nearly two centuries.

The John Company was slowly capturing political power in the Indian subcontinent and was exerting hard to extract more and more revenue in order to increase the profit margins. As much of their income was exhausting fast due to the huge expenses that were incurred, being constantly at war in different colonies, such as the First Anglo-Burmese War (1824–1826), First Anglo-Afghan War (1839–1842), First Opium War (1839–1842), First Anglo Marri War (1840), First Anglo-Sikh War (1845–1846), Second Anglo-Burmese War (1852–1853), and one of the most expensive wars of the world i.e. Crimean War (1853–1856). To meet the expense of wars, the company was constantly pressing the colonies to

---

[234]R.R. Heber, *Narratives of a Journey through the Upper Provinces of India*, Vol. 1, London, 1928, p.563.

[235]Blake, *Shahjahanabad*, p.180.

[236]Narayani Gupta, *Delhi between Two Empires: Society, Government and Urban Growth 1803–1931*, Oxford University Press, Delhi, 1981, p.6.

extract more and more revenue. The constant exploitation
made the people of the country rise against the company. The
infuriated groups rose against the British company on 10 May
1857 and soon the Sepoy Mutiny that started from the Meerut
Cantonment engulfed the entire north India. Historians have
explored extensively and located well the reasons for the rise of
'the first war of India's Independence'. But, they hold different
opinions on the nomenclature to be adopted for referring to
'the Great Uprising', which is also called 'the Revolt of 1857'.
The significance of the uprising lies in the fact that 'it was
the largest anti-colonial uprising anywhere in the world in the
nineteenth century'.[237] The extent of the uprising can also be
sensed from the participation of the soldiers. According to the
official figures the Bengal Army consisted of 1,35,000, 'native'
sepoys. Out of this, only 7,000 remained loyal to the company
and 1,25,000 went up in armed revolt against the colonial
masters. Delhi was the most crucial centre for the uprising of
1857, as the forces came to the city from all the major centres
of the revolt, declaring, shouting and announcing Bahadur
Shah Zafar as the king of India, unanimously. They accepted
the leadership of the ailing Mughal emperor and wanted to
fight the British under his leadership.

A committed literary stalwart of nineteenth century Delhi,
Ghalib witnessed the Mutiny of 1857 and noted:

> This year, at midday on Monday 16th Ramzan, 1273
> AH, which corresponds to May 11th, 1857...the gates
> and walls of the fort and the battlement of Delhi were

---

[237]Irfan Habib, 'Remembering 1857', in *Delhi in 1857: Studies, Images
and Documents*, Souvenir Indian History Congress: 70th Session, Delhi,
2010, p.8.

suddenly shaken...on that inauspicious day a handful of ill-starred soldiers from Meerut, frenzied with malice, invaded the city—every man of them shameless and turbulent, and with murderous hate for his master, thirsting for British blood—they were humble, quiet men who passed their days drawing some modest sum from British bounty...no men among them knew an arrow from axe...such men are made to people the lanes and by-lanes, not to grid up their loins and go out to battle... when I heard the noise and uproar, I would have made enquiry, but in the twinkling of an eye...every street and every lane was full of galloping horsemen, and the sound of marching men, coming wave upon wave, rose in the air. Then there was not so much as a handful of dust which was not red with the blood of men whose bodies were like the rose...and it seemed that every corner of every garden was stripped of its leaves and fruits, the graveyard of a hundred spring times.[238]

The sepoys instantly resorted to killings. The city suffered much loss as the soldiers started plundering the inhabitants for meeting their own expense within a few days of declaring the mutiny. The streets were piled with the dead bodies. Charles John Griffiths has also recorded the sight of a streets: 'The portion of the town we passed...had been pillaged to the fullest extent... Each street was filled with a mass of debris consisting of household effects of every kind...much of this wholesale destruction was, no doubt, attributable to the action

---

[238]Ralph Russell and Islam Khurshidul (trs.), *Ghalib: 1797–1869*, Vol. 1: Life and Letters, George Allen and Unwin, London, 1969, pp.135–36.

of the sepoys and rabble of the city.'[239] Corpses of people were lying on the streets and owners had left their birds in cages, he adds.[240] Both the abovementioned narratives indicate to a dreadful scenario that pounded upon the city and haunted it with the brutal killings and loot which was set in through the rebellion of 1857. Many other contemporary sources such as the writing of Ghalib that has been mentioned above also confirm the killings, uprooting of peace and decline in security around the city. The aftereffect of the munity was very cruel on the inhabitants. The inhabitants went under the trauma of house arrest, beggary, vacant houses, confiscation of property, proof of innocence to be produced, hunger, homelessness, etc.[241] Although, the uprising was crushed soon by the technologically advanced British forces, its different dimensions have affected the entire country. The most major shift after the war of 1857 was the transfer of power to the crown under the Proclamation of 1858. It was also called the Magna Carta of the People of India.

After seizing the city, the British were not sure whether it should be retained or destroyed. Charles Trevelyan pleaded to John Lawrence that the city be spared and rebuilt into the metropolis of India.[242] In May 1858, the Secretary of State decided and agreed with Lawrence 'that the political object to be gained by destroying the palace will be gained by occupying

---

[239]Charles John Griffiths, *A Narrative of the Siege of Delhi*, John Murray, London, 1910, pp.198–201.

[240]Ibid.

[241]Gupta, *Delhi between Two Empires: Society, Government and Urban Growth*, p.6.

[242]J. Lawrence to C. Trevelyan, 16 December 1857 (Lawrence Papers, F. 90, 12), pp.173–74.

it.'[243] The Lahore Chronicle of 15 May 1858 reported that the destruction of the city would be 'symbolic of the invincibility of British Power.'[244] The shift of the power from the John Company to the British Crown was not smooth. The killings and the losses that happened in the uprising of 1857 paved the way for this transfer of political authority. In the year 1859, *Lahore Chronicler* published views and suggestions of Trevelyan about the fort that the palace (Red Fort) would be destroyed and a fort Victoria would be built.[245] In March 1859 'a good deal of blowing up' was going on as noted in the *Delhi Gazette*. Many changes were made in the city as per the military and administrative requirements of the company. The proposal for blowing up the seven-miles-the long city wall was also made, but the insufficient quantity of gunpowder in the city didn't let it proceed further. Thus, the stones of the wall were removed, one by one; manually.[246] India didn't have many things to gain after Queen Victoria's Proclamation of 1858. The conditions of the proclamation were not very positive but definitely it was a step ahead in the direction in which Indians participated in the making of their nation. The Independence struggle gained momentum in the late nineteenth century and in the beginning of the twentieth century. It attained some significance and laid the foundation

---

[243]Secret Letter No. 68 of 1857 (*Indian Office Records*, India and Bengal Secret Dispatches, India Public No. 63 of 1858, 5 May).

[244]*Lahore Chronicle 1858*, 15 May 1858, p.309.

[245]H. Tervelyan, *The India We Left*, p. 66 and *Lahore Chronicle 1858*, dated 26 March 1859.

[246]National Archives of India, Foreign Secretary, 25 January 1858, F. 11-15, p. 51, Chief of Staff to Officer Commanding Meerut Division, 27 January 1858.

of the struggle for Independence. The Independence struggle
had its own losses and gains. The leaders went through thick
and thin but continued to resist against foreign yoke.

The Twentieth Century of Delhi

The next major tragedy that came down to India as a 'nation'
was only after the gap of ninety years from the uprising of 1857.
This time it was clubbed with Independence. The tragedy fell
upon the citizens in the form of Partition and the formation
of Pakistan, a separate nation for the Muslims of India. It
was the year 1947 when the Partition of a Nation (India) was
announced with the declaration of its Independence. It was
the first incident of its nature in the history of the world
that a nation was bifurcated on the very day of its liberation!
With this Partition, the worst and most painful episode of
displacement human history set in, where millions of people
were supposed to migrate to a new land, leaving behind their
belongings and homes. It was not a unilateral process; the
movement of the inhabitants was bilateral, as Muslims from
the newly demarcated India headed to the Islamic Republic of
Pakistan, whereas the Hindus and Sikhs from the territories
of Pakistan moved for India. Those who participated in the
struggle for Independence wondered about the formation of
the new nations, which they had never imagined. Some were
wondering if they had demanded the two separate nations in
the disguise of freedom.

Anyhow, the nations were formed and the tragedy of
Partition came as the worst episode in human history where
millions were rendered homeless and thousands were killed
or raped and missing human beings went unreported. In this

tragedy the irony was the killing and raping of one's own brothers and sisters. Many times I ask myself, is it really difficult to be humans in testing times?

A noted historian Gyanendra Pandey notes, 'In the context of 1947, a moment of quite incredible uprooting and violence, displacement in its physical sense refers generally to evacuation and migration.'[247] The total population of the city would have gone down to about 5,70,000 due to migration before it began to grow once again rapidly; so rapidly that by 1951, within four years of Partition, it had risen to 1,744,072. It was a little more than a million in four years, or a quarter of a million every year.

J.E. Welldon, a bishop of Calcutta noted:

> The disappearance of the British Raj in India is at present...and must for long time be, simply inconceivable. That it should be replaced by a native Government or Governments is the wildest of wild dreams...as soon as the last British soldier sailed from Bombay to Karachi, India would become the battlefield of antagonistic racial and religious forces...the peaceful and progressive civilization, which Britain has slowly but surely brought to India, would shrivel up in a night.[248]

Within a few days after the declaration of Independence and the Partition, India proved itself apt to the comment of Bishop Welldon.

[247]Gyanendra Pandey, 'Partition and Independence in Delhi: 1947–48', *Economic and Political Weekly*, Vol. 32, No. 36 (6–12 Sept), 1997, pp. 2261–2272.
[248]Ramchandra Guha, *India after Gandhi: The History of the World's Largest Democracy*, Picador, India, 2007, p.3.

As Partition set in, Delhi saw riots on an unprecedented scale. A middle-class migrant from western Punjab said, 'Partition changed the course of many lives which would otherwise have run in their familiar channels.'[249] Looking at the problems of his staff (whom Mountbatten wanted to shift out of Shimla), Mountbatten wrote to the prime minister and defence minister:

> I must admit that I am more shaken by the events which have touched my own staff than by the events one reads about in the newspapers...the night train from Kalka to Delhi to be stopped on two successive nights and all the Muslim passengers to be butchered in front of the guards is so serious...that the defence minister really must act strongly.[250]

These letters speak a lot about the riots that were indiscriminately falling upon many innocents. Many leaders were shaken by looking at the deaths, which became the fate of the innocents.

The rise in the population was a concern for the authorities and the newly formed government. The most important task before the government was to ensure that no communal riot should break-out. This was the scenario of change that was tapping the city of Delhi during its wake of freedom. The rise in population was at a breakneck speed. Besides this, the numbers of the Muslims looking for transit to Lahore were

---

[249]Pandey, 'Partition and Independence in Delhi', p.2261.
[250]*Indian Office Records*, R/3/1/172, Mountbatten to Baldev Singh, 2 September 1947 and Mountbatten to Prime Minister on 2 September 1947.

on a constant increase in the city. The city was growing and it was being filled by the arrival of refugees in tens of thousands from Punjab, Sindh and the North-West Frontier Province (NWFP). The increase in population resented the pressing needs for shelter, food and hygiene. The refugee settlements and the camps for Muslims were all short of supplies and the approaching winters were about to make it worse. The condition of the Purana Qila refugee camps was put before the Delhi Government's Emergency Committee by Zakir Husain as 'those who have made it to the camp had escaped from sudden death', to be 'buried in a living grave'.[251] The incidents of stabbing, looting and clash between the Hindus, Muslims and Sikhs were evident in Delhi long before September. These were also fuelled by an uncertainty of the future. Trains full of slaughtered bodies arriving from the NWFP further added ignition to the already veritable flood of blood. In her memoir, Begum Anees Qidwai of Lucknow notes, 'September came bringing with it unnumbered troubles...India had not been independent for fifteen days when violence and killing began in Delhi'.[252] The city went through a tough time where the people were thirsty of each other's blood and wanted to kill in the name of religion. The newcomers were prepared to do anything to earn money. They trauma of loss made them resort to violence on the slightest pretext. Shahid Ahmed Dehlavi in his work *Dilli ki Bipda* (Disaster of Delhi), mentioned that both the 'Hindus of Delhi' and the 'Muslims of Delhi' suffered. The Hindus lost the businesses and the Muslims were living in

---

[251]Abdul Kalam Azad, *India Wins Freedom*, Orient Longman, Chennai, 1988, p.233.

[252]Pandey, 'Partition and Independence in Delhi', p.2268.

fear. Further he writes, 'the scars of this separation will never disappear...this separation is like torture, like nails being pulled out of the flesh...Delhi has become like *dayan* (witch)...even though she has become witch, she still remained a mother'.[253] The riots spoiled the harmony of the city and the neighbours who had lived for years with each other and shared cultures, have turned into foes overnight. The fear of killing, looting and raping made every one suspicious of each other. All this that was happening in Delhi was sending shockwaves throughout the nation. Philip Ziegler, the auto-biographer of Mountbatten analysed the decision of Partition that tore the soul of Indian culture:

> Once the principal of Partition had been accepted, it was inevitable that communalism would rage freely. The longer the period before transfer of power, the worse the tension and the greater the threat that violence, would spread. Today it was Punjab, tomorrow Bengal...where Hindus and Muslims lived cheek by jowl. Two hundred thousand (dead) could have become two million, even twenty million.[254]

The riots were not stopping and finally Gandhi gave a call for the fast unto death. This call had a lightning effect on all the religious mobs and everyone came forward to surrender and promise that they will not indulge in violence.

The riots stopped but the reconciliation was not easy, the bitterness and hate towards the fellow beings became deep

---

[253]Gyanendra Pandey, *Remembering Partition: Violence, Nationalism and History in India*, Cambridge University Press, Cambridge, 2004, p.135.
[254]Philip Ziegler, *Mountbatten*, Collins, London, 1985, p.439.

rooted and continued to survive. In one of his speeches in October 1947 Gandhi said, 'Delhi has a long history behind it. It would be madness even to try to erase that history.'[255] On 26 January 1948, at a prayer meeting, Gandhi put forward that 'the worst is over' and hoped 'that Indians would work collectively' for the 'equality of all classes and creeds, never the domination and superiority of the major community over a minor, however significant it may be in number or influence.'[256] On the 4 September 1947, C. Rajgopalachari made another request to the citizens of India:

> Refugees are (being) sent all over India. They will scatter communal hatred on a wide scale and will churn up enormous ill-will everywhere. Refugees have to be looked after, but we have to take steps to prevent the infection of hatred beyond the necessary minimum which cannot be prevented.[257]

These words coming from the top leadership of country do indicate the intensity of the communal riots and the hatred that were spurting out in the different pockets of the country. This was while the refugees were yet struggling to secure the basics necessities of survival and meet their families.

Initially, the refugees headed towards Delhi but they saw there was not enough space and on social grounds a lot of resistance was working against them. More so, they faced resistance being outsiders. While the Hindus did not want the homeless to move in, Muslims who had chosen to stay

---

[255]Pandey, 'Partition and Independence in Delhi', p.2267.

[256]Guha, *India after Gandhi*, p.21.

[257]Ibid., p.84.

back were afraid of the refugees. They knew that most new arrivals had suffered on the way and lost family to the mayhem in Punjab. Many of the incomings people were surely looking for revenge and hence, there was fear, anguish and anger in the air. In order to control the situation, a joint delegation of senior citizens of the city met Mahatma Gandhi, who asked Jawaharlal Nehru to talk to the home minister and ensure that the incoming people should not be settled in the old city without the local residents' consent. Thus, the state organized to accommodate new comers into newer areas. The old city, despite having lost almost one-third of its residents, could not have managed millions who had come. It is also then that the city began growing in every direction. Forty years later Ebadat Barelvi, a Professor of Delhi college noted in his memoirs *Azadi ke Sayee mein*, that Delhi had become a veritable 'refugee-istan'.

All available spaces were occupied—there were tented accommodations in old forts, deserted mosques, ruined medieval structures, fields and even under the shadow of the wall around the old city of Shahjahanabad. After the appointment of Mehr Chand Khanna as Minister for Rehabilitation, various schemes for accommodation, education, employment and compensation claim processing were started. Besides, schemes to find missing people, mostly young women, was also initiated.

Those who came with property papers had an advantage and those who could not arrange for the documents ran from pillar to post, begging for a roof. Accommodations came up at newly created residential areas, virtually overnight in Lajpat Nagar, B.K. Dutt Colony, Malviya Nagar, Amar Colony, Tagore Garden, Uttam Nagar, Moti Nagar, Rajinder Nagar, Keshavpuram, Raja Garden, Rajouri, Ramesh Nagar, Tilak

Nagar and Hari Nagar, Ashram, but all these were cramped constructions. Or, were the jobs done in haste? This was the fate of millions who came leaving behind the massive and illustriously built *kothis*, *havelis*, mansions and houses at Lahore, Ghazi ka Thana and Islamabad. Many agricultural lands were acquired, and hectic constructions began initially for makeshift arrangements and then to build permanent structures.

A large section of the Sindhis, poor peasants and petty traders had walked across from Karachi, Thatta, Tharparkar, Umarkot and Sukkur into Rajasthan and Gujarat and settled there. Many later moved into Maharashtra and Madhya Pradesh. Hindus and Sikhs arrived from the NWFP, Dera Ghazi Khan, Dera Ismail Khan, Peshawar, Kohat, Chinyot, Islamabad and many other cities. The refugees brought with them their cultures, and this made inroads into the streets of the city. Its effect can be sensed through the fact that till the mid-1960s, the Peshawari *salwar kameez* and the Afghan male headgear with its golden peak was a common site in the streets of Delhi. The headgear led many to respectfully label them as Multanis, even Hindus with this headgear were called *Pathan saab!* They found shelter in far-flung areas and built thatched huts in localities like Nabi Kareem. They moved into refugee camps at Kingsway, Hudson Line, Outram Lines and Rides Lines. Today, these areas form the western side of the University of Delhi, and these areas also shelter the students who come to Delhi to study. A major share of revenue from these areas is channelized by the students, who pay hefty rents to stay near the campus. Haqiqat Nagar was developed later and many refugees were shifted to this location. Gujarwalan Town also came up during the same time that is the decade of the 1960s. The city was still trying to accommodate the influx even after twenty years of Partition. No one knew what was happening on the other side of the new border. The people there must have been living with same despair and sense of loss. The sense of loss might have been haunting them also, as it is still looming over the people who came to India in 1947. Even after seventy years of their arrival to this land they are unable to forget the tragedy and associate with their erstwhile lands nostalgically. Casual walks in the areas of Vijay Nagar, Tilak Nagar, Haqiqat Nagar, Kingsway Camp, Adarsh Nagar are sufficient to see some elderly who are in their mid-nineties. Many are inspired by some zeal to share and narrate the painful experiences of Partition and migration. Experience and memory both are made in complex ways; they depend upon the cultural heritage and the modes of recording, telling, repetition, accumulation either individually or collectively.

The refugees built houses on the allotted lands and also on the land acquired from land sharks. While a few moved to Mukherjee Nagar in the late 1970s and early 1980s, others were allotted houses in Rajinder Nagar and Inderpuri, where a settlement came up on agricultural land acquired from the village Dus-Ghara. A large section of the Sikh population settled in Inderpuri. Patel Nagar and Rajinder Nagar came up on lands acquired from the villagers of Shadipur, Khanpur and the surrounding villages and became home to large populations of Hindus and Sikhs, and also for the people who came from the NWFP. Many who came from the frontier province later established Kohat Enclave and Derawal Nagar, while some chose to live in Jangpura and Bhogal. Many settled down in Lajpat Nagar, Amar Colony, Malviya Nagar, Bhogal, Jungpura, Tilak Nagar, Ramesh Nagar and Bali Nagar. Rajouri Garden gradually turned into the quintessential Punjabi locality with their own subset of dialects, their own block-level festivities and outlets specializing in region specific snacks and Punjabi street food. Many tried to reflect in these colonies the life that they lived in the NWFP. The Punjabi diaspora rose steadily from the mid-1950s and its gradually ensured the major share in the commerce of the city. Certainly, 1947 with the twin events of 'Independence' and 'Partition' was a turning point in the history.

Meanwhile, the process of amalgamation of cultures, lifestyles, food, music and attire that has defined Delhi for thousand years continues unabated. Thus, Delhi is not only a site, or a stage of events which is inert, unchanging, un-historic, unimagined or meaningless bowl of history. Today, Delhi is more than 'a dream to attain' and has to be cherished as a city that has been seen and aspired by its citizens! What defines this city today, are not merely the events that have shaped it but its *admiyat!*

8

CONCLUSION

In the last fifteen hundred years, Delhi has seen the most extreme events, be it heinous crimes against its rulers and people or coronation celebrations, extravagant marriage processions and lavish *darbars*. Although the horrors as are discussed in the book were brutal enough to strip the city of its soul, none of them were able to do so. The city, its spirit and records have served as living experiences for many. Politically, it was a space of significance since the eleventh century as is proven by tangible evidences so far. With the construction of Shahjahanabad in the seventeenth century, it reclaimed its imperial grandeur with political assertion. The social and economic organizations that were at work around the capital city made it a centre of economic importance; this preference was further accentuated by its geographical location at the centre of the Indian subcontinent. The efforts of the sultans and the Mughal emperors made this city a hub of economic and cultural activities. Its diverse cultures gave it a cosmopolitan nature. Religious synchronization too was attained through the efforts of the Sufis. Later, important events relating to Sikhism added to its religious glamour; the various gurdwaras in Delhi stand testament to this. Christianity made its presence felt in the city only in the nineteenth century. The St James Church (also known as Skinner's Church), built in 1836 by Colonel James Skinner, is the oldest church in Delhi. With all these developments, Delhi attained a special status for itself.

The long association of various imperial powers in this city gave the territories of Delhi a rich heritage in terms of its historical monuments. Being the seat of the imperial capital, the city was home to seven imperial cities that were erected by various dynasties. Even during the modern times—to be precise, in the twentieth century—many political leaders from different ruling parties contested for this space as their final resting place. During the twentieth century, state funerals were organized for nearly all popular members of the parliament. This became a norm and led to an immense rise in the demand of the funeral grounds for the political iota. Many illustrative memorials were dedicated to a large number of political leaders in the mid-twentieth century. The desire for memorials was pushed for by many of their political followers. However, during the late 1990s, this practice was curbed after it came under pressure from the public and the other agencies that highlighted the constraint of space in the city, and wanted the government to act wisely on this issue. The decision taken by the state limited the scope of funerals and burial sites to be arranged by the state. It also limited exclusively dedicated memorial grounds for popular leaders. The discontinuation of state-funded mass funeral arrangements helped save the city from becoming bespeckled with restricted memorial gardens. The popular memorial gardens around Rajghat are Shantivan, Vijay Ghat, Shakti Sthal, Samta Sthal, Veer Bhumi, Ekta Sthal, Karma Bhumi, Sangharsh Sthal, P.V. Ghat, Jannayak Sthal, Smiriti Sthal and Kisan Ghat.

The other popular side of Delhi is its markets and various proliferating shopping hubs. The most popular kernel for shopping for a large variety of goods such as intricate

jewellery, clothes, furniture, light fixtures, perfumes, shoes,
fabrics, tools and paper is Chandni Chowk. This is followed
by Connaught Palace due to its international clientele.
Connaught Palace is less a market and more of a commercial
hub. An exclusive lane known as Baba Kharak Singh Marg is
allotted to all the states of India to display their indigenous
handicraft products and craft items. It is also situated in
close proximity to Old Delhi and its wholesale markets are
Chandni Chowk, Katra, Dariba, and so on. Many other
popular markets cater to the needs of the city's inhabitants as
well as tourists. Some of these include the markets at Lajpat
Nagar, Kamla Nagar, Janakpuri, Tilak Nagar, Rajouri Garden,
Sarojini Nagar, INA Market, Saket, Malviya Nagar, and the
most crucial one is Janpath. The most popular market which
gives a sense of the diversity in the country, and showcases
the art and craft of its different states is Dilli Haat. The
success of Dilli Haat located in INA has led the Delhi
government to inaugurate a few more such hubs around
the city. The sprawling examples of it are the Dilli Haats
located at Pitampura and Janakpuri. These hubs are popular
centres during the festive celebrations of Karwa Chauth,
Diwali, Janmasthmi and Shivratri, among others. The Delhi
government has also taken other initiatives to showcase the
handicraft of India. The Dastkar Melas organized throughout
the year in different parts of the city are living examples of
this. Interestingly, all the markets of Delhi are able to attract
a large number of customers due to the large-scale variety
of goods that are sold in these markets. A lot can be written
on the markets of Delhi but after highlighting these popular
centres of trade I would like to deviate a bit.

The city carries a lot of charisma, and holds many

attractions for people across age groups. Many of these attractions are discussed in Chapter 4. Here I would like to grasp the attention of the reader towards the engagement of the military in the city. There are many defence setups in the city such as the Cantonment area, Gopinath Bazaar, Bara Square, Subroto Park, Research and Referral Hospital, the headquarters of the different forces (Indian Air Force, Indian Navy and Indian Army). Many subsidiary and paramilitary forces also find representation in the capital through bodies such as the Coast Guard, CISF, Home Guard, National Guard, and so on. All these forces are engaged in providing twenty-four hour security to the city along with the Delhi Police which is directly under the command of the home ministry under the central government. The recent long squeal by the serving chief minister (Shri Arvind Kejriwal) was enough a reminder for all to know about the tussle of power-sharing which each layer of government wants to hold over the Delhi Police. All these forces are very integral to the city of Delhi and its existence as the National Capital Region. These forces are not always visible in the city but their discipline, grandeur and valour gets reflected in celebrations of Republic Day and Independence Day. Immense effort is put in by a large number of soldiers who participate in competitions on behalf of their regiments.

Overall, it can be said that Delhi is a city of immense diversity. It has stood well throughout history as a cohesive unit with different hues of politics, economy and social inclusion. In order to experience the soul of Delhi, one has to spend some time in the city and with its inhabitants. This allows us to sense its inner strengths and weaknesses along with its sorrows and joys. A dive into the *admiyat* (humanity) of this city will only hint that it is a city of *dilwalas*!

Delhi is not for immediate enjoyment, it's a possession forever!

APPENDIX I

THE MISTRESS OF EVERY CONQUEROR
BY KHUSHWANT SINGH

Delhi, the mistress of every conqueror of India, Aryan or Afghan, Persian, English or Mogul...debris of her many pasts, relics of her dead and gone masters... Yet Delhi lives... outgrown habitations, as she has crawled northward from Tughlakabad and Lalkot, through Dinpana and Ferozabad, till the long, red lizards of the ridge barred her way, and now she suns herself, a raffle of narrow and congested byways, beneath the crimson walls of Shah Jahan's great palace-fort... Delhi is more than her streets and temples...go round about her and count her towers; you may tramp from the Jumma Masjid to the Fort, from Fort to the Pillar, from the Pillar to Humaion's Tomb and the great Minar; and when all is seen you will understand that these things do no honour to Delhi... Inscrutable and undeniable, her claim is different from that of all other towns of India, for she has no rival in the greatness from the mountains to the sea, and all men know that whoso holds Delhi holds India...

Beyond the hard white shaded road—the only serviceable and well-kept thing in all the landscape...Some servant of an Emperor, some Emperor himself...who sleeps soundly in his grave, all unconscious that the city he believed so abiding and so loyal has drifted far from him and his all-powerful dynasty, and now darkness the northward sky with the smoke factory chimneys, and of locomotives straining across the iron-bridged Jumna...the south still stands the shaft raised by the slave-emperor from Turkestan and underneath it the iron pillar of an earlier 'conqueror of universe' bears witness yet to its Royal maker's foolishness. Tughlakabad...is given over to the jackals and the cobra and the owl-the very bats have found in it no ceiling for their foul nesting. Lalkot lies a weed-grown fold of scattered halfhewn stone and mud...Indraprastha is there still, but she has given up the struggle against the fate... Grand Trunk Road endures between and beneath the shadows of the heavy banyans above, whose leaves are whitened daily by the dust-shuffling bullock-carts, just as when Shah Jahan's vast equipage trailed slowly in to his new capital... A few minarets have pierced the skyline...Delhi, that is, of today-rises flat and uncomely behind her long, low, fortified and battlemented walls.

—Perceval Landon
Under the Sun

APPENDIX II

THE CITY OF SCENTS

Delhi is the city of scents as well as the city of doves. In the hot weather evenings the perfumes from the neams and oleanders and a myriad other gorgeous tropical blooms are almost overpowering. In no other of the world's cities have I known nature so to stimulate an exquisite perfumer's shop. Walking beneath the arcades of neams, with their blooms like green feathers, and the oleanders, tossing rose du Barri in the air; the perfumes are sweet to cruelty if the inner life is void of delight. And all round the city raises the glad chorus of thousands of doves happy in love and the companionship which the summer and the scent have brought. In no other eastern city that I know are the doves so glad as in Delhi. There, where human lovers have known the greatest heights and depths of passion, so also seems the animal creation most exultant in its love.

—Walter Tibbits
The Voice of the Orient

APPENDIX III

THE ROME OF ASIA

Probably there is no town in India that the travellers approaches with more expectancy than Delhi—the one-time capital of the country, the sacred city of India, Rome of Asia and the scene of the most critical episode of the Indian mutiny.

—Frederick Treves
The Other Side of Lantern

APPENDIX IV

THE PEACOCK THRONE

It should be stated that the great Mogul has seven magnificent thrones, one wholly covered with diamonds, the other with rubies, emeralds, or pearls.

The principal throne, which is placed in the hall of the first court, it nearly of the form and size of our camp-beds; that is to say, it is about 6 feet long and 4 feet wide. Upon the four feet, which are very massive, and from 20 to 25 inches high, are fixed the four bars which support the base of the throne, and upon these bars are ranged twelve columns, which sustain the canopy on the three sides, there not being any on that which faces the court. Both the feet and the bars, which are more than 18 inches long, are covered with gold inlaid and enriched with numerous diamonds, rubies, and emeralds. In the middle of each bar there is a large *balsas* ruby, cut *encabuchon*, with four emeralds round it, which form a square cross. Next in succession, from one side to the other along the length of the bars there are similar crosses, arranged so that in one the ruby is in the middle of four emeralds, and in another the emerald is in the middle and four balsas rubies surround it. The emeralds are table-cut, and the intervals between the rubies surround it. The emeralds are table-cut, and the intervals between the rubies and emeralds are covered with diamonds, the largest of which do not exceed 10 to 12 carats in weight, all being showy stones, but very flat. There are also in some parts pearls set in gold, and upon one of the longer side of the throne there are four steps to ascend it. Of the three cushions or pillows which are upon the throne, that which is placed behind the King's back is large and round like one of our bolsters, and the two others that are placed at sides are flat. There is to be seen, moreover, a sword suspended from this throne, a mace, a round shield, a bow and quiver with arrows; and all these weapons, as also the cushions and steps, both of this throne and the other six, are covered over with stones which match those with which each of the thrones is respectively enriched.

I counted the large *balsas* rubies on the great throne, and there are about 108, all *cabuchons*, the least of which weighs 100 carats, but there are some which weigh apparently 200 and more. As for the emeralds, there are plenty of good colour, but they have many flaws; the largest may weigh 60 carats and the least 30 carats.

—J.B. Tavernier
Les Six Voyages de J.B. Tavernier

BIBLIOGRAPHY

Al-Biruni, *Al-Hind: The Making of the Indo-Islamic World, Early Medieval India and Expansion of Islam, 7th–11th Centuries*, tr. Andre Wink, Vol. I. (Oxford University Press: New Delhi, 1999).

Ali, Ahmed, *Twilight in Delhi* (Oxford University Press: London, 1966).

Ashraf, K.M., *Life and Conditions of the People of Hindustan*, 2nd edition (Munshiram Manoharlal: New Delhi, 1970).

Azad, Abdul Kalam, *India Wins Freedom* (Orient Longman: Chennai, 1988).

Beg, Sangin, *Sair-ul-Maazil*, (ed.) Sharif Hussain Qasimi, Ghalib Insitute, New Delhi, 1982.

Banerjee, A.C. and D.K. Ghose, *A Comprehensive History of India* (People's Publishing House: New Delhi, 1978).

Blake, Stephen P., *Shahjahanabad: The Sovereign City in Mughal India 1639–1739*, South Asian Studies 49 (Cambridge University Press: New Delhi, reprint 2017).

Brunt, P.A., 'Thucydides: The Compassionate Scientist', in C.M.D. Crowder (ed.), *Histories and Historians: A Selection of Articles from History Today* (Oliver & Boyd: Edinburgh, London, 1968).

Carr, Stephen, *The Archaeology and Monumental Remains of Delhi* (Ludhiana, 1876).

Chakrabarti, Dilip K. and Nayanjot Lahiri, 'A Preliminary Report on the Stone Age of the Union Territory of Delhi and Haryana', in Upinder Singh (ed.), *Social Science Press* (New Delhi, 2006).

Chattopadhyaya, B.D., 'Indian Archaeology and the Epic Traditions', in Upinder Singh (ed.), *Social Science Press* (New Delhi, 2006).

Chenoy, Shama Mitra, *Shahjahanabad: A City of Delhi 1638–1857* (Munshiram Manoharlal Publishers: New Delhi, reprint 2015).

Crowder, C.M.D., *Histories and Historians: A Selection of Articles from History Today* (Oliver & Boyd: Edinburgh, London, 1968).

Dalrymple, William, *City of Djinns: A Year in Delhi* (Penguin Books: London, 1993)

Daly, J., Bowles, *Indian Sketches and Rambles* (Patrick Press: Calcutta, 1896).

Delhi in 1857: Studies, Images and Documents, Indian History Congress: 70th Session Souvenir, 2010.

Digby, Simon, 'The Tomb of Bahlul Lodi', *Bulletin of the School of Oriental and African Studies*, Vol. 38, No. 3 (1975), pp. 550–61.

Dudney, Arthur, *Delhi: Pages from a Forgotten History* (Hay House India: New Delhi, 2015).

Elliot, Henry, *Memoirs on the History, Folk-lore, and Distribution of the Races of the North Western Provinces of India: Being an Amplified Edition of the Original Supplemental Glossary of Indian Terms*, in John Beames (ed.) (Trubner & co.: London, 1869).

H.M Elliot and Dowson J., *History of India as Told by Its Own Historians*, Vol.II (Cosmopolitian: Aligarh, 1952).

Elphinstone, Mountstuart, *An Account of the Kingdom of Cabul and Its Dependencies in Persia, Tartary and India* (Richard Bentley: London, 1842).

Fanshawe, H.C., *Delhi: Past and Present* (John Murray: London, 1902).

Farooqui, Mahmood, *Besieged Voices from Delhi 1857* (Penguin Viking: New Delhi, 2010).

Ferrier, J.P., *A History of the Afghans* (John Murray: London, 1858).

Galbraith, V.H., *An Introduction to the Study of History* (C.A. Watts & Co. Ltd.: London, 1964).

Gascoigne, Bamber, *The Great Moghuls* (B.I. Publications in association with Jonathan Cape: New Delhi, 1971).

Guha, Ramchandra, *India after Gandhi: The History of the World's largest Democracy* (Picador: India, 2007).

Gupta, Narayani, *Delhi between Two Empires: Society, Government and Urban Growth* (Oxford University Press: Delhi, 1981).

Griffiths, Charles John, *A Narrative of the Siege of Delhi* (John Murray: London, 1910).

Grover, A.K. and P.L. Bakliwal, 'River Migration and the Floods: A Study of a Section of Yamuna River through Remote Sensing', in Upinder Singh (ed.), *Readings in History, Delhi: Ancient India* (Social Science Press: New Delhi, 2006).

Grover, A.K. and P.L. Bakliwal, 'A Study of Yamuna River through Remote Sensing', *Man and Environment*, Vol.9 (1985), pp.151–53.

Habib, Irfan, 'Remembering 1857', *Delhi in 1857: Studies, Images and Documents*, Souvenir Indian History Congress: 70th Session, Delhi, 2010.

Habib, Irfan, 'Economic History of the Delhi Sultanate: An Essay in Interpretation', *The Indian Historical Review*, Vol. IV, No. 2 (January 1978), pp. 287–303.

Hamilton, Norah Rowan, *Through Wonderful India and Beyond* (Holden & Hardingham: London, 1915).

Hasan, S. Nurul, 'The Morphology of a Medieval Indian City: A Case Study of Shahjahanabad', in Indu Banga (ed.), *The City in Indian History* (Manohar: Delhi, 1991).

Hearn, Gordon Risley, *The Seven Cities of Delhi* (W. Thacker & Co.: London, 1906).

Heber, R.R., *Narratives of a Journey through the Upper Provinces of India*, Vol. 1 (Carey, Lea & Carey, Philadelphia, 1829).

Jha, D.N., *Ancient India: In Historical Outline* (Manohar: Delhi, 2007).

Joshi, M.C. and B.M. Pande, 'A Newly Discovered Inscription of Asoka at Bahapur, Delhi', *The Journal of the Royal Asiatic Society of Great Britain and Ireland*, No. 3/4 (October 1967), pp.96–98.

Kaul, H.K., *Historic Delhi: An Anthology* (Oxford University Press: New Delhi, 1998, 2nd Impression.

Khan, Dargah Quli Khan, *Muraqqa-i Dilli*, Department of Urdu, University of Delhi, 1985.

Kidwai, Saleem, 'Dragah Quli Khan: Portrait of a City (Persian)' in (eds.) R. Vanita and S. Kidwai (eds), *Same-sex Love in India* (Palgrave Macmillan: New York, 2000).

Koenigsmarck, Count Han von, *A German Staff Officer in India* (London, 1910).

Kumar, Sunil, 'Transition in the Relationship between Political Elites and Sufis: The Thirteenth and Fourteenth Century Delhi Sultanate', in Karashima Noboru and Hirosue Masashi (eds), *State Formation and Social Integration in Pre-modern South and Southeast Asia: A Comprehensive Study of Asian Society* (The Toyo Bunko: Japan, 2017).

Kumar, Sunil, *The Present in Delhi's Pasts: Five Essays*, 2nd reprint (Three Essays Collective: New Delhi, 2017).

Kumari, Savita, *Tombs of Delhi: Sultanate Period* (Bharatiya Kala Prakashan: Delhi, 2006).

Lahore Chronicle 1858, 15 May 1858, p.309.

Landon, Perceval, *Under the Sun* (Hurst and Blackett: London, 1906).

Law, Jean de Lauriston, *Memoiressur Quelques Affaires del Empire Mogol, 1756–61* (Alferd Martineau: Paris, 1913).

Lawrence, J. to C.Trevelyan, 16 December 1857 (Lawrence Papers, F. 90, 12), pp. 173-4.

Leslie, B., 'Delhi, the Metropolis of India', *Journal of Royal Society of Art*, Vol. 61 (1912).

Mani, B.R., *Delhi Threshold of the Orient: Studies in the Archeological Investigations* (Aryan Book International: Delhi, 1997).

Mackenzie, Colin, *Life in the Mission, the Camp, and the Zenana or Six Years in India* (Richard Bentley: London, 1853).

Malcolm, J., *The History of Persia*, Vol. II (John Murray: London, 1829).

Mani, B.R., 'Excavations at Lal Kot 1991–92 and Further Explorations in Delhi', *Puratattva*, No. 22 (1991–92), pp.75–87.

Manucci, Niccolao, *Mogul India*, 4 Vols, translated by William Irvine (Low Price Publication: Delhi, 1907–08, reprint 2005).

Merewether, F.H.S., *A Tour through Famine Districts of India* (A.D. Innes: London, 1898).

Metcalf, C.T., 'Delhi 1815', *Home Miscellaneous Series*, Vol. 776, Indian Office Library, London.

Mukherji, Anisha Shekhar, *The Red Fort of Shajahanbad* (Oxford University

Press: USA, 2003).

Nangia, Sudesh, *Delhi Metropolitan Region: A Study in Settlement Geography* (K.B. Publication: New Delhi, 1976).

Nath, R., *History of Sultanate Architecture* (Abhinav Publication: New Delhi, 1978).

National Archives of India, Foreign Secretary, 25 January 1858, F. 11-15, p.51, Chief of Staff, to Officer Commanding Meerut Division, 27 January 1858.

Pandey, Gyanendra, 'Partition and Independence in Delhi: 1947–48', *Economic and Political Weekly*, Vol. 32, No. 36 (Sept 6–12), 1997, pp.2261–2272.

Prasad, Pushpa, *Sanskrit Inscriptions of Delhi Sultanate 1191–1526* (Oxford University Press: Delhi, 1990).

Phillimore, R.H., *Historical Records of the Survey of India 1800 to 1815* (Survey of India: Dehradun, 1950).

Rana, Safvi, *Where Stones Speak: Historical Trails in Mehrauli, the First City of Delhi* (Element, 2015.

Roberts, Earl, *Forty-one Years in India* (Macmillan: London, 1911).

Rumi, Raza, *Delhi by Heart* (Harper Collins: India, 2013).

Russell, Ralph and Khurshidul Islam (tr.), *Ghalib: 1797–1869, Vol. 1: Life and Letters* (George Allen and Unwin: London, 1969).

Sadique, M., *History of Urdu Literature* (Oxford University Press: Delhi, 1964).

Sanderson, Gordon, *Delhi Fort: A Guide to the Buildings and Gardens* (Asian Educational Services: New Delhi, 2000).

Sarao, K.T.S., 'Delhi as It Was Known to the Buddhist', *Historic Delhi: Indian History Congress*, 52nd Session, 1992.

Saraswati, Swami Dayanand, *Satyarth Parkash*, Chiranjiva Bharadwaja (tr.) (Star Press: Allahabad, 1927).

Sarkar, J.N., *Fall of the Mughal Empire*, 4 Vols (M.C. Sarkar & Sons Ltd.: Calcutta, 1950).

Sauda, Mirza Muhammad Rafi, 'Masnavi Dar Shidi Faulad Khan, Kotwal, Shahjahanabad', *Kulliyat-i Sauda*, 2 Vols (Allahabad, 1971).

Secret Letter No. 68 of 1857 (*Indian Office Records*, India and Bengal Secret Dispatches, India Public No. 63 of 1858, 5 May).

Sen, Surendranath, *Delhi and Its Monuments* (A. Mukherjee & Co. Ltd: Calcutta, reprinted 1954).

Sharma, A.K., 'Prehistoric Delhi and Its Neighbourhood: Physical Features' in Upinder Singh (ed.) *Readings in History, Delhi: Ancient India* (Social Science Press: New Delhi, 2006).

Shrimali, K.M., 'The Origins: From Indraprastha to Dhilli', *Historic Delhi* Indian History Congress, 52nd Session, 1992.

Siddiqui, Iqtidar H., *Perso-Arabic Sources of Information on the Life and Conditions in the Sultanate of Delhi* (Munshiram Manoharlal Publishers: New Delhi, 1992).

Singh, Khushwant, *Delhi: A Novel* (Penguin Viking: New Delhi, reprint 1990).

Singh, Malvika, *Perpetual City: A Short Biography of Delhi* (Aleph Book Company: Delhi, 2013).

Singh, Upinder (ed.), *Readings in History, Delhi: Ancient India* (Social Science Press: New Delhi, 2006).

Singh, Upinder, *Ancient Delhi*, 2nd Edition (Oxford University Press: Delhi, 2010, 3rd impression).

Smith, R.V., Delhi: *Unknown Tales of a City* (Roli Books: New Delhi, 2016, 2nd impression).

Smith, R.V., *Lingering Charms of History: Myth, Lore and History* (Niyogi Books: Delhi, 2015).

Smith, R.V., *Delhi: Historical Glimpses* (Aryan Book International: Delhi, 2010).

Spear, Percival, *Delhi: Its Monuments and History* (Oxford University Press: Delhi, 1994).

Srivastava, A.L., *The Sultanate of Delhi 711–1526 AD*, 5th edition (Shiva Lal Agarwala & Company: Agra, 1966).

Tavernier, J.B., *Les Six Voyages de J.B. Tavernier*, 1677.

Tervelyan, H., *The India We Left*, and *Lahore Chronicle 1858*, dated 26 March 1859.

Thakran, R.C., 'Protohistoric Archaeological Remains of the Union Territory of Delhi', in Upinder Singh (ed.), *Readings in History, Delhi: Ancient India* (Social Science Press: New Delhi, 2006).

Thomas, Edward, *The Chronicles of the Pathan Kings of Delhi Illustrated by Coins Inscriptions and Other Aniquarian Remains* (Trubner: London, 1871).

Tibbits, Walter, *The Voice of the Orient* (The Theosophical Publication Society: London and Thacker & Co.: Bombay, 1909).

Treves, Frederick, *The Other Side of lantern* (London: Cassell & Co., 1906).

Triveda, D.S., 'Visnudhvaja or Qutb Manar', *The Chowkhamba Sanskrit Studies*, Vol. XXIV, Chowkhamba Sanskrit series Office, Varanasi, 1962.

Wood, Oswald, *Final Report on the Settlement of Land Revenue in the Delhi District Carried on 1872–77 by Oswald Wood and Completed 1878–80 by R. Maconachie* (Victoria Press: Lahore, 1882).

Vibart, Edward, *The Sepoy Mutiny as Seen by a Subaltern from Delhi to Lucknow* (Smith Elder: London, 1898).

Wyman, E.F., *From Calcutta to the Snowy Range* (Tinsley Brothers: London, 1866).

Ziegler, Philip, *Mountbatten* (Collins: London, 1985).

ACKNOWLEDGEMENTS

By its very nature, history as a discipline requires a lot of rigour to trace the source of the historian's study, and then to see it through a critical eye in order to get a reasonable glimpse of the past. Although as a student of history, I have not done anything extraordinary in this work, the journey of the exploration and writing would have never been accomplished without some people, who were always around to motivate, help and discuss. Thus, I owe to express my gratitude to them.

At the beginning, I would like to express my gratitude to my teachers who have introduced me to the processes, principles and ethics of research. I would like to thank Prof. R.P. Rana specially for his kind guidance and intellectual generosity and for being a constant mentor in my many journeys of research. I would also like to express my gratitude to Prof. Sunil Kumar who instigated my interest in the history of Delhi. Here, I would like to confess that his excessively informative lectures on the history of the Delhi Sultanate which I attended during my post graduation days are responsible for the germination of this research. The intellectual commitment, style and passion with which he carries forward the narratives of the Delhi Sultanate are remarkably outstanding! I have faith that these credentials must be guiding many more.

I would also like to warmly thank many people who have offered me their invaluable time and assistance. At Indian Institute of Advanced Study (IIAS), my sincere gratitude to Mr Prem Chand (Librarian, IIAS, Rashtrapati Nivas, Shimla) for providing the generous support in the library and most importantly for making rare books and articles available to me. It is his assistance that helped me complete the manuscript on time. I am deeply indebted to him. The extremely helpful and kind library staff at IIAS deserve mention and their efforts are worth commendation. They not only offered me generous assistance but the support of this remarkable community helped me to attain intellectual engagements.

I would like to express my heartfelt thanks to Prof. S.Z.H. Jafri, who has been a guiding light in times of darkness.

The journey of this book was made enjoyable by many friends. A few deserve special mention here because they were always curious to know about the progress of this work. Their curiosities served as silent and passionate motivators. So, dear friends—Shubhra Kathuria, Sudhir Sharma, R.B. Azad, Aadya, Kavita and Shams Tabrez: thank you for all the support and confidence you have in me. I owe respect to all of you. I owe gratitude to Col. (Dr) Vijay K. Tiwari as this book took its final shape after innumerable long discussions with him. His interest in the anecdotal history has helped to locate many episodes that have been narrated in this book. Special thanks to Ashutosh Bhardwaj for his conscious intellectual support and constant inquiries on the subject.

I dedicate my love and gratitude to my family who have always stood with me. My father, Shri Devi Singh Kuri, has been a source of inspiration and he has taught me well to stand through tough times. My maa, Smt. Rameshwari, is a luminary and there is lot to learn from her, especially her ability to sense the dilemmas of other persons. The loving presence of my brothers, Sachin and Rishi, is always a cocktail of fun and work, loaded with a lot of thinking. Both being good readers are always able to see the episodes of our discussions through a critical lens. My sisters-in-law, Monica and Kanika, are fun people, and their presence has always been refreshing. Both have helped build the subject as per the backgrounds of their academic expertise. My sister Kiran and brother-in-law Omparkash are people of infrastructural support and have always stood by me whenever I needed them. Durga and Rajeev are lovely souls who always work as *jinns* to make the impossible possible!

Aditya, Maira, Abhimanyu, Mira and Chotu-Vani (Dhani) are stars full of enthusiasm, energy and love. Their innocent gleam inspires me a lot. I thank them for their presence which boost me up. Rio and Shibu are kids of other species but definitely their presence is significant for me in many ways!

I owe a real debt of gratitude to the editorial team at Rupa Publications for their insight, support and kind treatment of the changes that I made till the very end.

At last, once again, I would express my thanks to the Indian Institute of Advanced Study and its staff for providing the real academic environment and support on all the fronts. The academic environment that is available at the institute in the midst of Shimla's lovely weather has been a real motivation to complete this monograph.

Dr Manisha Choudhary
Shimla
October 2019